HERMANN VASKE
Preface

Standing on the shoulders of giants.

Isaac Newton is recognized, along with Galileo and Einstein, to be one of the world's true geniuses.

However, when asked about his achievements, he said "I have done no more than stand on the shoulders of giants."

If learning from your predecessors is good enough for one of mankind's greatest thinkers, surely it's good enough for the rest of us.

That's why I've interviewed some of the masters in the various fields of advertising, arts and film, and put them together in this collection.

Instead of starting from scratch, and trying to reach the same heights that they have, we can assimilate their knowledge and give ourselves a head start.

Then perhaps we can reach higher than them.
By standing on their shoulders.

Hermann Vaske
May 2001

About the Author
Hermann Vaske

Hermann Vaske is an advertising creative, author, director and producer.

He's one of the most awarded German creatives and the only one to win an Art Director's Gold medal, Cannes Awards, and Gold Awards at Clio for his commercials and the Grimme Award, Germany's TV Oscar, for his groundbreaking film "The A-Z of Separating People From Their Money" which stars Dennis Hopper.

After graduating in Communication from the University of Fine Arts in Berlin, and studying film directing at the American Film Institute in Los Angeles, Hermann spent 2 years at Saatchi & Saatchi in London and Frankfurt.

He then spent a further 3 years at GGK, Springer & Jacoby, and Lowe & Partners working with blue-chip companies such as IBM and Mercedes-Benz. At Lowe & Partners he became Creative Director responsible for the Opel/General Motors Account.

Later, he became FCB's Executive Creative Director. Here, he worked with a range of clients, including MDR, Colgate, ARTE.

Hermann's independent career started when he founded Hermann Vaske's Emotional Network and became its Executive Creative Director working with clients like Deutsche Bahn, Audi, Volkswagen and ZDF.

His recent clients include BMW, Hugo Boss and Bayern 4 Classic.

Hermann Vaske's Emotional Network is an advertising agency and production company in Frankfurt which combines Hermann's own writing, producing and directing talents with those of other highly creative people such as Wim Wenders, Paul Arden, Mike Figgis, Tony Kaye, Mark Williams, Stein Leikanger, Malcolm McLaren, Julian Schnabel and Hugh Hudson.

The services and talents of Hermann Vaske's Emotional Network are used by advertising agencies, TV-stations and in fact all clients to create, write, film and produce outstanding creative work, from conception to completion. In the last few years Hermann Vaske's Emotional Network produced commercials, together with Wim Wenders, for Deutsche Bahn and the EXPO in Hannover, and with Paul Arden for Audi.

Hermann's previous television films include features on David Bowie and Yohji Yamamoto, as well as the feature length documentaries "Best Sellers" and "The Ten Commandments of Creativity" starring Dennis Hopper as Moses and Peter Ustinov as God. Shown around the world, from BBC 2 and Bravo (USA), to Hong Kong.

His latest book "Why are you creative?" (published by Verlag Hermann Schmidt Mainz) was released in 1999. His "Why are you creative?" TV series will be launched on the the ARTE channel in 2001/2002.

Hermann's major project for the third millennium crosses two genres: investigative creative documentary, and pulp detective movie.

It's called "Who Killed the Idea?".

Hermann is a frequent speaker at creative and marketing conferences and seminars in Germany and abroad, and a professor at the University of Applied Arts and Sciences Trier.

ACKNOWLEDGEMENTS
Hermann Vaske

Thanks to Almap/BBDO, Alta Light Productions, Anton Corbijn, Arden Sutherland-Dodd, Bartle Bogle Hegarty, BBDO, BMP/DDB, Charles Bender, Cliff Freeman & Partners, Colleen of Joe Pytka Films, DDB, Dentsu, Harold Weiss, Headlab, Jerome Person, Julia Feldmann, Ania Bakowski and Karina Arndt of the Emotional Network, Lars Hinsenhofen, Leagas Delaney, Lois USA, Louise Higgins, Lowe Lintas & Partners, Michael Conrad, Nick Hay, Nils Petermann, NSF, Ogilvy & Mather, Paul Weiland Films, Radical Media, Research Studios, RSA, Sebastian Durbant, Timo Breidenbruch, Tina Schembecker, Toshiaki Runze, Saatchi & Saatchi, Sedelmaier Films, Studio Toscani, TBWA, Tony Kaye Films, Veronique and Catherine of The Philippe Starck Office, Walsh Trott Chick Smith, Walter Scheuerl, Wieden & Kennedy, Wim Wenders Films.

Special thanks to Keith Reinhard, Marcello Serpa and Joe Pytka for the inspiring forewords, to Walter Lürzer for the unique platform Archive, to Michael Weinzettel for wonderful editorial work, to Der Stern (especially Torsten Bardohn, Jan-Piet Stempels, Ulrike Woltering and Andreas Schilling for wanting to publish my collection of interviews as a book) to Robert Klanten, Hendrik Hellige, and Thorsten Geiger of Die Gestalten (for the great design and layout advice), and to Anette Krischer (for networking and initiating the contacts).

Extra special thanks to the BMW-Group, who helped us to make the Cannes presentation of the book possible, to the digital artists of DAS WERK: Christian Leonhardt, Klaus Braumann, Stefan Jung, Joachim Sturmes, Ralf Drechsler, Stefan Jonas, Ben Losch, and Oliver Kehler, also to Marcus Weyrauch of Avid Media Online and Jochen Wenke of Tongalerie Frankfurt, who sorted out the digital part of the presentation. To Roger and Romain Hatchuel of the International Advertising Festival for the great and friendly support over the years and last, but by no means least to Angela Krejci (without her inspiration the project would not have been possible).

And finally, thanks to everyone who's been interviewed, nice talking to you.

FRANK LOWE
It's very difficult to tell a joke in 30 seconds

In the seventies Collett Dickenson Pearce was undoubtedly the best agency in the world. Two men were mainly responsible for that. One was, unsurprisingly, the creative director, Colin Millward. The other was, unusually, the managing director, Frank Lowe.
Frank was not only an account handling powerhouse, he was something hardly ever seen: an account man with more creative judgement and energy than most so-called creatives.
Until CDP in the 70's, no one had even dreamt of challenging New York's creative superiority. Frank Lowe almost single-handedly grew a generation of creative talent that made London the best in the world.
After CDP, Frank opened Lowe Howard-Spink, which became Lowe Lintas. His agencies have probably won more awards than all the rest put together, at least that's what it feels like. I talked to Frank Lowe at his London headquarters.

▷ Hermann Vaske: Frank, is advertising art?
◁ Frank Lowe: It's the commercial art, not the fine art. But I think it's very difficult to work out the difference between the two. This is a question everybody asks "is it art or is it commercial art" and I always think, well it's commercial art because it has a financial end in mind. You're doing something to be paid money, that's not pure art. But then you look back and I think, "Well, hang on a minute, Mozart was a commercial artist", he was told he had to compose something. You know "I want a new sonata for Wednesday and then the King of so and so is coming, could I have a little welcoming piece on Friday?" I mean Michelangelo was painting for money. You know, they were all paid, so I'm not sure really what the distinguishing line is. Perhaps the biggest difference is, it is not enduring art. Modern advertising doesn't endure very much.

▷ That's all fine and good, but didn't your campaign for Smirnoff come close to art?
◁ Well, that was wonderfully crafted advertising, a beautiful mixture. In a sense, Tarsem was painting images through film. So, in that sense, it was wonderfully artistic, and it is a piece of art. I think, one must leave an individual to judge what it is. It's very difficult to be precise, because I started collecting photography many, many years ago and for many years there was this debate about whether photography had value, because of course photography is not designed to be a one-off. You can produce more prints. I think generally today, people would accept that photography is art, and this is the reason of course, sadly, why the prices

of so many of the great photographers have just been going up and up, and why the exhibitions get more and more, and they are attended better and better, so perhaps things change. Perhaps advertising is a modern form of art in quite a pure sense.

▷ You started to work in advertising the sixties. Do you have any explanation why the sixties created such a creative renaissance in England?

◁ Britain did spawn, at that time, a group of photographers, a group of artists, a group of designers, a group of film directors, who have endured and have become known for the things they do and, I think, also that inspired young people. It's lucky, but I think it's because we are all the same generation now, we're getting older unfortunately, but we're all the same generation.

▷ You have a special relationship to the "Famous Five": Tony Scott, Ridley Scott, Adrian Lyne, Alan Parker and Hugh Hudson (the five commercial directors from Britain that conquered Hollywood). Can you elaborate on that?

◁ Yeah, Alan worked very closely with me when I was running CDP in the very late sixties and we did "Bugsy Malone" when he was still working there. He wrote it there and, I remembered, he came round to my house for dinner. I don't know how old he was then, probably about, I don't know, 23, 24, very young, and he was leaving me this stuff he'd written, the whole thing at dinner, just the two of us. And I said to him, "You know, I know just the composer for this," and because I happened to have an album of the composer, and I played it, and he said "Oh that's a good idea". So I saw him a few days later and I said "What did you do with that music?" He said "I rang him up he's going to do the music". So, ever since then, I've gone to one day of shooting on every film Alan's made. I have finished up in some very funny places I can tell you. I finished up on "Mississippi Burning" watching him film at three in the morning when they had one of the terrible hanging and burning scenes, and I finished up in Malta when he was shooting "Midnight Express" (and got food poisoning, I remember, which was not a highlight). And I remember New Orleans, when he was doing "Angel Heart", we went to Dublin when he was doing "The Commitments". I'm very fond of him, I think he's a great director.

I think it is very important that these people who set the standards come to our agency and talk. I mean every time Alan Parker makes a film, before he shows it almost to anybody except the studio, he brings it to the agency and he shows it to us, and he's available to talk about it afterwards. And I think that kind of thing is a very stimulating thing for young creative people: that you should be able to stand around and chat with people like Ridley, I think it's very important.

▷ So, basically, he gives the agency an exclusive sneak preview?

◁ Yes, and to our clients. Yes, absolutely a sneak preview. People see it months before it comes here, and normally two or three weeks before it launches in the United States. And I think they feel that that's kind of special and I think it's quite nice to see a film, good or bad, before anybody has commented on it. Before the critics have commented. There's nobody saying "oh you must go and see", you have to make up your own mind. You have no outside influences. Nobody's told you it's great or told you it's terrible and that's a good thing for the kind of critical faculties.

▷ Are commercials well told jokes?

◁ No. They're not the most well told jokes, I've never really understood this debate. I think it was David Ogilvy who said humour doesn't have a place in advertising. I think the reason David said that, I'm sure, was because he had no understanding of television advertising because he was brought up before television advertising, he understood press. He didn't understand television. And there's another school of Ted Bates people saying you should, basically, just shout your message louder and louder. But you know that theory, it's rubbish. Absolute rubbish. If you think of campaigns like Hamlet, like Heineken, running for twenty-five years, building huge brands on wit and style and humour. There is no way on this earth the client would put money behind them for twenty years if they didn't work, so that's just a nonsense. And I think the people who decry it are basically the people who can't do it, because it's not easy. You know, 30 seconds to be witty is very, very difficult. I mean, just think in terms of telling a joke, it's very difficult to tell a joke in 30 seconds, they normally take longer, so that's the first thing. You know, when I first went to New York I got a job as a salesman, I was about 22, selling carpets in one of the stores on Fifth Avenue and I was able to sell carpets I think principally because I had an English accent, and it was quite smart to have an English accent in those days. But when I was selling you just didn't go up to somebody and say "Good morning, I'd like to tell you about our new carpet, it's made of this, this, this, this, this and this and so it is of wonderful value, I suggest you buy one now" because they'd just walk away. You wouldn't do it, you'd say "Good morning Madam, can I help you?" "Well, I'm looking for this that and the other". You know, and you would engage them in conversation. And any salesman going in to sell something to a store doesn't go in and say "Good Morning here's the latest offer from Coca Cola, if you buy twenty four dozen you can get

Stills from Lowe's
"Water in Majorca" commercial
for Heineken

one dozen free." He says "Good morning Harry, how are you? How is the family? How are the kids? Did you hear the funny story about the man and the hippopotamus ?" or whatever. It doesn't matter what it is, what matters is that they engage with the person, that's how we live our lives. So why shouldn't television be a one on one experience? Television doesn't talk to ten million people, television talks to one person who is actually watching. There may be three in the room but each person is watching it as an individual. Why wouldn't you engage them, why wouldn't you charm them, why wouldn't you make them smile, just as you do in selling anything in life?

▷ Especially your Heineken commercial with the dog that paints the kitchen wall. That made people smile and created a lot of talk. How important is word of mouth?

◁ You'd be amazed how many people actually wrote in and asked how did you teach the dog to paint, they didn't realise it was a person, I mean people are very strange.
I thought "My God, they don't really think you can teach a dog to get up on its two legs with a paint brush and paint.", but they did.

▷ Is good advertising only advertising, if it works in the long run?

◁ Yes, I think in general advertising isn't going through a wonderfully rich period. I don't think there is a lot of wonderful advertising that builds enduring campaigns being done. But then I think that's part of the business, clients think short term, I don't think clients are so involved in building brands as they used to be, or investing in brands as they used to. The quarterly earnings are crucial for most companies, particularly in America, but now even all over Europe they have to get sales by the end of the quarter. And I can't say "I know you're trying to build a long-term image" because, as a client said to me once "In the long term I'll be out of a job" and therefore that is a problem.

▷ Regarding longevity, you did a great job on Heineken, for instance.

◁ I mean it's been a good experience on Heineken, because we've been working with Freddy Heineken for a long time, and his name's on the door: his grandfather founded the company, it was his product, and he's devoted his life to making it something. Most clients don't devote their lives to making it something, they do a job for two or three years and then say, "Well, I'm off to Colgate now, I've got a better offer" and suddenly their loyalty is totally transferred to something else. That's not the way founders work. Clarence Birds Eye invented frozen foods. I remember, after working on it for ten years, I'd been working on Birds Eye longer than any single person in the whole of the marketing department in Birds Eye.

Frank Lowe

▷ Could you have done Heineken if it wasn't man to man, and if you had to sell it through hierarchies instead?

◁ Well, I think not. I think first of all it would have frightened them, secondly it's an important brand, and clients take less risks on bigger brands.

▷ How important is the briefing?

◁ Well, if you get a briefing from the top it's normally simpler. But, by the time it gets through the ranks, everything's in there, the kitchen sink, the whole thing: it does this, it does that, it's a new design, the trunk's this big, it's got a so and so engine, it holds five people, it comes in three different styles with a hatchback, it's got a sunshine roof, two airbags, and so on and so on.
You can't remember all that in a piece of advertising.

▷ CDP was the basis for your success. Does your style of advertising still thrive on that experience?

◁ I learned many things from John Pearce, who was my old boss, and from Colin Millward, who was the best creative man I've known. Bill Bernbach was wonderful too, but Colin for me was great. John used to say to me: "Remember Frank, if you listen to your clients long enough, it'll help you write the advertising." I don't mean to say I let them write the strategy, but I did say "Talk to me, tell me about your product, tell my why you're making it, tell me who you're talking to, tell me what you're trying to say". And they go on and on and on, and eventually they'll say something that is important to the consumer and on which you can create a piece of advertising. Because, at the end of the day, unless you can create a piece of advertising from the strategy that is memorable, the strategy isn't really worth much. You know saying "I don't care if it's dull, that's the strategy" doesn't work. Because then you just run thousands of ads and, particularly with the zapper, they just zap, zap, zap, and they're gone very quickly. You know, I saw a statistic the other day: 50% people in Britain use the remote control to avoid advertising, 50% is wasted, terrifying. Whereas before they had no choice, because nobody would get up off their sofa, walk over to the TV, change channels and then have to go all the way back.

▷ Yeah, that's why you have to be attention-getting and memorable.

◁ You have to entertain and you have to make them enjoy it. One thing many clients hate to hear, is that people didn't buy the television to watch your adverts, they bought the television to watch the programmes. That's why, if you're going to go in their living room in their home, where they're having their dinner or sitting round, you really ought to leave

them a little bit richer for visiting them, and you ought to have made it a pleasant experience, and not shout at them. I know, the television companies deny that the TV commercials are louder than the programmes. They say "No, no, no, this is all checked and they aren't". They are, we know it, I know it, you know it, when they come on they're always louder. And I hate that because then I have to look for the remote control to turn them down and that's stupid. I mean, will you pay any more attention if I shout at you? No, you just won't, it doesn't work.

▷ How do you regard David Ogilvy's sentence "If the client moans and sighs, make the logo twice the size."

◁ David wrote that a long time ago. I mean, we wouldn't have had Elvis Presley, because we would still be listening to Mozart, if we didn't realise that rules are made to be changed, and life changes and people change. And I'm sure the kind of views I have of advertising 25 years from now, many people will have many different views, I'm sure many of them will be better, or different at least.

▷ British humour often features subtle soft sell. How would you define British humour?

◁ What's the reason behind the British sense of humour? If you look at the history of humour in Britain, it started at the beginning of this century. Queen Victoria said in her famous line, "We are not amused". There was very little wit, it was a serious country of serious business. The middle class and the aristocracy basically fulfilling their duty to God by running the world, this was how they saw themselves. They had this responsibility, they'd conquered the world and they'd better run it properly and take it very seriously.

I think that what happened then was when Britain started to lose the opportunity to run the world, countries we had ruled became independent, we had wars, and we'd got no money, and suddenly we weren't very powerful. The only mechanism we could find to cope with loss of power was to laugh at ourselves, because otherwise we'd have cried. So we started to tell jokes, we started to make fun of ourselves.

And anyway, it's much easier, as Jewish people do, it's much easier to make fun of yourself than to allow somebody else to make fun of you, because that you can live with.

Stills from the Heinekens
"Lip Sync" commercial

▷ Why are you creative?

◁ I think it started in 1967, I was a young account man and I bumped into John Webster, who was working in the same agency, who was the art director. We formed a bond to try and do good advertising at that time, and we did some very nice work. I think it was to do with the fact that I do like to feel that, when somebody sees the ads that I'm involved in, I'm

Frank Lowe

not ashamed to admit to having been part of them. And my sternest critic is my young son, and he's always the first to say, "Dad, did you do that?" Or "Hey dad, I like that..." Children have no shades of grey, they don't understand the marketing director's problem, or the fact that the client's a very big client and we have to be careful. He just says "It's great" or "It sucks" but I think that's most people's judgement of life actually, I really do. There are only three reasons for being in advertising.

The first is, in my opinion, to do work that works and you're proud of. The second is to enjoy doing it. And the third is to make some money.

Now sometimes you can do advertising you're proud of which doesn't make you much money, but it's great for the creative people and you're proud to do it, and other clients are attracted.

And sometimes you can have a client going through a difficult period, but you still like the relationship because you're bonded and trying to solve it together. And sometimes agencies, for particular reasons of growth or building, won't handle a client as good as it should, but it may still be worthwhile doing so for the sake of the company as it grows.

Those are the three reasons, and if you've got two of those, one of those even, it's alright, but if you had none of them, then you shouldn't have the client.

Tesco was perfect in many ways. When we got the Tesco account, everybody rang up and said "Oh that'll finish you: supermarket, pile it high, sell it cheap, crap advertising". Well of course, ourselves and David Abbot have proved this is not true. The toughest category in the market probably does some of the best advertising. Tesco have been a very nice client to work with. They've encouraged us beyond belief, beyond most clients, particularly most packaged goods clients, they've been much braver than other clients, so that's been wonderful.

They've allowed us to do really good advertising, which we're proud of and which has worked, because, as you know, they've overtaken Sainsbury's and they're now Britain's number one, and, contrary to what people might think, they have paid us properly.

▷ How did you hit that extraordinary idea doing the Tesco campaign with Dudley Moore?

◁ Well, you remember we talked about going to the client and talking? Well, it came absolutely out of that, in this case. We'd arranged for the writer, who's now a creative director, Paul Weinberger, to go and visit them and find out every single thing he could. We wanted a campaign to say that they would go to any length throughout the world to buy the best products. Because they had a reputation for cheapness and not quality and they wanted to change it.

And he came in to me one day and he said "I think I've found it", he said "I've found out that they've bought the whole production of a farm that makes free range chickens in Normandy, and I want to base a campaign on a man who goes to try and find the free range chickens and he never finds them, but he keeps on finding other things and he looks all throughout the world". And you could see instantly it was a great campaign.

▷ A single minded idea.

◁ People, in 30 seconds or 60 seconds, find it very difficult to grasp more than one idea. And if you feed them more than one idea, then they don't get any of it. And this is a question that has been asked a hundred times and the best way I can illustrate it, is: here's a tennis ball, catch it, thank you, here you go. Here's four. Catch them.

▷ I got one.

◁ Right, so even though I threw you four, you only got one.

▷ That's a perfect analogy. But is that enough to defend ourselves against the avalanches of images that we are bombarded with today?

◁ Today's images have come down to sports, music and sex. Maybe sex was always an image. But, particularly today, the sports people have become the great idols of the day, and I suppose, to a degree, pop music. I think the worry about all that is that there is a great temporary feeling about all of it, and therefore they are very transitory images.

And I remember a story: my son was obsessed with Michael Jordan, even though he's never seen a basketball game because he lives in Europe. But Michael Jordan was a hero. Then Michael Jordan retired. And I was sitting in this very room, and somebody from Sports Illustrated or Newsweek rang me up and said "I'd like to talk to you about the retirement of Michael Jordan". And I said "Yes?". And he said, "We're doing an article, and I wanted to ask you, since you're involved in sports and advertising, how do you think the world is going to cope with the loss of Michael Jordan?" And I

Stills from
The Independent campaign

put the phone down, I walked over to the window, I looked out: it all seemed fine. So I came back and I said, "I think we're gonna be all right after all." And he said "You're not taking this seriously."

It seemed to me an extraordinary thought, that today the retirement of a sports-person, or the retirement of a band or a rock group, or whatever, is something very very significant.

It seems that, years ago, the images of the painters, the musicians, the sculptors, the architects, those were, perhaps, images that will live forever. Today, I think we live with transitory images, brought on by the media, because they're got to write something. That is, I think, one of the great problems: our children are obsessed with transitory images.

Frank Lowe

18

▷ Your agency has won the Grand Prix in Cannes for The Independent. A hymn for free speech?

◁ You start with the idea that the newspaper is called The Independent, and that in itself gives you the lead. It talks to people of independent spirit. Most of the newspapers come from a point of view: you shall be a Conservative, you shall be a Socialist; you shall approve of this, you shall not approve of that. The Independent tries to give a balanced view. And that was what the advertising was all about: we live in a world where you shan't do this, you shan't do that, don't walk on the grass, don't this, don't that, don't the other. What we're saying is that we like people to make up their own mind, by reading what is in the newspaper. And it finishes up "...don't talk, don't read." Which is another problem, I feel that reading is absolutely crucial, and reading unbiased unprejudiced, factual information allows people to make up their own minds, and resolve their own feelings, resolve the conflicts that they have within themselves. Whereas my parents, when I was a child, made up my mind for me, which is probably why I rebelled rather a lot as a child.

▷ You know, I like George Lois' comment on trends when he once said to me "When I see a trend, I run as fast as I can to the other direction."

◁ Well, you're absolutely right. It's the same thing that Bill Bernbach said "When everybody zigs, zag". I think one has spent one's whole life doing that, and in our business you have to do that. Because the minute the consumer starts to really feel they understand exactly what you're up to, they're bored. So you've got to take them and then twitch them a bit. And they think "Hello, I didn't expect that! This is interesting, this is new information."

Will you be as fortunate finding a second career?

Heaven knows, you are going to need a second career more than this gentleman.

Compulsory retirement at 55 is on its way.

No matter how long your service, no matter how high your position, you could be out of a job, come your 55th birthday.

The company car will disappear.

The expense account will disappear.

The private health insurance will disappear.

Sadly, your mortgage won't. You may well find yourself repaying that until you are 60 or 65.

Civil servants should be alright. They have indexed-linked pensions, courtesy of the poor old taxpayer.

Members of trade unions should make out too. They often have an army of negotiators to battle on their behalf.

No, it's the private sector business-man who will be in trouble.

His retirement age is going down, but his life expectancy is on the up and up. Today's 40 year olds can expect to reach 80. You could easily be faced with 25 years in retirement.

How will you manage?

That fixed company pension that looked oh-so-generous ten years ago, won't be worth much in another ten year's time, never mind twenty or thirty.

State pensions aren't famous for keeping up with inflation either.

Of course, with the two added together, you may just have enough to survive.

But is that all you want to do?

Survive?

Wouldn't you prefer to do something positive with the second half of your adult life?

Albany Life and the Inland Revenue can help you.

Start salting away a regular sum each month. £15, £50, whatever you can spare.

We will bump up your contributions by claiming back from the taxman every last penny of tax relief we can.

We will then invest the total amount on your behalf.

We receive what is arguably the best investment advice there is. We retain Warburg Investment Management Ltd., a subsidiary of S. G. Warburg & Co Ltd., the merchant bank.

Start saving in your thirties or forties and you will amass a considerable sum, well before your 55th birthday.

When you are pensioned off, you will have a wad of tax-free money to cushion the blow.

Enough to set up shop in some sleepy Devon village.

Enough to pursue some half-forgotten craft, like working with cane or stained glass.

Enough to buy you a stake in some successful small business near your home.

Whatever you decide to do, you'll be better off mentally as well as financially. People vegetate if they have nothing but the garden to occupy their minds.

There is no reason why you shouldn't be active and working at 73, like Mr. Reagan here.

Though hopefully you won't have to carry the worries of the world on your shoulders.

Take the great photographers, like Penn, or Avedon, they've always tried to do different things. The great painters of the modern era like Rauschenberg, they've always tried to do some things that are different. I think creativity is all about doing things that are not quite expected, that are different from what we've seen before. The impressionists moved forward as photography developed. That's the difficulty, unless you're a natural genius, like Mozart or somebody.

▷ Is being different the key to commercial success?

◁ Advertising is commercial art, but then you could argue, of course, that Michelangelo was commercial art "Paint the ceiling and I'll pay you this". Was it commercial art? Well, he was paid and he had to paint it, so you could argue that. Now I wouldn't compare what we do with Michelangelo. But nonetheless it is commercial art, and you do have to follow a brief. But nonetheless, I do think it is part of the environment. This is something I've believed in so strongly all my life, that advertising is an absolute part of the environment, just as architecture is. And I think it is absolutely vital that we have respect for the consumers.

Remember what David Ogilvy has said "Remember the consumer; she's your wife." You know, the respect that when you go on people's televisions, when you go in their homes, they didn't invite you. And of course, nowadays, you know, with a zapper, fifty per cent of people kick you off. So you'd better be amusing, you'd better be charming, you'd better be witty.

▷ Your Olympus campaign is still running? And there's a new one with Joan Collins?

◁ The problem with cameras is, they are all essentially, seriously dull. They're all the same shape and size, and they all have a zoom that goes in and out, and lenses, and to show pictures of cameras is massively boring. So what we tried to do was use Joan to bring interest to the camera, because the camera itself has no interest within itself.

Instead of her promoting it, and saying 'I always use an Olympus', which is really dull (because everybody knows that what you've done is paid her a lot of money to say 'I use an Olympus').

But if she's against it, she's fighting against it and shouting, 'Don't you dare take my photograph', and running away, that's much more interesting. Consumers are so cute today, they know that when Michael Jordan says 'I wear these things' somebody paid him several million dollars to say it. They're not stupid, even my kids worked that out!

Stills from Olympus campaign with Joan Collins

▷ What is the better method for creative people to get these great ideas, obsessive work or a day off once in a while?

◁ Well, I'm sure they're all different. For me, to work, I have to take time off. I have to take time off just to let my brain relax, to go with my kids, to go and hit a golf ball or play a game of tennis. But other people like to work hard. Take Amadeus Mozart, he must've written every minute of his life, otherwise he couldn't have written all that stuff and died at the age of thirty-five. So I think it affects people quite differently. I think, also, it's a question of money, too, probably, you know. A couple of hundred years ago somebody probably said 'I'll give you twenty crowns if you'll do me a little piece of music about the Thames', so Handel wrote the Water Music.

Well, he had to have it ready by Sunday because the king was going down the Thames. So there wasn't the time to take any time off, but I don't think there's any given rule about how these things work. I'm sure you will ask other people, and I'll bet they'll all have different ways of working.

▷ Is advertising a life long learning process?

◁ I was having lunch with somebody today, from one of our very large clients, Unilever. And they said "You've been in advertising so long, are you still interested?" And the answer is "Yes I am still interested". And probably the reason is because it's enabled me to meet so many interesting people, and there's always new stuff to learn, and there's always new ways to do things. And, strange enough, it gets harder and harder to do things that are new, but I am absolutely still interested.

But the great benefit, to me, it has enabled me to be able to find out anything I want about whatever I want. I suppose if I was a plumber, nothing wrong with plumbers, rather vital actually at times, but you wouldn't elicit the same information that you do. Robert Hughes came and gave a talk to us, and at the end of it my head ached; it was so intense, on art from Leonardo to Ferrari, and it was so intense, in an hour and a half, that at the end of it, my head ached. But I felt I'd been in the presence

Frank Lowe

of somebody from whom I had much to learn, and that was a great thing, you go away thinking "God, I know nothing about art. I'd better really start thinking about it." Whereas I'd gone in the room thinking "Well I know quite a bit about art", actually I knew nothing.

▷ Advertising and popular culture influence each other. What is the difference between homage and a rip-off?

◁ Oh, well I think it's very relatively simple. A lot of people today simply see pop videos and they think "I'll do that, that'll be great," without an idea. Now I remember, many, many years ago, I was doing an advertising campaign for Birds Eye, the frozen food people, and it was for a product which unfortunately was called Dinners for One (which is a rather miserable thought in itself) I mean people were slightly embarrassed, about getting a dinner for one, because it said you were not a very social person. So they did change the name to Ready to Eat Dinners, which was fine. But we had the idea, which Alan Parker shot, and which was the first of its kind, where we took the film "Brief Encounter".

Now, if you remember, at the end of Brief Encounter, where Celia Johnson goes off on the train, and Trevor Howard is left alone to walk home and he had his Dinner for One. That was a perfectly fair use of the medium, and of the story. It wasn't just a rip-off. And there is a big difference in that. The Hovis campaign, that is not a rip-off. That bread was made and cooked, originally, at that period of time, by those bakers, in those old cobbled streets. That's a homage.

And there are too many rip-offs today. And truthfully, you get a lot of rip-offs which you actually could put the name of almost any product on the bottom of. It doesn't really make any difference. Well, I think if you're borrowing from popular culture, and it is self-evident in advertising that you are borrowing from popular culture, and everybody knows what you're doing, that's fine.

I think that if you're gonna make Psycho II (though God knows why anyone would want to make Psycho II, since Psycho I seemed to me entirely adequate as a film) that isn't stealing, that's just kind of I'll make an up-to-date version, and why bother, one asks. What I hate, however, is people stealing within advertising, from other advertising they've seen before.

▷ Awards: which ones count and which ones are masturbation?

◁ I think it is always important, just as you have the Oscars in the film industry. I think it is always important, not only to honour people who try very hard to do something very special, I think that it does act as an inspiration to others. And of course, sometimes you get a film that wins all the awards, that maybe shouldn't. I mean the idea that "Titanic" would get more awards than "Gone with the Wind" is rather nauseating, actually, because nobody'll watch "Titanic"" in twenty years, but people'll watch "Gone with the Wind" in two hundred years.

But those aberrations come about, and perhaps it was a consequence of how much money they spent on Titanic, one is always slightly suspicious of that in advertising. The awards that are important are where the judges are people of quality, calibre and impartial. So there are problems, but nonetheless, I do think it is important that people are honoured, because they try so hard, and I think it sets standards, and I think it makes people try to do better work. And I'm all for anybody doing better work. Otherwise, what's the point?

▷ Eisenstein once described creativity was to bring two things together to form a third. Does that apply to the merger of Lowe and Lintas?

◁ Eisenstein, one of my serious heroes. Well, you know, we've done this merger, in a sense it was creatively a take-over. We have offices now in eighty-two countries; we have over two hundred offices. So that means that any client who comes and talks to us, and says 'Can you do our advertising all over the world?' Yes, we can.

Because Lintas was the Unilever agency, and Unilever are all over the world, and that's why it started, as you know. I believe that, with the creative reputation that the Lowe Agency has, it's going to have, and is having, more influence. And it seems to me that the Lintas clients are welcoming this. I just had lunch with Unilever, they're welcoming better work and the Lintas staff are welcoming the chance of doing better work. So, what I believe it will finish up as, is what I always dreamt of, which was a global agency with good ads, because I couldn't bear it if we didn't do good ads.

□

INTRODUCTION TO GIANT COPYWRITERS

Introduction

BY KEITH REINHARD

Chairman DDB Worldwide, New York

In the beginning was the word. (Pictures came later.) And the word became spoken, and printed, juxtapositioned against images or deftly placed a top musical notes. And the words (no matter how original) were called "copy." And those who crafted them were called "copywriters," the poets of commerce, the highest calling in advertising. A picture may be worth a thousand words, but it is those thousands of words that people find stuck in their humboxes and flowing as everyday catchphrases from their tongues – "You Deserve a Break Today," "Where's the beef?" "Whassup?" I'm well past my deadline as I sit down, finally, to write a few lines of introduction to the section of this book that celebrates copywriting. When Hermann Vaske asked me to do this piece, I quickly agreed, then found all the usual reasons to avoid actually doing it. There were e-mails to answer, phone calls to make, ceilings to stare at, windows to peer out of – dozens of distractions of my own making. After more than 40 years of writing copy in one form or another, I still shrink, as most writers do, from the numbing terror of a blank page or an empty screen. And the awesome responsibility that goes with it. To choose the right words – usually plain and simple words, then arrange them in fresh and unfamiliar ways. In order to surprise and excite, to create feeling or knowledge, to create a sale, or a brand, or a whole new category of business. To change a mind, or maybe in some small way, to change the world.

Anyone who doubts the power of words to change a life need only recall that the legendary David Abbot had no intention of entering the advertising business until he chanced to read a 1957 advertisement for El-Al Airlines written by Bob Levenson. Levenson's copy so inspired Abbot, he resolved to become a copywriter himself and went on to craft the ads and campaigns that, in turn, inspired millions more. A few years ago, at a dinner in Levenson's honor, David Abbot paid tribute to Bob and the power of words by first recalling the story and then reciting (from memory!) all 581 words from the El-Al ad that inspired his own distinguished career and so enriched the history of our business.

I was asked for advice by an aspiring young copywriter not long ago. My first suggestion was: Write. And write. And write. Every day write 300 words that convey how you feel about something you care about. Let your passion show and don't polish too much. Then show what you write to someone who likes you well enough to tell you the truth.

Be curious about everything. Eavesdrop on everybody. Develop an eye for what moves people and an ear for what resonates. Study history, philosophy, anthropology, biology, psychology, art, music, sports, drama and literature. See lots of movies, go to plays and go on hikes. Ray Bradbury describes this process as stuffing your brain with seeds. When you least expect, those seeds will sprout into wondrous things you could have never imagined.

And read. Read everything. Read six different magazines every month. Read the sports columns to develop a reporter's eye. Read critical writing for economy of language and cutting wit. Read Tom Wolfe to learn how to paint vividly with words. Read Shakespeare to learn rhythm, and James Joyce to learn how, as one critic said, "to use words like a blowtorch ... or like a violin." Read Hemingway to learn the difference between the right word and the almost right word which, as he put it, is "the difference between lightning and the lightning bug." And read about the legendary copywriters on the pages that follow.

As for me, I will try to follow my own advice. Because after all my years and all my jobs in advertising, I still aspire to live up to my very first title: Copywriter.

Keith Reinhard
May 2001

DAN WIEDEN
I'm just the writer

The advertising agency Wieden & Kennedy, and Nike-founder Phil Knight, have turned the sportswear manufacture Nike into a myth. The courageous small agency out of Portland, with reception areas in New York and Amsterdam, has produced breakthrough and attention-getting advertising since it was founded. In Cannes I talked to the creative mastermind of the agency, copywriter Dan Wieden.

▷ Hermann Vaske: Have you been on many juries?

◁ Dan Wieden: Really, working in the agency is like being on a jury every day.

▷ Interesting viewpoint.

◁ Not with a festival in mind, but with the audience in mind. We say in the agency that we would like our things to contain two elements. One is scope, there should be something in our communication that gathers as many people as possible in a relevant way. That's why we very often use real-life situations, human frailty and things like that. And the other thing is, a commercial should have depth. Once we know we have an audience, we should engage them with something other than just flat lifestyle advertising. They themselves should have to contribute something to it. Either with a humorous reaction because they recognize what they would have done in a similar situation or with sympathy, empathy, things like that. I think that's the main thing with truly good advertising – it engages people. It is impossible to remain uncommitted to what has taken place.

▷ There is something of this type of reality in the Kaurismäki brothers' films. You know what I mean?

◁ Yes, absolutely. I was once asked, why do you have so many ugly people in your commercials? Ugly people, what do you mean? Well, look at them. That's what people look like when they're not picked off fashion or model agencies catalogs.

▷ There was some controversy surrounding your Dennis Hopper commercial for Nike. How did that come about?

◁ It's for a line of cross-training shoes for Nike that are based on football cleats. The creative team looked for somebody that is a type of football fan. And Dennis Hopper plays a sort of a crazed ex-ref.

▷ Is creating controversial advertising one of the ingredients of Nike advertising?

◁ It seems to be a by-product. It wasn't something it set out to be. It becomes part of it. Making a commercial is not about being safe or acceptable, but being provocative. It's a lot easier being provocative when it's not your money.

▷ Exactly.

◁ That's why good plans are so valuable, plans that have courage are very rare.

▷ If you look back in Nike history, what was the most shocking thing that happened in this very long relationship with the client?

◁ You mean in terms of ads?

▷ Yes.

◁ Yes, probably the Revolution spot with the Beatles.

▷ The black and white one. I remember that.

◁ At the time it was a very new and controversial technique, even a point in history where Nike had lost their number one ranking behind Reebok. They came out with a great product and they were bankrolling everything on this product and this commercial. They allowed you to shoot a commercial before. There was a lot of risk taken at a critical point in time and it worked.

▷ But it basically came to the conclusion that nothing can be accomplished without taking risk.

◁ Yes, I would think that's true.

▷ That's also one of the components of the Nike advertisements.

◁ That doesn't mean that risk always works either. Sometimes you have a failure if you're taking a risk, it's just part of the game. You just hope that there is enough attention being paid, that you win more than you lose.

▷ Michael Prieve, your creative director, told me that one of the interesting things about your company is the corporate culture. How would you describe it?

◁ It's a little hard for me to describe it accurately because it's a little like talking about your family. You are so much a part of it that you can't see it objectively. It's a very close but very explosive, very emotional group of people, very talented. There's a lot of freedom. The reason for the kind of freedom is, because everybody there is just pushing themselves more than anybody else could push them.

▷ Michael said that some of the interesting things about it is that you and Mr. Kennedy allowed people to basically be themselves.
◁ Yes.

▷ Another thing he was saying was that you were somebody who was always good with swear-words. He said that you and your partner said that, "well, if that's him and he's good at this then just let him be himself. Just let him do it." What he summed up as the Nike slogan: Just do it.
◁ I think generally most creative people will create their own rules for themselves. And that's how they have to be judged. That's what they have to be held accountable to. It's not something that should lay on top of them, but something that comes from within them. Everyone does it, I believe. A discipline is inherent, it may be different to the next fellow's, or the next woman's. The important thing is to find out for yourself, to find out what works for you. And be held accountable for it, but also be allowed freedom.

▷ Instead of showing off all the awards you have won, the reception of your offices in Portland and Amsterdam shows pictures of the people working there. I think that also says a lot about the company and the people that run the company.
◁ I think the awards are interesting, but they're not the reason for people to do what they do. It's the process that is far more fascinating than the results of the process. If you get obsessed about awards you end up buying the right to create ads to win awards. It's, like, ludicrous.

▷ You mean it becomes like masturbation?
◁ It becomes very inward-looking. When I first met Phil Knight, when we first started working with Nike, he made it very clear that he hated advertising; and when Kennedy and I started creating ads we kept running into roadblocks about what we thought were great pieces of ad crap. They were rejected out of hand as being phoney. And what we learned slowly over time was to quit talking to other writers or art directors or creative directors and not write ads for judges at Cannes. But to write for tennis players or basketball players or runners.

▷ That should be the motivation.
◁ Because otherwise the real people you're writing to are just listening in to you talking to your buddies and not talking to them. That's pretty

Nike by
Wieden & Kennedy

much not the point. I thought it was really interesting if you look at the work that won all the medals, it must have been 90% of it was humorous purpose, it was joke after joke after joke. Nothing against humour, obviously one of ours that won was a humorous spot full of self-irony. But it was just astonishing, like a stand-up convention or something.

▷ Do you think this is becoming a trend?

◁ Well, no. I think it seems so to me, and I am not much of a scholar of advertising, but it seems to me that each award show has it's own sort of slant. Like, there is a certain kind of ad, a sensibility, that tends to dominate. So I don't know whether it's the international nature of humour that seems to bridge gaps easier than other things or whether it's just the dynamics of the location or the group of people that get together that reenforces. By the way, did you notice that both of the commercials that won here were not entered by us but by the production companies?

▷ Would you have entered if they hadn't sent them?

◁ I don't know. We produce, especially for Nike, such an amount of commercials, you enter what you think is your best work. Luckily, production companies have a different view of that.

▷ I once did an interview with George Lois years ago and he said whoever enters work at an award show is a fucking fool...George is quite an intense person.

◁ Oh my god, I've heard stories.

▷ You seem to be more of a laid-back type of person. Is that the West Coast mentality?

◁ It's West Coast mentality and jet lag. Actually the intensity is usually focused around the day-to-day work. That provides the energy, the adrenaline to the agency. It doesn't make any sense for me to try and top that. I have to provide some kind of centre.

▷ Do you have sport facilities in your agency?

◁ We took out the ceiling in part of the building and put in a basketball court.

▷ How do you like Portland?

◁ It's a very pretty little city. It's very human in scale. That's what I like about it.

▷ It even has a film festival.

◁ Yeah, the international film festival. In fact some fellows, Steve Sandoz and Warren Eakins, who worked for us, produced a commercial for the Festival that won a Lion in Cannes.

▷ You said that when you met Mr. Knight he hated advertising. Does he still hate advertising basically?

◁ I brought him around and he brought me around. I think he found that it's a fundamental engine to his business now. The debate would be whether what we do is advertising. I suspect that it is probably closer to advertising than I would want it to be.

▷ Could you explain that?

◁ I like to think of our advertising as being a lot more unconventional than I'm afraid it is.

▷ Why unconventional?

◁ It is more conventional than I wish it were.

▷ What about new and unconventional means to reach target audiences? I'm thinking of superhighways and interactive.

◁ I think that's a really interesting issue because in some ways it may provide the impetus to re-think what it is we are all about, what is advertising, what is an advertising agency, what services does it provide? To really get at the heart of the problem we've got today, which is how to talk to people in a way that is meaningful. The change has to come from a basic motivation of what you're trying to do, whether you're trying to manipulate or whether you're trying to share information. That's a fundamental issue for the industry.

▷ That's basically the difference between descriptive communication or propaganda.

◁ The larger the industry has become the bigger the amount of money that's on the table. Once one's market share point starts equalling millions and millions of dollars, people tighten up and suddenly it's about not losing money. So there is all this research and all this testing based upon buying and manipulating, making sure things happen and not letting things happen with things you introduce to the market. The problem is that after a while, people you are theoretically trying to manipulate get wise to that whole thing, they don't play the game the way they're supposed to, and you've broken their trust and destroyed the idea of a brand. I think that whole line of approach is sort of running into a dead end right now. Nobody really knows what to do about it.

▷ How do you cope with it?

◁ What we're just trying to do is probably best shown by the work with products that need to be pushed. We have the same sense of urgency that every other agency has with their client, but when we sit down and do the actual piece of communication we put that aside for a moment and generally get excited about what it is that we have to say. And most of the staff are sports nuts, very enthusiastic. So their sense of humour or their sense of awe or whatever it is, is really critical in communication and they just share that joy and that emotional connection with that sport, with the audience. But, it's not necessarily about the shoe, it's

Nike by
Wieden & Kennedy

often about the emotion or about the spot of insight somebody always has in that sport. If you're honest in that way you do build a brand and you do work that creates longer – lasting relationships with your customers than if you're basically trumpeting the latest technological gimmick. In many ways I think that Nike's relationship with their customers is an on-going dialog. You may say the same thing over and over, but you say it in a way that is different, refreshing.

▷ Why are you creative? What drives you?

◁ Quite honestly, what drives me has actually nothing to do with me. It has to do with other people that I worked with. A long time ago, when David and I first started the agency, we were, like, maybe 12, 13 people, it must have been about 11:30 at night and I had fallen asleep listening to some voice tapes and I woke up and I had this existential crisis about why the hell am I doing this. I have a family, I have four kids that don't see me enough. We invested whatever money we had in buying typewriters, chairs and nonsense. And it's the most insecure business you could ever possibly wanna go into. It's sucking up all my time and what's the point of it? It's very funny, because almost instantaneously I had this understanding that this had nothing to do with me or with David. It had to do with creating a place where people could come and live up to their potential. Where the bullshit of the business was held to a minimum and where our work would come first and affect the marketplace. So that's sort of the reason I'm doing it, it is still working, people still find the agency a healthy place to work. It's basically my job to make sure it stays that way.

▷ That's an interesting story you just recalled. Can you put that in a picture?

◁ Kennedy is the art director. I'm just the writer.

▷ If you were to describe yourself, what attributes would you give yourself?

◁ Although I'm over 50 I'm very naïve. I'm very illiterate about the industry I operate in. I'm an obsessively curious person. And, I would suspect, a compassionate person.

▷ Could you give an example of you being a curious person?

◁ One of the things most curious to me is how organisations grow and grow, people inter-relate and how people can remain powerful inside of larger organizations. I've just read this fascinating book, called "Leadership and New Sciences." It's about social organizations, business organizations and how they relate to the developments and the discoveries in quantum physics. So I am also curious about how the business itself works, how agencies relate to clients and how clients go about making

Dan Wieden

34

things. I spent a year and a half of my early life writing about toilet paper with Georgia Pacific. I suppose if you can be curious about toilet paper for a year and a half you can be curious about anything.

▷ Seems to be like a civil service in advertising. Was it like direct marketing?

◁ No, I was inside the company. So I was writing sales promotion pieces. I'm not sure if I was actually curious for a year and a half, but I tried.

▷ So now you're a real expert on the quality of toilet paper?

◁ Yes, basically the world can be divided into two kinds of people: folders and wadders. And the wadders are best because they use a lot of toilet paper.

□

DAVE TROTT
Postmodern advertising is bollocks

The British press once compared advertising by Dave Trott to a brick flying through the consumer's window with the client's name attached to it. Trott's style is different to most English advertising because, in the late 60's, he studied advertising at New York's Pratt Institute. On his return to England in 1971, he started to work as a copywriter for Boase Massimi Politt in London. Ten years later, he left that agency to found his own: Gold Greenless Trott. During that decade it was voted 'Agency of the Year' by London's Campaign magazine, and 'Most Creative Agency in the World' by Ad Age magazine in New York. In 1990, he founded Bainsfair Sharkey Trott, which he says was 'a total disaster'. 4 years later he opened his current agency: Walsh Trott Chick Smith, where he's much happier. I interviewed Dave Trott in London and Berlin.

▷ Hermann Vaske: Is advertising art?

◁ Dave Trott: Well, it's probably not something you can call pure art with a capital "A". It's more like applied art. Like you've got pure math and applied math. So I think you get guys, like the painters and sculptors, and nobody has ever given them a brief. They just do what pleases them. Similar to pure math, where people experiment with new thoughts just for the sake of it, just to discover things, not to do anything with them. But then they put it into the field and the applied mathematicians come up and find ways to use it for practical purposes. So you've got pure art, which is people like sculptors and painters who don't have a brief, they make just what pleases them. And then, once they've come up with it, that's the end of the process as far as they're concerned. I mean, there was no reason why they created it for an art gallery, because there didn't have to be a reason in an art gallery. And then you have got people like me, who would be more like applied artists who work to a brief. You use things to an end rather than just experimenting.

▷ Does a brief need a USP? Or does the product need a USP?

◁ As you know, USP stands for "unique selling proposition", and the two important words there are "unique" and "selling". It is easy to find out if a product is unique. The name of the product doesn't matter. If I go to a store and ask for the product that does X, and if there is only one product they can give me, it's unique. The other important word is "selling". The product may be unique, but does anybody want to buy it? So you have to check that your supposed USP is both unique and selling. If it genuinely is, then a unique selling proposition is the best thing you can have. If you haven't got that, you have to do branding. You have to separate yourself from everybody else somehow. And it's either USP or branding. If you don't do

Everyone's got a favourite Abba song.

either of those, what you do is just entertainment: a nice piece of film with someone's name on the end. It may be a nice piece of film, but it isn't advertising. What they call "postmodern advertising" at the moment is based on the premise that all products are like all other products, so the only difference is the advertising. We are now no longer selling the product, we're selling the advertising. Postmodern advertising is bollocks. If you don't have a genuine USP, absolutely the first thing you must do is make the people remember who ran the ad. If you can't do that then you haven't done your job. Because if they can't remember who it was for, then what does it matter whether they like it or not? I think of sports shoe advertising at the moment. Nike became very successful just by advertising sports. So, everybody else thought "Nike became number one just by advertising sport. We must copy Nike." So now they all do sports advertising. But Nike is number one, and it's okay for them to grow the market by just doing sports advertising. Now the rest is copying Nike, and you can't tell a Reebok ad from an Adidas ad from a Puma ad. And all that they do is just grow the market for sport, and Nike picks up more sales. Because, if you don't change the dynamics of the market, you contribute to maintaining the status quo, and only the brand leader benefits. Nobody is actually telling you, which is, "Hang on, don't buy Nike, buy our brand".

▷ Speaking from your personal experience, what are some of the differences between British and Americans advertising?

◁ Well, I was taught in New York, and most English advertising people were taught in England. In England, "selling" is a dirty word, in New York it isn't. In New York it's right up there with being a doctor. People aren't embarrassed about selling in America the way they are in England. Consequently, there is much more openness, there is much less sneakiness about selling in America, much less embarrassment about pretending this isn't an advert, this is a piece of entertainment, like an ad in England. What is there is open. I'm going to sell you and as I talk to sell you, I'll leave an opinion. But your starting point is that I've got something to sell you, and I think after I tell you the facts, you'll have to buy it. That's the starting point in America. But if I tell you the facts in a boring way, you won't remember them. So I'll tell you the facts in an interesting way and you'll remember. That's not the way it works in England, it works the other way round. You aren't going to buy it anyway, so that's why I am going to simply concentrate on entertaining you, and just sign off with my product's name. At least I'll have good tracking statistics and everybody will remember the ad. They won't remember what it's for, but they will remember the ad. And, even if it doesn't do anything for the client, maybe it'll win an award and make the agency look good. And what people in England do because they are ashamed of selling, all they do is technique. Now I think they do technique superbly well. But what they make is lovely pieces of film. What they don't make is adverts. In the States, if you're going to sell something, you say "Here is this object and here is this object, they are identical, except this one is fifty percent cheaper. Which looks better to you?" That should be your starting point. Then, what you add to that is your personal creativity. But what they do in England is, they never get that far, they just think straight into the creativity and what happens is you've got a lovely little film with no sales point. Now what P&G do, on the other hand, is they stop at the sales message and never get to the creativity. They stop at the side by side demo, or the before-and-after, whatever it is, you know.

▷ Is there a before and after concept you like? Or which is very effective?

◁ The Hamlet campaign I used to love a lot, that was before and after. Because that came out of a real life situation. You know, the "Happiness is a cigar called Hamlet" where you get someone in a disastrous situation and there is nothing that you can do, so they'd smoke a Hamlet and at least they'd cheer up little bit. It has a very boring brief, but the ads that were written were absolutely superb. And you couldn't have written them without the premise of why you buy the product.

▷ It's sort of a drug-like promise, isn't it?

◁ Yes, it's what came out of research. People were asked, "Why do you smoke cigars?" And they said, "Well, you know, whenever anything goes

WHAT LINE DO YOU TAKE ON EUTHANASIA ?

IT'S MY RIGHT.   **I'VE CHANGED MY...**

talk
radio
1089am / medium wave
THERE'S A GOOD ARGUMENT FOR LISTENING.

wrong, you light a cigar, you relax and suddenly things don't look so bad." And this is the premise with which you start your advertising which is when the creativity kicks in, and now you can go as wild as you want and know that you're hanging off a really good proposition as the selling proposition rather than merely an entertainment proposition.

▷ So, Freud is wrong and right at the same time: "A cigar is not just a cigar."

◁ No, the quote actually said, "Sometimes a cigar is just a cigar." I thought it's great, that's the way it came from Freud.

▷ What was the selling idea of the Toshiba campaign?

◁ Toshiba was a great case where everybody at that time was doing better technology for pictures. Sony owned the market at that time because of Trinitron. And everybody else was doing better pictures. Because that's what Sony did. They were the market leader, and it's not much of an advertising idea to say, "Let's copy the market leader," although that is what happens most of the time. The basic idea behind this is, when the market leader is doing it, it must be right. What we did instead was ask ourselves what would make people buy a TV on a Saturday morning in Dixons? People had 200 quid in their pocket, or 300 quid, and they come along and they say to the salesman, "What is the biggest telly I can get for 300 quid?" They don't say, "What's the best technology?" So he says, "Well, these three tellies." Well, two of those don't match with our furniture. They're dark wood and our furniture is light wood. So, let's forget the dark wood tellies and stick with a light wood telly. Up to this point the TV is a piece of furniture, not a piece of technology. Now, what you come down to is, of these three tellies that we're left with, which ones have we heard of? "Well, Sony, I've heard of that. Hitachi, I've heard of that. But what's this one: Makamichi, Sanyo, whatever? I never heard of that, so the company might not be around next week, so rule them out. And now

HOW DO YOU SEE GERRY ADAMS...

STATESMAN ?　　　　　　　　　**TERRORIST ?**

talk radio
1089am / medium wave

THERE'S A GOOD ARGUMENT FOR LISTENING.

we're down to two, let's turn them on and see what the picture is like."
And at that point, technology is important. But not until that point. And
so we looked at the whole process of where we could affect the purchasing
decision. And what it was, it wasn't due to technology – we can't make
our picture look better than the other one, everybody judges completely
differently. And some people like their colours as bright as neon. We
couldn't affect how they made the TV sets, whether they had dark wood
cabinets, you know, light wood cabinets or whatever. All we could affect
was "Have you heard of this make of telly?" So we had a six week stretch
of commercials, and at that point we needed to make the name so
famous, so talked about, just the name. That was all advertising could do.
The problem was, how do you get the name of Toshiba into the English
language? It's just another Japanese name like Sensui, Sanyo, Mitsubishi,
they're all just Japanese names. There is no English side to it. Now, in
English, tosh is just a name that your uncle calls you when you're a little
boy, it's just a friendly name. So we take Toshiba and we make it Tosh:
"Hello tosh, gotta Toshiba." Then, in order to make it modern and high-tech,
we made it a blueprint. This blueprint character comes on and talks
about it, but people thought that was a little cold, so in order to make
it more friendly, we got Ian Dury's voice which is cockney, and that's a nice
counterpoint to the high-tech blueprint. Because you think if the blueprint is going to talk, it'll talk like a robot. But if you have a Cockney talk,
"ello", it's quite another matter. So that was kind of how we did it.
Within six weeks, they had gotten the same awareness as Sony, and at
the moment they are joint number one in TV with Sony. By value, not by
volume. Because they are at the top of the market. So they don't sell as
many tellies as Sony, but they sell them for more money. So they now
make as much money in TV as Sony.

▷ As for print ads. What's more important, the word or the picture?

Talk Radio

◁ As I understand it, the look of a page is what makes you stop at it. What the headline actually says is what makes you read it. So the look , if it's a functional look, of course the look is more important. If it's just decorative, non-functional, just following the current fashion − then I think it's not important at all. If you've got a good line, then that's going to be more important than the art direction. But if you've got a brilliant visual, you almost don't need a headline. Remember that pregnant man ad that Charlie Saatchi did, do you remember that? It almost didn't need a headline. Just the shot of a man, pregnant. Now take another of his ads "What happens when a fly ends up on your food? First, it's on your food, it sucks it up, then it defecates back on your food. Then, when the fly is finished, it's your turn." You don't even need a picture for that.

▷ What do you think of celebrity advertising?

◁ I think it's lazy. I think it's all very lazy. It's money instead of thought. It's very reassuring to get a celebrity. It's reassuring to do a million pound commercial. And it's all lazy. I don't think a lot of it works. I think it works where you've got an idea. If you haven't got an idea, if all you have is a celebrity, then it doesn't work. If you take any of the commercials around on British TV at the moment, it's all just "Grab a celebrity and stuff it in a commercial." And what you do is you sell the celebrity, not the product.

▷ What about the way Hollywood is marketing films? Isn't it cultural imperialism, when you have things like Rambo in every Third World country? Is Hollywood just another brand that these countries are force-fed, as with McDonald's and Coke?

◁ I don't see what's the problem. You've got that, and that links everybody internationally, and then you've got local differences. You know, I don't have a problem with that. Yes, everybody has McDonald's everywhere. So what's the problem? It's food, everybody can eat. You can do films that everybody can watch, I don't have a problem with that. And then you've got local differences. The global stuff doesn't preclude the local stuff. You've got an international conduit like in a lot of Hilton hotels. And if you're the kind of person that wants to go and stay in a Hilton hotel, you'll never see the local colour. You're not going to say every little village in Africa has a McDonald's. I think they are in the big cities and I don't have a problem with that. You know the kids can go there, the kids can eat what they are happy with. And I think that's pretty good. We've got global stuff which links everybody and then you've got local stuff which is different. My wife speaks English but she's Chinese. And when she sees her family, they speak Chinese together. But in Singapore, where she's from, they pick English as their language because it's the most widely spoken language in the world. If a German airliner flies over Japan, the

Dave Trott

pilot talks to ground control in English. Would it be better if the pilot spoke German and the ground control spoke Japanese? Of course not. Going to a foreign country, you know there'll be a couple of things that you recognise and that you can cope with. And then, if you want to explore more, there'll be the country itself and the foreigners. And otherwise, if you just have the foreigners, then you put ordinary people off travelling. And, except for backpackers and stuff like that, the families can't do that. I see the good effects of a lot of that stuff, of tying the world together. And that is not to say making it all the same. It's giving it more accessibility. And it's the same with Hollywood movies, you know. There's a common thread that we can all link on, and there's the local differences. America is global. That doesn't necessarily mean they dominate everything and they are out to own everything. But I think it brings the world closer together in terms of having links with each other, the English language for one. And it's not because of England that the world is linked by the English language, it's because of America and Hollywood.

▷ What about the common thread that is religion?

◁ I think religion is superstition. If you listen to all the great men, religion is what happens when a great thinker dies and the civil service takes over. The classic illustration of that was Buddha. Buddha was a Hindu the way Christ was born a Jew. Buddha was born a Hindu, and eventually, because of the course of his life, he realised what Lenin says, that religion is the opium of the masses. It's like "Knock on wood, then I'm safe." I don't want to think. If I go by superstitions, I don't have to think. And Buddha said, "You worship all these little gold idols, the little pieces of wood, the little statues, and it's actually keeping you enslaved. You're not thinking, you're not using your brains, you're just worshipping these little pieces of wood. Stop it, destroy them, think for yourself. Free yourself." So they built wooden Buddhas and put them on altars and worshipped them. Don't you think they kind of missed the point of what the guy was saying? And that's kind of where religion is at. Religion is probably the exact opposite almost of what the guy that you're supposed to be worshipping is saying. You take Jesus, you take Mohammed, Buddha, what they were all saying was "Free yourself, don't worship something, free yourself." So what you then do is you worship them. That's where religion is at.

▷ How come there are still so relatively few women in advertising?

◁ You know what's interesting, my partner here, Amanda Walsh, is the managing director, and she was talking about why you don't get many women in the creative departments. It's about 5% only. I was thinking about it, and I was saying to her, "You know in this agency we've got 50%

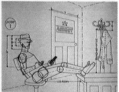

One of Trott's commercials for Toshiba

to 60% females, and they are in TV production and account handling and press production. And you get women in planning, too. You do get fewer women in the creative department." And the lazy way to think about that is that it's because men don't want women in the creative department. I don't think this is the truth. I think if you look at the way mens' and womens' heads function, women are more about responsibility and men are much more about play. If you've got children, you can watch that from the time they're born. Women are about responsibility and men are about play. And so women naturally gravitate to the areas where we cannot take a chance on things going wrong, like account handling, like TV production, like press production, like planning, areas of serious responsibility. Men gravitate more to the areas of just play. The creative department. You know, you don't think up exciting ideas by being responsible. You think up exciting ideas by being silly and thinking, "What is the most outrageous thing we can do?" That's not a thing a woman would say. A woman would say, "it's got to be there by this time. And it has to have covered all these points on the brief. And we mustn't go over budget." That's what a woman would say. That's why women are in those positions of serious responsibility, whereas men are in the position of play like "What can we do just to create a lot of outrage?" I don't think it's anything of a conspiracy to keep women out of the creative department. I think women are too responsible, too sensible for the creative department. And the creative department should be the antithesis of responsibility. And that's why you need responsible people in account handling, to allow the creative department to be irresponsible.

▷ Why are you creative?

◁ The only difference between a creative person and anybody else is, everybody has the same idea, everybody has lots of good ideas, but a creative person does it. And that's the only difference. You know, anyone can say "Let's stick a real shark in a giant tank of formaldehyde." There's nothing especially brilliant in an idea like that, anyone could have done it, loads of people probably have. But then they thought of some reasons why it wouldn't work, or else they just couldn't be bothered. At least 1,000 people will have the same idea, 999 of them won't take it any further, the one that actually does it will be seen as a creative. Webster's Dictionary defines being creative as "Bringing into being something that didn't previously exist." And that's all there is to it. And someone said to Damien Hirst in a recent interview, "Your pictures and things, I could have done that." And Damien Hirst said, "Yes, but you didn't, did you?"

And that's exactly all there is to it. A creative person does it and everybody else talks about it, thinks about it but doesn't do it.

□

I couldn´t rely on being a sweet kid

After he graduated as top student from the Australian Writers & Art Directors School in 1987, David's assault on the Australian ad industry was immediate. He joined OMON (a new agency) and so began his career as a writer. His very first TV commercial received a D&AD silver nomination and a bag of Australian awards. .

In 93 he was promoted to joint creative director (at 23, he was Australia's youngest CD). The following year the agency was named "Australian Agency of the Year."

In mid 1996, he was appointed Executive Creative Director of Saatchi & Saatchi Singapore, and Regional Creative Director of S&S Asia. Still only 27, he was forced to tell some clients he was older. As time went by his Singapore office has gone from strength to strength, dominating every award show and competitor in sight.

And consequently Saatchi & Saatchi Singapore was named the "Ad Age International Agency of the Year." Soon Droga was appointed Executive Creative Director of Saatchi & Saatchi London. I interviewed David Droga several times, in Cannes and London.

▷ Hermann Vaske: So David, what's the rush?
◁ David Droga: I guess I'm just trying to keep up with my own expectations. I mean, why the hell do anything at someone else's pace? And that's what's so brilliant about any creative industry, your success isn't restricted by age, rules or regulations. Nothing is or can be predetermined; it's all about what works. Fortunately, at the end of the day it does just come down to talent and commitment. I'm one of seven children, so I was born into a competitive environment. From day one it was about standing out from my brothers and sisters. I couldn't rely on being a sweet kid. I had to think laterally to get attention, and I guess that's what advertising is all about. So I don't think of myself as a person in a hurry, just as someone who doesn't like to waste time.

▷ So who or what is your creative god?
◁ Well, assuming I've interpreted your question the right way, I would have to say inspiration is my creative god. It's such a precious and sought-after commodity. I mean we look for true inspiration everywhere and in everything we do. Walking down the street, at the cinema, from our loved ones, at art galleries and, more often than not, at midnight staring into a blank layout pad.

You could say that when you are inspired it's kind of divine. Yet how often are we really inspired? It can become an addiction. I know that's

Stills from Droga's
Toyota commercial

what drives me. The constant search. I don't know if that actually answers your question. I think it might.

▷ If so, then what inspires you David?

◁ Well, where do you start on that one? I'd say emotion is what inspires me the most. All types of emotions, good and bad. After all, emotion defines a moment. But I guess that's too easy a response. It's hard to list things that inspire me, because it's usually things you can't predict that are the most inspiring.

▷ Can advertising inspire?

◁ Absolutely. Isn't that what clients are paying us for? Ads have such potent potential. They can redefine a product or help elect a government. I honestly believe we underestimate its power. But the sad reality is that most ads produced aren't inspiring at all. It's just the client and agency going through the motions. They lack originality and genuine creativity. However, every so often I see something that rekindles my faith. And usually they are the simplest ideas of all. Simple, relevant and unique.

▷ Well, here we are in Cannes. Do you think awards are an evil or good for the industry?

◁ I think awards are definitely a necessary evil. It's important we recognize and celebrate the individuals who push this business along. However, the big question is which awards show. I mean there are definitely too many award shows. And some are nothing more than direct marketing companies. You know, you spend half your money, and instead of sending you back a gift they mail you an award. It's actually kind of pathetic that certain award shows attract entries. But I guess some agencies will only enter the ones they know they can win. It sort of defeats the purpose a little. If my house was full of trophies from school athletics races, I could hardly claim to be a world class athlete. Personally, I try and only enter a few major awards. Obviously Cannes or I wouldn't be enjoying your company today. The One Show, D&AD and the Clios. These are probably the main ones. But then again, even those awards have a different value against one another. But, at the end of the day, awards shows should be for inspiration, not your sole motivation. We have to be careful we don't get caught up too much in our own hype. I remember while judging the Clios this year, one particular incident helped put everything into proportion for me. During one of our frequent coffee breaks I decided to sneak up to my room to make a few calls. As I entered the elevator I was greeted by a large group of people participating in another convention within the same hotel. I could tell by the identity badges they were all wearing. Similar to the one I had clipped to my chest. As it turned out they had all gathered for an international symposium on bathrooms. Seriously. Anyway, as I stood

Dave Droga

48

Droga's campaign
for the MTV program
"Jackass"

silently in the lift I couldn't help but overhear their conversation. They were talking about bathrooms, Italian tiles and vanity mirrors with as much passion and vigor as any advertising judge I'd ever heard. That's how we must sound to the average punter. Scary, isn't it?

▷ Saatchi & Saatchi Singapore were voted "Ad Age International Agency of the Year" and you won many Lions in Cannes. How did you feel about that?

◁ Great. Winning the "International Agency of the Year" award was definitely the highlight. Because it's about more than just one or two good campaigns. It's about what the agency stands for. Doing good work for every client. Not just the small entrepreneurial clients but also the large, more conservative ones as well. A lot of agencies spend their time trying to write ads for only a small percentage of their clients. My objective has been to try and do it for all our clients. Although we still have many battles ahead, I'm proudest of the work we've produced for our biggest brands. BBH London won it, so I needn't tell you how thrilled people were even to have got on the bandwagon. I guess that answers your question about inspiration. As for the Lions, well naturally that's a bonus. In fact there are eight creative teams in our Singapore office, and every single team has won at least one Cannes Lion in the last two years. If every client can be pushed, so can every creative team. It's not about having one star team. It's about building an expectation and contagious momentum within the office.

▷ So if you were to walk down to the beach and find your creative dept dancing around and worshipping a large Golden Lion, what would you do?

◁ Damn, I'd not only tell them to get a life, I'd inform them that they are probably missing the Young Creative's party further down the beach.

▷ How do you think advertising in Asia compares to that in other parts of the world?

◁ I imagine there are more simularities than differences. The same emotions and factors usually motivate people from all walks of life. Love, religion, money, family, opportunity and an overwhelming desire to improve oneself. But how that is conveyed varies from country to country and culture. Asia is such a magnificently diverse region. Outside of Singapore Thailand's ad industry is perhaps the most admired in the region. Not because it wins at global award shows but because they have forged such an incredibly strong identity of their own. Sure, I don't find all their ads funny, but then that's not the point, is it? And then you have places like Vietnam, where advertising is still considered by many as Western propaganda. Hong Kong on the other hand is one of the most mature ad industries of all. They have a style of ads unlike any of their neighbors. Almost every TV ad produced in Hong Kong carries a deep and philosophical message.

▷ So what is the future of advertising in Asia?

◁ You just said it. Asia is the future of advertising. Not yet, maybe not even for quite a while, but with the current growth rate and increase of local talents, it's destined to forge ahead. I mean, you're talking about a region that contains almost two thirds of the world's population. Now that's a hell of a lot of consumers. Which means expats like myself will become less and less relevant.

▷ So, David Droga, why are you creative?

◁ Maybe because I grew up in the mountains of Australia. So I had to use my imagination to entertain myself. Or maybe just because it beats having a day job.

□

CLIFF FREEMAN
Self-irony can be very winning

No one has sold as much fast food as Cliff Freeman. Zillions of pizzas and hamburgers have been consumed due to his efforts. But his commercials for Wendy's or Little Caesar's are anything but advertising's equivalent to fast food - they have become milestones in the history of advertising. There is something about his work that stays true to the great Bernbach revolution of the 60´s. When everyone else is obsessed with style for its own sake, Freeman´s is advertising that gets into the language. It´s self-confident enough to be self-deprecating, this makes it simultaneously intrusive, memorable and appealing. His work has such a quintessentially American style, it has creatives all over Europe saying "Why can´t we do work as funny over here?" I interviewed Cliff Freeman in New York.

▷ Hermann Vaske: Why are you creative?
◁ Cliff Freeman: Luck. I was lucky...lucky to be born with certain abilities.
▷ Also with the ability to fill out your timesheets?
◁ Yes. I have filled out my timesheets. If I don't, I have no idea what I worked on.
▷ Mr. Freeman, the spots for Little Caesar's have long been gems of American humour. What's the story behind that campaign?
◁ Well, you know, pizza is a fun product. Everyone sits around and eats pizza together, so you've got to have fun for it when you advertise it, you certainly can't treat this seriously. I mean everybody in this category tries humour of a sort, but not always successfully. But humour's a kind of staple in the fast food industry, and of course it is something we do a lot. When we first got the business, we did a lot of very competitive commercials against mainly Pizza Hut. And I think when you're slamming the competition people find it kind of hard to take unless you do it in a way that is really fun. Then they are able to accept it. Americans really are not totally receptive to dumping the competition unless it's done in a certain way. So we started to do this fun thing due to the competitive nature of these early commercials and, you know, people seemed to like it, so we just kept it up.
▷ Does humour have to do with the unexpected and the surprising?
◁ Absolutely, yeah. I think one of the keys is having something happen that the audience does not expect, When that little bitty woman opened her mouth and out came that gruff "Where's the beef?" that is something that took the audience totally by surprise.
▷ You were on this famous spot for Wendy's?
◁ Yes. On that and the Russian Fashion Show. That whole series directed by Joe Sedelmaier.

Stills from Freeman's "Where's the beef" commercial for Wendy's

▷ So you're the one who wrote that famous line?

◁ Yeah.

▷ It's one of the best lines in the history of advertising.

◁ Big stroke of luck, I'd say. A lot of things coming together. But you know I had a dinner speech on Friday night and it's interesting. That commerical was shown on a reel with fifteen other commercials we did, and it does not get the laughs the other commercials do. I mean, I look at it now and it does not seem all that funny to me, but at the time it was tremendous.

▷ What made you think of this line? Did you go to hamburger places where you got cheated in terms of meat quantity, or what?

◁ Actually the account guys came up with the strategy. At the time Wendy's had a product called the Single, you know, one patty of beef, and it actually was more beef than McDonald's Big Mac or Burger King's Whopper. These just sounded big but in fact they had less beef than this Wendy's thing modestly called a Single. And that was just the strategy and the whole idea of the big bun and that is just something that I dreamed up.

▷ For Little Caesar's you dreamed up the idea of the pizza cooks trying to consumers into believing that they to offered two pizzas for the price of one.

◁ Yes, it was basically the old idea of the flimflam man, the con man, a very American idea with some rich comedy stuff to draw from.

▷ Have you ever been the victim of a con man?

◁ Na, not really, but it is a typically American genre. When you think of the Candid Camera shows. There was this great bit where they took the motor completely out of the car and they coasted it into a service station and asked, "Could you check my oil?" And the mechanic comes back and says, "You don't have a motor in there." And the customer goes, "What do you mean, I don't have a motor? I just drove here." I mean this is a very American way of dealing with these absurd situations, nobody overreacts, everybody stays very polite while they're doing this stuff. So that is the tenor behind these Little Caesar's spots you're talking about.

▷ Is advertising the fine art of separating people from their money?

◁ I guess it is. It sounds bad but I think it probably is. There are very few things you absolutely need. I guess you need shelter and you need food and you need love ... but you don't need a lot of things that we sell. But they're part of what makes life worth living, I suppose.

▷ Is self-irony an ingredient for good humour in commercials?

◁ I think if you've got what might be thought of as something negative about a product, that you can sort of take lightly or make fun of, not taking yourself seriously and being honest about your shortcomings then – again a very American thing – consumers find that very appealing. Self-irony can be very winning. You know, many of the movie stars have this kind of personality, it can be very charming that self-deprecating kind of thing.

▷ What do you think about using celebrities to sell products? Does Hollywood sell?

◁ I think they do if you use them right. You see, celebrities represent something to people. They represent certain character traits. You know, they're friendly, they're grouchy, they're cute... they're, you know, like your nextdoor neighbor, they're like some stuffy rich guy, etc. So if you use them in a way people perceive them to be, and you use them naturally with the product, it can work out very well. But quite often, they're not used that well.

▷ What do you think of your competitor Pizza Hut's commercial that starred Anthony Quinn?

◁ Er, you know, I don't like to critique other people's work particularly. I think it's a pretty tough business to be in and, you know, I don't know what the Pizza Hut client is like, so...

▷ What about Anthony Quinn as an actor?

◁ Well, what about him? He was great as Zorba the Greek, I don't know about pizza sales. Anyway, we also did something with celebrities for Little Caesar's but we did the reverse, we took old, you know, has-been celebrities that would work basically for nothing. We used them to demonstrate that since we charge so little for the pizza we had no money left over for expensive celebrities, so we just went for the cheap guys.

▷ So who did you use?

◁ We had Evil Knievel, the motorcycle guy who was a celebrity in the 70s. And we had this guy who played little Eddie Munster in "The Munsters," you know that was his claim to fame in his whole life, so we had him dressed up like little Eddie – he"s in his late thirties now, so that was kind of funny.

▷ With the walls between the disciplines breaking down, with feature film directors making commercials etc, do you find it easier to get celebrities to work in commercials?

◁ I remember when I started I once wrote a jingle and I called up Neil Diamond to see if he would do the lead, this was in the seventies, and he was disgusted and appalled that I would even suggest such a thing. But boy, you know, times have changed and I think people are probably more realistic about life now than they used to be because life is a little bit more precarious, things are not as easy anymore and if you can make a

buck doing something, you think, "OK, what the hell."

▷ You did an enormously successful campaign for Prodigy, an online service. The director on that was Tony Kaye. How did you find working with him?

◁ It was a great, great experience. I had worked with Tony before once, on some commercials for the Comedy Channel. I met him again in Los Angeles, and we had a nice chat, and David Angelo and I and some other people here came up with this Prodigy campaign, which was a great advertising idea. I think, simplifying a very, very complex service, an online service. We showed buses that represent the communities you can find online with groups of people on it that had the same interests, you know, like music, pets and fly fishing. And these buses drove around and picked up people who had these same interests. It turned out to be a huge shoot, with potentially a hundred and twenty principals put on three different buses. But Tony has a great sense of the camera and that thing about surprising you with the way he looks at things. He's just a very intuitive thinker and a lot of fun, and this was very much one of these organic processes, you know, where an awful lot came about when we were shooting, a lot of stuff that was not on the boards originally. Also, some outrageous things happened, like we had this pig that collapsed in the heat and just about had cardiac arrest.

▷ Sounds dramatic.

◁ Yeah, they had to whisk this pig off the set and, I'm not making this up, about three or four hours later the pig's lawyer came. It was out in the desert, it was like 115 degrees and out there came this lawyer roaring in his big black Mercedes, with a big doughnut and pulled up. The producers run over there, the car window comes down, the guy in there says. "I'm representing this pig." He had suspenders on with dollar signs going all up and down and there was this big hush conflab about whether the pig was going to survive this, ... the heat problem, and if he didn't, what this was going to mean. It was just so surreal all the while with Tony up in his helicopter shooting this elephant for five hours ... But it was great fun, a lot of fun and we were very happy with the result.

▷ What happened to the pig?

◁ He did not die, but we had to use a stand-in pig who wasn't as cute but, you know, that's life, you just go on. We go on to the next problem.

▷ Earlier, we talked about humour as a selling tool. How about shock tactics?

◁ Well, if you mean by shock tactics the things Calvin Klein did in his campaign, being extremely provocative – I don't know if one can call

Real people casting – Cliff Freeman's award-winning ad for the "comedy channel" it shocking exactly - yeah, absolutely, I think everything should be provocative in a way. I'm using provocative in the sense of surprising, you know, and that can be a great tool. We did this "Body Shot" campaign for SauzaTequila where you see a shot of tequila, the urn and the salt, and it was put on people's naked bodies. That was considered shocking by some. It was all naked bodies after all. So it was shocking, it was sexy but it was also elegant. This campaign did very well.

▷ So what did you think of that "kiddie porn" campaign for Calvin Klein?
◁ Well, my opinion is that it was absolutely dead on. They totally nailed what I believe their objective was. When I saw it, I kind of liked it. I mean, many of the kids weren't very attractive but I thought it was quite successful ultimately even though he had to pull it. I was certainly not offended by it in any way. I didn't take it that way. I knew where he was coming from, it was sort of pornographic but to me he was just trying to mimic something and he did it so well, I thought. I find most of his stuff very effective except perhaps for some of those Obsession commercials.

▷ You're talking about the ones that David Lynch did?
◁ I don't think it was David Lynch who directed the ones I'm thinking of. Perhaps Avedon did them, I don't know.

▷ Would you like to work with David Lynch?
◁ Yeah. Maybe. But, you know, I don't think these feature film people do very well at commercials. The Coen Brothers did it and their feature films are great but I don't think their work was very good in commercials. I don't know why.

▷ You mentioned this other campaign you did with Tony Kaye as the director for the Comedy Channel. These feature some of the most extraordinary casting I've ever seen.
◁ Well, we just cast here in New York and we used a lot of real people. Or what they call real people. I picked this up from my work with Joe Sedelmaier. He would just pick any good face, any good voice he could find. I guess that's where I learned it, with Sedelmaier. I do it all the time now, I find people who are the part, you know, not who are acting the part. There is a certain naive quality in these people that you can never get from a performance. One of the people in the Comedy ad is a neighbour of mine, she has the most outrageous laugh like a Polish washer woman, she never stops laughing. So that's all she had to do - laugh for this entire commercial.

▷ What else do you want to achieve in your life?
◁ Well, I guess I'm mostly focused on the agency now and the growth of the agency and the continually new challenges coming in, solving new

problems. Also, I want to get into slightly different areas with the agency. We're so well known for comedy and certain kinds of things, yet there are so many other things we are capable of doing that we haven't really done. This is really a very collaborative business, we really work here as a team. And it is such a joy, the group coming together, its like making a movie. When we did this Prodigy thing, it was ten people working together for a month...five or six weeks actually, it was a long time with the editing process and so forth, and you know when you do something that you're really proud of and you have to part with, it's kind of hard, it becomes almost like a little family. And this agency's like that, and that's kind of where my focus is now.

▷ You're from the South originally?

◁ Yes, I was born in Mississippi, last stand of the confederacy, Vicksberg, Mississippi. That is where the final battle took place.

▷ Do you own a confederate flag? I once interviewed Alan Parker and he had one in his office.

◁ Oh no, I have no particular feeling about the South, one way or another. I don't particularly feel part of any group, I don't even like the idea of being part of a group, the whole idea, really, except this group, this agency. And my wife and I are a group.

□

ED MCCABE
The prettiest girls were around the creative people

Ed McCabe is a master at one-upmanship. In 1973 he won more gold medals for his creative work than Doyle, Dane & Bernbach combined. Along with his partner Sam Scali he turned Frank Perdue into the chicke king of America. He had more to do with building Volvo than the factory in Sweden did. He was the youngest person to be inducted into the copy-writers hall of fame. He inspired a generation of creatives into selling with attitude. I interviewed McCabe several times in New York and Berlin.

▷ Hermann Vaske: How do you get your ideas?
◁ Ed McCabe: Every campaign I ever wrote that anybody thinks anything of, or that I think anything of that was successful, I did in a bar or a restaurant, every one of them. Because you can't sit in an office and have things happen, things happen going through normal life, and you'd just better be prepared to deal with them at that moment. I keep pencil and paper with me wherever I can, and if I don't have it with me I steal it or borrow it, or you know, I've ripped pieces out of old ladies shopping bags on the subway and bummed a pencil from someone else because I had to write something down. It's very perishable, and sometimes it's no good anyway. But you have to have it at the time, and then you look at it later, and you say, I don't know why I was so crazed about getting that on paper.

▷ Why are you creative?
◁ Well, why am I creative...
When I started out in advertising I was in the mailroom. I looked around the whole thing, and the people who were laughing the most and smiling the most and had the prettiest girls around were the creative people, so I decided that's for me.

▷ Why do you have that revolver on your desk?
◁ It is a speech memento from an advertising industry debate I participated in. It was what they gave everyone.

▷ Why?
◁ It was called a "shoot-out". It's another term for a debate. It was meant to be a debate between East coast and West coast advertising people in America. To see which coast created better advertising.

▷ Who won? Or was it academic?
◁ It was a silly topic. No one won.

▷ Regarding your background, did you, at some point in your life, consider advertising a silly topic?
◁ Like anything else, it depends on how you do it. It can be a very silly topic if you don't have a set of standards to guide everything you do. No,

I've never regarded advertising as silly. However, the way some other people practise it, I regard it as tremendously silly.

▷ Do you think that the sheer bulk of advertising we're confronted with today can be topped?

◁ I think there is more mediocre, insubstantial, inconsequential, confusing, wrongheaded, unfocused advertising today than there has ever been since the 1950s. And I think the reason is, there are a lot of people making advertising who don't have a clue about what they are doing. They haven't been properly trained. There are a lot of reasons for that. During the 70s and 80s, everybody was focused on getting senior people to do the work. Then, because of all the mergers and acquisitions and such, the middle management in agencies were decimated, fired, or given early retirement. So, for some time now, no one qualified has been watching. So you get a bunch of kids, just out of school, put them into a room, let 'em do something and they sell it to clients who are a bunch of kids just out of school who don't know what they are doing either. As a result, there is a lot of money being wasted on idiotic, ineffective advertising. Clients, generally, don't have much faith in the kind of advertising that is being done today. And they are right. They shouldn't have. So, they put money into couponing and promotions, things they think can help them make their numbers, and take it out of advertising. It's a horrible time for quality. And I think that whenever there's a horrible time for quality, it's a good opportunity for quality. That's one of the reasons I came back into the ad business.

▷ So what do you do to improve the advertising? You said that on the one side there is the client who does not know what he's doing. Which means there is probably a shitty brief to start with...

◁ Well, I don't even know if it is a shitty brief, or if it goes much deeper than that. I think it is that clients have never been educated in communications. If you look back at the 60s or early 70s, you'd find people on the client side who were educated in communications. Then came the whole brand management structure. Brand managers came in and were making advertising decisions. They didn't really know anything about advertising, but at least there were still people around, in those companies, who did. But that hasn't been the case now for the last 15 to 20 years. See, you've got people out there making decisions who have no idea what communications is all about, have no training in it, no faith in it, little interest in it. So the problem is education and training.

▷ Isn't that your own fault?

◁ Yes, partially. We all contributed to it by not paying attention. We whined a lot about what was going on with clients, about brand management and all of crap... but we didn't offer relevant solutions. I think some of the industry organizations could have put together some educational training. That would have been helpful. As for the creative side, by the way, I've been working on something. A Masters program in copywriting for the School of Visual Arts.

▷ Are you going towards a Ph.D. in copywriting, or what?

◁ No. A Masters is enough. At least it will put copywriters into the industry with enough basic understanding. Some of this mindboggling crap chat you see coming out would no longer be produced. This program will have some novel things to it. One of the courses, for example, is a course in salesmanship taught by top salesmen from many different industries. That hasn't existed as far as I know. Another one is the study of all the great copywriters from the past up to the present.
I don't think they quite do that, you know. Some students read David Ogilvys' book or something. But, this will have a whole class on each person as well as an in-depth study of their work and beliefs. Right now, many young people come into advertising and don't know anything about any-thing. They come in with no historical perspective. They come in throwing away a rule book that they have never read. And, you see, there are still important lessons in that book. I mean the biggest problem in advertising, from an effectiveness standpoint, is that much of it can't even be understood. You look at it and it's as though you have to be as knowledgeable about the product, use, and history as the copywriter. You have to be a marketing expert in order to understand the advertising. No one has taught these people that the public isn't walking around carrying that brief with them.

▷ So you would for instance do Gossage, read Gossage. Fine, that's like literature studies so far. You read someone like Faulkner and analyze his works.

◁ We're going to do them all. Leo Burnett, Bill Bernbach, Rosser Reeves, David Ogilvy, Gossage, everyone. But that's just a small part of it.

▷ And then what?

◁ That's just a small part of it. There would be another course in basic writing, a very fundamental course. Basic copywriting. Then there is a course on applying that copywriting to actual advertising exercises. The thesis. Students will have to go out and make real advertising on their own. It has to be paid for by somebody else. With no help from the faculty, except guidance.

▷ And that would be the thesis?

◁ Yes. They have to actually sell a client some form of communication that has to be produced by them and paid for by someone else. And they have

Maybe your second car shouldn't be a car.

VOLVOS LAST A LONG TIME. ISN'T THAT BAD FOR BUSINESS?

To some manufacturers, building a product that lasts is the height of foolishness.
But it's an idea that's highly respected among enlightened consumers.
So instead of designing our cars to fall apart so that you'll have to buy another one, we design our cars not to.
That way you'll want to buy another one.
How well our cars last is best summed up by this fact: 9 out of every 10 Volvos registered here in the last eleven years are still on the road.
And in a world where people are becoming increasingly disenchanted with the cars they drive, our customers are coming back for more. The car most often traded in on a new Volvo is an old Volvo.
How's business?
Well, Volvo is the largest selling imported compact in America today. And this will be our best year ever.
The Volvo policy of enlightened foolishness is paying off.

HOW I BECAME THE CHIQUITA OF THE CHICKEN BUSINESS.

Perdue chickens: Frank Perdue became 1972's most dazzling business success.

Some of McCabe's press ads for Vespa, Volvo and Perdue Chickens

to write a paper on what it's attempting to do, how it fits into a long-range plan. What it's all about. They have to bring in the final piece, either printed or if broadcast, a film on tape, and present it. So, part of it is teaching students how to be effective.

▷ You mean how to make a catch, how to pitch something, how to get something done?

◁ How to actually accomplish something. Today these kids come out with a portfolio of stuff they theoretically could do. But, they haven't really done anything. At least with this, they will have done something. They will have a solid piece of work that they can explain, hopefully. This program will be very hard to get into. And it's going to be even harder to get out of. (Laughs.)

▷ How long will this course last, altogether?

◁ It is one year.

▷ That's pretty short for a Masters course.

◁ For these students, it will be a long, tough year.

▷ Who will be teaching?

◁ For example, in the course on the Greats, I have people who knew them, who worked with them, giving the course. For example, Bernbach. The course on Bill Bernbach will be taught by Bob Levinson. And who knows, he may bring in Bob Gage for part of it. That will be 10 days, just on Bernbach, 10 days on Burnett. And the guy doing the Burnett course will be someone who spent a lot of time with Leo Burnett; not just someone who read up on the subject. It won't be just somebody's opinion. It will be someone who was involved, who really knew what was going on.

▷ Aren't you afraid of creating a bunch of Leo Burnett or Bill Bernbach clones?

◁ The objective there is not to get people to write like any of those people. Nor to think like any of those people. It's just to get them to understand the texture of what the business is all about. How it got where it is. What's right, what's wrong. That's what the problem right now is. You can't tell most of these young kids anything. I look at some of this advertising and say ... . What the hell are you trying to tell me? You could say that's an age thing. I don't think so. When we did great work in the 60s and 70s people could always look at it and know what the hell it was we were trying to do.

▷ What made you get involved in training the next generation? Was it just the quality of the work that worried you or was it also a personal matter?

◁ First of all, the School of Visual Arts asked me to do it because they felt there was a serious need for it. I concur that there is a big need. And as

Ed Mc Cabe

64

I've done some research in trying to pull this thing together, more and more I realized how great the need is. But it won't help everything. Only copywriters. You know, one thing that's happened that I have observed, in the big agencies? They have stopped making a distinction between copywriters and art directors. Now, everyone is creative. So, when they had to cut back, they fired a lot of middle management copy supervisors, so you get a situation where art directors are now Group Creative Directors, approving the work of copywriters. I've seen copywriters who have worked in big agencies for three years and no qualified, competent copy person has ever looked at their work. So, how can it possibly be any good? Even if it's only one word in the commercial and the rest is all pictures, who is making sure it's the right word?

▷ Yes, but as you know, a copywriter working on a film script has to deal with the pictures too.

◁ Absolutely. Absolutely. And sometimes there is still dialogue.

▷ You mean it's not a dying art form? Dialogue is still alive?

◁ Well, I think it has to be. It's been used and abused and badly done for so long. And people laugh at the motion of a "slice of life" commercial. But it is still possible to do one that is great.

▷ Yes, even in advertising you sometimes hear great dialogue.

◁ Very rarely. And that is usually contributed by the director.

▷ So how do you make a kid write great dialogue for a commercial?

◁ First, he or she has to learn how to write. There is no other way. One of our courses will be just writing and rewriting things. Over and over and over again. They don't know how to do it. I'll say to a young copywriter... Well, fix this line, and he'll look at me as if to say; "What do you mean, fix this line? I wrote it. It must be perfect." Sometimes it's only perfect after it has been written and rewritten a couple of hundred times. Any good writer knows that. Sometimes it happens automatically in your head. Even so, you spend a lot of time thinking about how to make it better. Nobody is being trained how to do that. I don't know if things are going haywire in general education or what. Poor education and lack of training: these are the reasons why advertising is so bad. And of course, as I said, the whole client thing. There are totally untrained people making advertising and marketing decisions. And that is another thing that brought me back.

You see and read about companies cutting back and downsizing. To me, it's only a matter of time before a company realizes that they don't need huge marketing operations. That can be gotten elsewhere. Either as a package from a number of different sources, or from one. And I saw a great opportunity in that. Building this business is not about making advertising. It's about making results. Sometimes results come from public relations and other disciplines. Agencies went at it and called it integrated communications. It hasn't panned out as a profit-making concept. But, that isn't what it's all about. It's about improving results of communications. If you're interested in excellent results, you'd better be able to do more than just advertising. The problem is they were all buying pieces and trying to put it together and it didn't work. So, here we are, integrating disciplines.

▷ When did you start?

◁ Two years ago.

▷ Could you tell us a little bit about your current clients and the campaigns you're doing?

◁ We have nine clients, and every client we have is outperforming their category in terms of sales results. Based on initiatives generated by us. That's what we're interested in doing. Every one of them is a success story.

▷ So you have nine clients and nine success stories?

◁ Yes. One of these clients is the Rally's hamburger chain. We helped turn around their sales, profits, stock value, everything. We generated one of the most talked-about campaigns in the country. Even though it wasn't seen in New York, it's been shown on Network Television, on shows talking about advertising.

▷ What was the concept?

◁ Well, it's really about what's wrong with fast food as it currently exists. The menus are too long and complicated. The service is too slow. It's not fast. It's got too expensive. We took everything wrong about fast food, and built the campaign around it. One of the things is it's a drive-thru, not a sit-down restaurant. When you go to a drive-thru in America, order a cheeseburger, French fries and a coke, get the bag, go down the road, you open it up, and presto! It's a fish sandwich. So we instituted a guarantee that we get it right or you get it free. We took everything that was wrong with fast food and restructured it. And the campaign theme was: "Rally's has it right." And, one by one, we've dealt with all of these issues.

▷ It sounds like it was you who briefed the client.

◁ Oh, we do that a lot of times. We give clients the brief. Generally, when they come to us, they say; "Help!" So we help. Sometimes they know. Some clients know. But, in my experience, they're in the minority. The problem ones are the ones that think they know. If they don't know, and say it, that's great. If they do know, and really do know, that's great. I mean I don't mind working for a client that knows what the brief should be. But so many don't.

Ed Mc Cabe

▷ So when you have a client that comes to you, let's say a carmaker...

◁ Like BMW.

▷ Yes, so BMW comes to you and says; "Help!" What are you going to do?

◁ Well, they did. We pitched them. We didn't get it.

▷ Who got it?

◁ Mullen in Boston. I rest my case. Look at the work.

▷ That bad?

◁ There are a lot of reasons why people change agencies. They don't all have to do with the work. There is politics, there is money, lots of things. There is this whole new mentality in advertising that I don't understand. That winning accounts is what seems to be the thing that matters. It isn't. If you have fewer accounts, the quality of the work is higher. This makes every one of your accounts a winner. That's all you need, right?

▷ In the long run it certainly is. Let's go back to my question. So the client says "Help!" What do you do? What happens next?

◁ You have to analyze the whole company.

▷ So you have your own planning department?

◁ No, I'm not a big fan of planning. I think it's a bunch of bullshit.

▷ So, do you let God analyze the situation, or what?

◁ We get all over and into a company. Our whole management team. We operate like a consulting company. We get into the company, we analyze everything. We don't leave anything to chance. We don't start anything until we know everything. The old adage in the advertising business used to be, "You do your job, we'll do ours." Bullshit. Unless we know how to do a client's job, how can we know how to advise their company what to do?

▷ And then?

◁ We go there. We get all the information that's available. We figure out what we need and we don't need. We go out into the field. We spend time talking to consumers, a lot of time talking to consumers. Before we did the fast food stuff, we lived fast food. We drove around the country going to fast food places, and realized what was wrong. We talked to people about it, and they talked about it. The campaign did itself, based on that.

▷ Did you try the product yourself?

◁ Oh, definitely. I had more heartburn than you could imagine. I was eating twenty cheeseburgers a day. I mean we went out for two weeks, all of us. A whole bunch of us. We went all over the country. We were eating fast food, examining the product, talking to customers. We talked to them a lot, you know. They're bugged by the high price. They're bugged

by the slow service. They're bugged by the incorrect service. They were all the things which we had the answers for.

▷ But that's not a formula, that's just common sense, it just takes a sharp mind.

◁ Right. But that's all there is to this business. (Laughs.) People invent things like planning. To me planning is a way of getting really bad advertising past ignorant clients. Because, you know, when you do something that is totally unprovocative and turn it into something that people really like, that is what planning gives to it. Planning is such a joke. They send some 26 year old English kid out to talk to consumers and they expect that that's the answer. And I don't think you can do it that way. I think the people that are actually planning the work and doing the work are the ones that have to go out and talk to the people. There are too many chances for errors. But in the end this is not a complicated business. It never has been. It's all about common sense. You don't have to reinvent the wheel.

▷ Sure, as we all know, you have to spot where the problem is and then you have to do something that's different and memorable.

◁ And that's not always a problem. Sometimes it's an opportunity. I always go back to Castrol Motor Oil which we did at Scali McCabe, Sloves a long time ago. I'm gonna use this example to explain the opportunity: Castrol Motor Oil was oil used by people who drove funny little cars like Triumphs, MGs, and other esoteric cars back in the 60s. They used it in their car because Castrol had this great English racing mystique. But in America, nobody knew anything about it. Now, we, the agency, perceived, because we had Volvo, that the car market was heading toward small

Stills from Rally's commercial

cars. Castrol had a heritage in small cars. That's where it was historically used. The mass of people couldn't see the need for an oil like Castrol. They were happy with their Quaker State and Pennzoil. We knew that the market was moving to small cars. So we said to Castrol, ,,Position your oil as the oil engineered for small cars." And they said, ,,What about the big cars?" We said, "Forget them." There aren't going to be any big cars. Forget them. Within three years, we were in a three-way tie for number one. Been there ever since. Quaker State, Pennzoil and Castrol. Three-way tie.

▷ The conclusion out of that would be: the more specialized you are, the better your advertising. The more high focused and single-minded you are, the better.

◁ No. It is the appearance of high focus and single-mindedness, when you know that 90% of the cars that are going to be sold in America are smaller than those existing at the time, it is easy to formulate a long-term plan to meet an opportunity that hasn't arrived yet. That's the secret. I mean, if you do advertising for today, you'll get nowhere. Today is going to be gone tomorrow. You've got to build toward something. You intersect your own future success. Whether it is 5, 10, 20 years out, you have to think that way. Fewer people in advertising think that way anymore. This quarter. That's all they can see. That's why promotions and merchandisings and coupons and premiums are taking away so much from advertising. The dummies want everything right now; which is at their expense later on. But, when you are focused on a long-term goal, you don't have to give anything up. If you've got the right plan, you'll be very successful in the short term, too.

▷ I read this big article on you. It was about you leaving SMS, saying „goodbye" to the business from one day to the next, getting married and stuff like that.

◁ That was about seven years ago. I tried to figure out if there was something else I wanted to do. After five years there was an opportunity, here, to start over and do it the right way.

▷ So you wanted to figure out if there was life after advertising?

◁ There was, but you know, it can be very complicated. To start over in advertising is hard enough. To start over in something else where you have no credentials is even harder. I was looking at producing pictures. Thought about a few other things. A lot of the ideas I had were for businesses where I'd been the client. But then I'd have ended up having all these people around me I didn't want to work with. You know, all those calculator types.

▷ So the conclusion is that advertising isn't all that bad.

◁ No, advertising isn't bad if you do it right. It's hard to do it right, you know. It's really hard.

▷ We talked about the Rally's campaign where you said it kind of did itself based on the information you had gathered. What can you do when you can't think of anything at all? What do people do?

◁ They go to the books. I've never gone to the books. That's not how I work. I came from the streets of Chicago. I didn't have any education. I never finished high school and I figured that the nature of advertising was to communicate with people like me. Yet, so much of advertising today I can't understand. I have to believe a lot of the world can't understand it either. So, advertising should be very simple, sometimes it's visceral, sometimes it's intellectual, but it always needs to be so simple and clear that anyone can get their heads around it.

▷ What part of Chicago are you from?

◁ I was born on the south side, raised on the north side. But it was a time when none of it was great.

▷ It was always a very high-crime city, wasn't it?

◁ It was a tough time.

▷ Did you get involved in any gang fights?

◁ Oh, yeah, constantly. When I was a kid. I mean they used to have race riots in Chicago every month. It was dangerous. Gang wars every night.

▷ Were you involved in a gang!

◁ Yeah, when I was really young. Before I went into the advertising business. But I've gotten involved with a different type of gang. (Laughs.)

▷ You said that your campaign for Rally's hamburgers received a lot of attention, was even talked about on the TV news. So you think that this kind of word of mouth is the best thing that can happen to advertising?

◁ Absolutely. It's the best kind of advertising. If you can create something that is all word of mouth, that's when you have the best. Like this campaign we did for Tom's of Maine, a cosmetics company. Not a big budget. First night that was on the air Jay Leno picked it up in his monologue. I mean he did a whole thing about it.

▷ Can you kick that kind of thing off?

◁ No, I don't think you ever kick it off. I think you let it kick itself off. If it's good enough then you push it all the way and you manage it. If you try to kick it off, then it's false. When it has natural interest and people do it automatically, you can extend it, you can explode it, you can magnify it. But if it isn't there, it's never gonna be there, and it's gonna be just hype.

▷ I'm sure it was a word of mouth thing when your famous Maxell campaign kicked off first time.

◁ And Perdue Chicken. When we launched that, everybody was talking about it. I mean, everybody was saying, „Did you see that guy that looks like a chicken?" I mean there was talk everywhere.

▷ That's one of the all-time great campaigns.

◁ Volvo wasn't bad either. Ha, ha.

▷ Do you miss the smell of a car? It's something special.

◁ It's something I know. I spent most of my career working on cars. I'm good at it. And I like it. I understand it. I also know what everybody is doing wrong. Once you know that it's invaluable. I can see where everyone is going. I haven't seen any good car advertising in a long time. Actually, a recent Infinity campaign I saw wasn't bad. It's not great, but it's not bad. It's very straight, which is a breath of fresh air. Everybody is trying to out-dramatic everyone else. Enough already! This is just a stand-up guy talking. He's got an interesting personality. He says some interesting things. They are all trying too hard.

▷ Is there a car account that you could go for and pitch?

◁ Oh, there are a lot. You know, these things happen in their own time. That's the problem with the advertising business. When you make advertising and you create campaigns for people, you make things happen when you want them to happen. But getting the accounts don't happen when you want it to happen. You have to wait, it's a different kind of game. A lot of agencies today are built for getting accounts, not for selling products. We're built for selling products. I don't worry too much about getting an account. We get 'em.

□

JERRY DELLA FEMINA

I didn't have the body copy

"What an Italian boy with chutzpah can do for Madison Avenue" was the headline of a story about Jerry Della Femina. As time went by, Jerry answered the question himself. After seven years of struggle as salesperson, messenger and newspaper boy, the son of Italian immigrants became one of the giants of American advertising. His books and campaigns were an inspiration for numerous young Americans to get into advertising. I met the legendary zampano in his office at Madison avenue.

▷ Hermann Vaske: Jerry, behind you on the wall I see the biggest dollar bill that I've seen in my life. Is advertising the fine art of separating people from their money?
◁ Jerry Della Femina: I think advertising is a way to make money. I don't know if we separate anyone from their money although I have the dollar bill there so that I can have something to pray to.

▷ Are you a hippie?
◁ If I am, I'm the oldest one. Well, I said to someone the other day that I probably am the oldest baby boomer (laughs.) I have lunch every Wednesday with some four or five very famous people in the United States, we have lunch every Wednesday. I'm the oldest one there and yet I'm the one with the youngest child.
So I guess I am the oldest hippie. God!

▷ But it's nice.
◁ Yeah, it is, I like it, I like it, I like the times. I thought that the sixties and seventies were very important times. I think that once you get past all the excesses – there were excesses everywhere – there was a real spirit and people were willing to take risks, there was a lot of taking of risks. I'm not a wild man but I am a risk taker, I love the chance to try things, to try things differently. I'm amazed at the number of people that come up to me and tell me, "I read your book and that's how I got into advertising."

▷ Bearing in mind all the discussions about Judge Thomas and office sex, you were really ahead of your times.
◁ I'm trying to remember... I think I talked about that there was sex in advertising.

▷ Is that the reason you went into advertising?
◁ No, I went into the business because I was lazy. Well, when I was young I was very poor. I didn't get a chance to go to college though I wanted to, I didn't have enough money to go to college so I found myself in a lot of jobs, I got married very young, and I just did anything I could to keep my family going, that was my job, my work. And so I was an insurance adjuster and I was a shipping clerk. I had twenty-two jobs, and one of the jobs was a messenger for the New York Times, I used to pick up advertising copy. And I would go into these buildings and, see, go in with my

Della Femina's commercial for Nathan's

advertising copy and sometimes I'd go, take it to that place, take it here, and I'd see these people up with their feet on the desk and relaxed, and I remember saying to myself, "What a wonderful job, I wonder what they do." I remember asking, "What does that man do?" and this man had his feet up on the desk, they said he was a copywriter, and I said, "How much does he make?" And at the time, I think he made $30.000 a year, which was all the money there was in the world in my opinion. And I thought that if one could put one's feet up on the desk and be paid something like $30.000 a year, that was the job for me. This is the job. So I started looking for my first job in 1954. And I looked until 1961, so I looked for seven years to get into the business. And I persisted at it, I just took other jobs, I sold bathrobes, I sold toys, and what I didn't realize at the time, I just thought I was doing this for my family, but I was getting a real education in selling things, in dealing with people and understanding a lot of it, a true education.

▷ How did you talk people into buying things?

◁ Well, one of the things I always did was when they came in to buy, I used to sell children's toys, and people would question and I remember it was always near the Christmas season, I worked for Macy's. At Macy's I sold toys and I sold bathrobes. I would always give them a real choice. I would always say, "You know, why don't you check out, or go to Gimbel's and see if their price is as good as this one..." and I think, invariably, they would not. First of all, two things would happen. Most of the time they didn't want to go across the street because it was crowded, but they always saw this as a sign that this was gonna be the best price and they would always buy it. And I would always have the best selling record of anybody there. I remember selling bathrobes to older people. And then I said, "They have a great selection of bathrobes over at the other store. If you want to take a look at that and then maybe you'll come back." And they'd say, "No, this is great, this is fine." and they'd take it. And I'd always find that worked instead of pushing people and having them resisting you. It's always easier to soft sell. But this was instinctive, this, no one taught me how.

▷ That's definitely a better method than putting the people under pressure saying, "If you buy it tonight you'll get it for $1500, if you come back tomorrow it'll cost $2000."

◁ I remember at one point a similar situation, there was a mother and a kid. And the kid was playing with everything and I said, "Well, instead of getting this" – I don't remember the toy he wanted – "we have fantastic stamp collections that cost even less than the toys, and they're really terrific, and I think it's an education too, because the kid would be able to see all the different places and it's important, it's the beginning of a wonderful hobby," and so she went in to buy one thing and walked out with something that cost less – a stamp collection that probably was more educational for the child. And that was that kind of selling I did, and I did it extremely well. I was their top salesperson. And I was a kid, I was 19 or 20. I got married at 18. That's when I met my wife, my first wife, I've been married twice. My wife asked me, "Why did you get married so young?" and I said that I just wanted to be the first one in my group to get married, and it was just that I had to get out of my house. I guess as a young person I was always seen as being a little bit different by many, I always tried to do things, there was something in me that wanted to do it differently.

▷ So how did you manage to get out of Macy's and into the business?
◁ Well, after seven years of looking, which was really a tough time, one day I decided that I was going to send ads to agencies and I wasn't going to sign them. The reason I wasn't going to sign them was that too often the process is the following: you tell them that you're good, then they open your book and then they have to decide whether you're good, whether you told the truth or not. I decided to reverse the process so that they got advertising which wasn't signed, so they didn't know who did it, so they would have to make the conclusion that whoever sent this advertising is really good. Then I'd call up and say that it's me, and that would change the process and maybe I'd get the job, and it worked. The minute I did it I got the job. I did five ads, internal house ads for an advertising agency, and what I would do is this: they would get these internal house ads, one on a Monday and it was signed JDF, and one came in on a Tuesday and it was signed JDF, and they were always different. I was told later on that when the director got one on a Thursday, he said, "Who is this JDF and what does he want?" And on Friday I sent him an ad and then I called him and said, "Hello, this is JDF, when can I come in for my Interview?" And he interviewed me and hired me right on the spot.

▷ What made you decide to open your own agency?
◁ I probably was difficult, difficult for other people to have to work with me. I have a real sense of what I think is right in advertising. And a real sense of what I think should be done, and I could see that when I was working at the Ted Bates agency, that I was... I did extremely well for them and they certainly grew, the work I did on Panasonic built that brand in the United States, but I was someday going to become unemployable because I was seen as a maverick. Someone who was a little bit different, a little bit different from the rest. And what advertising wanted in those days was people who performed and I was a non-performer in this kind of world. So I started my agency out of self-defense. Knowing that the day would come when people would say ...

▷ ... "this man is unemployable."
◁ ... "this man is unemployable." I mean I saw myself as becoming unemployable because I have very definite feelings about what should be

done. I also wanted to have a place where people would be treated the way I wanted to be treated. You know, where there would be less pressure on people, more moral enjoyment, more spirit. Everything in my book, as you'll see, says what was going on in the advertising world in those days. That people were really expected to perform. People were fired for stupid reasons – a man was fired because he was using the boss' elevator. This man worked very late that night, saw the elevator, an empty elevator, pressed the button, went downstairs, and the next day he was told, "You're fired," and he wanted to know why, and he was told, "You stole his elevator, the elevator has to be kept there waiting for him so that when he comes out he should not have to wait for the elevator."

▷ George Lois called your book of the advertising scene of the fifties cynical.

◁ That's strange. I'm a rebel, but you can't be a rebel and really be cynical. I think a rebel wants to change things in a visionary, enlightening way. Cynical is when you sit back and you watch it and you talk about it but you don't do anything to change it. The conditions that I wanted in my agency, was that the agency was really fun, lot of freedom. Everybody has the chance and the right to say anything they want to me, and they do. Our company culture is really good, and it has to be good because that's the kind of place that I would want to work at. When you came into France they give you a card that says that you have to write what you do, and I unconsciously wrote – I didn't even think –did not write "advertising agency chairman," I wrote "advertising copywriter." And I guess, that's what I really am.

▷ You're saying that working long hours and working over the weekend is OK. Don't you think it should also be part of a company culture that people finish in time and get home in time?

◁ If people are really enjoying themselves, if the work is good and they're having a good time, there are no hours. Imposing hours and saying get it done by a certain time is a deadline mentality. Then you get what I don't like – you have people looking at their watches. Again, I'm not going to criticize other people's way of working. I just don't think that people can feel as much about the company if what it is is 9:00 to 6:00, or 7:00, whatever the hours are. What I like best about it, we have a woman who's the president of my agency. We're the first agency to ever have a woman elected president and have her name put on the masthead. McNamee is a woman. Without her having founded the agency herself. Mary Wells founded her own agency but Louise McNamee came to work at our agency as a researcher. Someone said,"How could you do that?" and I said,"Because she is the smartest person I have." And I think that that's the mentality. If I know one thing, it's that she will always be there. Sometimes I'm looking for her, I have to talk to her about something and

I'll call on a Sunday, she's in her office, and that inspires other people to be in their office. So if you love your job, working all the time is not a hardship, it's a pleasure. If you don't love your job then somebody better give you real strict and visible hours so that you could come in and then you could leave. It's too bureaucratic for me. All we have to do is get out our work, and make it. The other thing we have to do is we have to be brutally, brutally frank with ourselves. I'm tough on our creative product, I don't think our creative product is as good as it was in the seventies.

▷ What are the components of rebel advertising?

◁ There's a little bit of - what's the word I'm searching for - danger, there's always danger. It's always on the borderline, but it always has to be in good taste. But let's get back to rebel advertising. There's a certain amount of risk involved in it, there's also a greater chance to fail, it's a little bit cheeky, a little arrogant, there's a touch of arrogance, chutzpah. Chutzpah's a good word. Is chutzpah a German word?

▷ It's Yiddish.

◁ Really? Interesting because someone, ... the first story anyone ever wrote about me was what an Italian boy with chutzpah can do for Madison Avenue. It took me weeks to find out what chutzpah meant. It just described something that I'd said as chutzpah, and I said I didn't quite understand what that meant. Yeah, chutzpah, there is a lot of chutzpah, it involves a little bit of - I don't want to say arrogance - but it's close to arrogance.

And what happens is when it works, it really, really works, it really gets people's attention, because it's unusual, it's different. A lot of advertising gets done, but never makes it because it's perfectly safe, and it's perfectly in line and it doesn't do anything but it also doesn't offend anyone. Rebel advertising is filled with risks. The real thing is, with rebel advertising you fall down a lot. But you also get up and you're better for it and the advertising's better for it. I think that what's happened in the States is that we've become very research-oriented, my agency included, and lost a part of that rebel spirit. We've stopped for the most part, and this is in the States - I always have to include my agency as part of this - we've stopped listening to our stomachs and started listening to peoples's numbers, which means we have very good safe advertising but there isn't the same excitement, there isn't the same fun.

▷ How did you come upon the Joe Isuzu concept?

◁ By accident. It was originally an ad that was going to a small group of dealers in the Los Angeles area. One-shot commercial, one commercial, and it was such an unimportant commercial because in terms of - we only had, I think, $ 30,000 to spend on production. We had two young people, the copywriter was 22, the art director was, I think, 23, I'm not sure, but they were really young, first commercial they ever did, they

One of Della Femina's
commercials for Isuzu

came up with this liar. And I saw it, because I see everything that Isuzu does, and I saw it and thought it was a fantastic concept that we should do tomorrow. It was funny, it worked, I liked the way it was performed. And the minute it was done I put it on our reel. Why would I put this small commercial on our reel? It had everything going for it.

▷ It's a great send-up of car dealers.

◁ It's saying this is what people think car dealers are, but let's twist it. It's got the twist, it's got the humour. And Joe has evolved, the commercial that won the Gold Lion was Joe chasing a bullet. We could say the most outrageous things about Isuzu and have people just staring at the screen because they want to see the truth. And it's interesting, because this Isuzu advertising has been extremely effective. To think that Isuzu came to the United States in 1979 during the recession that was being blamed on Japanese cars, their total budget was 7 million dollars, which is what some car companies in the United States spend in a week. We had a full year to spend $ 7 million. We had a name that no one could pronounce – Isuzu is a very difficult name to pronounce – our car models were three years behind the times, they were not new, they were undistinctive, and we managed to build – they now spend $ 100 million – and we built a brand taking it away from Subaru and taking it away from the other Japanese cars. They would always over-exaggerate Joe, we put him into everything. We have him on the autobahn, have you seen the commercial where he's on the autobahn? And he passes the Mercedes? Oh, it's wonderful! There are two Germans riding on the autobahn and they look behind them and they say, "Look behind us could it be?" And the guy says, "No, it couldn't be. Step on it, let's lose him," and the faster they go the closer he's coming and they say, "He's gaining on us," and he comes by and it's Joe Isuzu and he looks in the car and he says, "Guten Morgen!" And the guy says, "I hate Joe Isuzu", and he passes him.

▷ What do you think sells more cars - clever and smart reality (like Volvo in the UK and Mercedes in Germany) or a funny over-dramatization of reality like Isuzu?

◁ I think the over-dramatization is always funny if you can do it and get away with it.

▷ The Volkswagen in the sixties was not that serious.

◁ In Volkswagen it's always fun, they're warmer. All the Volkswagen owners would wave to each other because it's like seeing, like being part of some odd club or something. It was a very unusual experience to say the least. When I had a Volkswagen, half my friends wouldn't talk to me and the other half wanted to know what this odd thing was.

▷ Why are you creative?

◁ Why am I creative? There are so many things I can't do, all that's left to me is to be creative. I'm creative because it's probably an extension of my lifestyle and the way I think. I look at things and see them in a different

Jerry Della Femina

78

**YOU'VE GOT A SHOT
AT THESE COPS.**

Columbia Pictures Television

way. I think that I'm not a person who's very concerned with order and bureaucracy or the way things are done, and I think that when people are concerned with the mechanics of things and the order of things they can't see the fun of it. I think differently than a lot of other people, I'm willing to take chances and I think that's a very great part of creativity, I think that creative people have to always be on the edge of disaster. Probably the best thing that happens, the thing that makes you most creative, is that you don't fear failing because if you fear failing you don't have the gift. There are so many things one can do that keep you from being creative, and you can't always do it right – there hasn't been a single creative person that was always right. But there have been bureaucrats who have always been right. They don't have to care about anything. My sensibility, my sense is that I know that I'm gonna fail a lot. I'm gonna make mistakes, things that aren't gonna work. But at the same time, I'm gonna reach even further and try, and that makes me creative and that's why I worked so hard to get a job in advertising because it seemed like a good place to fail. I think even surgeons can be creative, I think the great ones are creative, but they also see more of their patients die, but in the end if the surgeon is creative he's a great surgeon. He's the one who makes the operations no one thought could be performed. So, the thing is there's creativity in every area except, I guess, in bureaucracy ... and the electricity business, which God knows I'm not qualified in. But I think that what happens is that creativity is a wonderful opportunity to try to be different. You succeed a lot but you also fail a lot and you're also out there, when you fail. You don't fail in a small room where nobody can see you. People who invent things are creative. And when you fail in advertising creativity it's public and there's something exciting about that. It might be more exciting than have people see you win all the time.

▷ Helmut Krone says that he always had the fear of failure and that kept him going.

◁ That's interesting because when he – he sort of preceded me by a few months – and when he first started, or when he was hot, at the top, I could never imagine him ever fearing anything in the world. He was my hero. I would look at him and say, "This is a man who fears nothing." You don't know what's going on inside.

▷ That's right. What goes on inside Jerry Della Femina?

◁ Not the fear of failing, I mean it's really not part of my make-up. If anything, yeah, the need to have fun. The need to enjoy. You can see by my choice of wives! That I like the job of living on the edge. There is no boredom. Not even in my marriage.

▷ I feel the thrill of failure always on last-minute rides to the airport. I always reach the airplane at the last second.

◁ The last second. Everything has to be at the last second. The most fun I've had was writing a campaign in a taxicab on my way to the client because he said, "It's gotta be ready," and you know that's the ultimate pressure. I never would have the body copy ready. And this client always said he wanted the body copy. And I remember once he said he was gonna fire us. The client was Fuji Film. And the client said he was gonna fire us if I didn't have the body copy ready and my partner and I were sitting there and I read him the headline, I didn't have the body copy, and he said, "That's great, that's wonderful," he says, "What's the body copy? I picked up a blank piece of paper, it was blank, and I started reading the non-existent copy. And it was – I must say this and my partner said so too – it was brilliant copy. I was making it up as I was going along. And I read a full, I mean I read an ad that was so, so good and when it was over the client said, "that's just great! Can I see it?" And I said, "No, no, we're gonna have it, we'll have it for you." I was holding a blank piece of paper and my partner was shaking his head and the meeting was over and he said, "I can't believe you did that," and I said, "I can't believe I did that." I just had, I actually read him probably one of the best ads I had ever written. And my partner said to me, "Do you remember what you said?" And I said, "No, I haven't the slightest idea." And I never could recreate it, I tried, and the second time I showed him the paper, the client said that it sounded much better before. Never got it. But the adrenalin, the excitement of having to make it up right there, including having to read him the coupon on the ad.

▷ Jerry, everybody knows that you are bald. How do you cope with that?
◁ Oh, I love it, I love it. It's attention and in the end, I like that a lot. I need it. Not having hair to me was a very definite thing, I had a little hair left. And, you know, the thing to do is to shave it off, so then it becomes distinctive, it's different. Unlike a lot of other people who are desperately trying to spread whatever hair they've left on their scalps. I used it even for advertising. I had to advertise a man's hairpiece. They gave me one to put on my head, but I hated the fact that it wasn't real. The very first ad my agency ever did was for a hair product and the headline was, "Are you still combing your memories?" And then I wrote about what it feels like to be bald. Looking in a three-way mirror when you buy a suit and really seeing how bald you are. And how you take a few hairs and you try to put them on one side and you try to put them on the other side. All the things you do, and in the end you have to say to yourself "I am bald." And it's a horrible thing for a man to accept. There is not anyone who is comfortable or happy with it. "Are you still combing your memories?" was a very successful ad.
What it said was that people are really fooling themselves.

▷ Assuming there was an effective remedy for baldness, would you try to advertise it rationally or emotionally?
◁ Always emotionally. I think that it is so underrated as a problem that men feel. When you first start losing your hair you are in your early twenties sometimes and it's dramatic. So I think it's an emotional issue. I think you can get them by talking to them about how their life will change. And I think men think that they are not attractive anymore when they start losing their hair. Interestingly enough, there are statistics that show that among men who are fooling around and have as many women as they can find there are many balding men. For them it's almost...
It's a compensation. Men who are short compensate by being overly aggressive. Men who are balding compensate by saying to themselves, "I'm gonna be attractive to women despite this," and they work even harder at being attractive. That's why people say bald men are more sensual. Not that they are more sensual, they just try harder.
□

PHIL DUSENBERRY

The best advertising is a dramatization of the truth

Phil Dusenberry got into advertising via radio. As a disc jockey with WBBI, a local radio station in Avingdon, Virginia, he wrote his first copy. Many radio scripts later, he landed a job with a station on Long Island and, finally, started to work as a copywriter for BBDO New York. There, he worked on accounts such as B. F. Goodrich, Dodge, and Pepsi. In 1977 Dusenberry became Executive Creative Director. Under his creative leadership BBDO was transformed into a major contender, not least on account of the many creative awards it garnered. In 1990 and 1991, for example, BBDO won more Clios than any other agency. During the 80s, Phil Dusenberry also made a name for himself in Hollywood, when he co-wrote the script for "The Natural", starring Robert Redford. He also worked as a copywriter on the "Tuesday Team" the ad-hoc agency that created the campaign for Ronald Reagan's re-election in 1984. In 1986 Dusenberry became Chairman and Chief Creative Officer of BBDO New York, and in 1988 Chief Executive Officer. I spoke to this exceptional creative in his "oval office" about Bob Dole, Pepsi Cola and why the Gettysburg address would have been a great commercial.

▷ Hermann Vaske: Phil, is advertising all about dramatizing the positive?
◁ Phil Dusenberry: Advertising is about dramatizing the truth. There's an old joke about two kids talking about what their fathers do for a living and one kid says, "My father lies for a living. He's in advertising." Well, maybe in some yesteryear there was some basis in reality to that, perhaps there was some fabrication of the truth going on. The nuances that are the fine line between truth and fiction still exist. But, I think, the best message, the best advertising, is a dramatization of the truth – not necessarily a dramatization of the positive. You can take anything and make it positive, but you can't take anything and make it the truth. I think that people are aware of this. And nothing will put you out of business faster than trying to dramatize a lie or dramatize a fabrication. The same is true of products themselves. Bill Bernbach said that nothing would put a bad product out of business faster than good advertising. That's true because people would rush in and buy the product. They would try it. They would discover that the product does not live up to the promises the advertising made and, therefore, they would not return to buy it again. That's what good advertising does ... it advertises a basic truth about the product. Consumers will appreciate that you are, in some manner, telling the truth about that brand or that product or that service.

▷ You mentioned Bernbach. His "Lemon" ad for Volkswagen was a good example of how you can even dramatize the negative when telling the truth and, through the use of irony, turn it into something very positive.

"Always larger than life" –
Pepsi with Cindy Crawford and
Malcolm McDowell

◁ Sometimes self-deprecating humor, as in the case of Volkswagen's "Lemon," really works because people are disarmed by the basic truth. In this case they were saying that this particular car, this one issue of an entire assembly line, wasn't good enough to be sold and that's why they called it "Lemon." They talk about the procedure they have on the assembly line and how close the scrutiny is. I think people understood that this is a true story. People respond to that and they like the humour of it. You can tell the truth in a humorous way and that can be very, very effective. We have been doing that for years on Pepsi. What we're saying on Pepsi is the truth about this particular product; Pepsi has a very young way of feeling, a very young way of thinking to it. We dramatize this truth in a humorous way. It comes across because there is a basic reality, and the best humour comes from reality anyway. It comes from something you can relate to. Something you can understand. In the end, the best kind of emotional message is something based on truth.

▷ And the best kind of humour is based on personal experience?

◁ Sure, it's what I like to call the shock of recognition. The surprise of "Oh yeah, that happened to me once," or "That happened to my family or someone I know"

▷ Like that commercial you did for Pepsi in which the Pepsi cans stick to people's lips because it is so cold.

◁ Yeah, that's an example of what we are talking about. If you drink something that is very cold and you drink it up in the Yukon, the can will stick to your lips. We decided to dramatize this truth and it became a very engaging, humorous way of dramatizing how much people love Pepsi-Cola. As that commercial ends, everybody in town has Pepsi sticking to their lips. People who watch that commercial can appreciate the fact that this has probably happened to them at some time or another in their lives. You recognize that and, as a result, it becomes very relevant to you. You can relate to that on a very personal level. Which brings us to the subject of emotional purchases. So much of what we buy, I believe, is bought on the basis of an emotional level. When a housewife walks down a supermarket aisle, there are 20 to 30 different brands in any given category from which she or he can choose. And what is it that makes that person reach for your brand? Make that brand decision in a matter of seconds? I believe it's made on an emotional level because people don't remember the messages each product has put out there in their advertising. They never go to the store, walk down that aisle and say, ,,Yes, this is the product that I'm going to buy because it's got this, this, and this." They do in some cases, but in most cases that product decision was made on an emotional level.

Phil Dusenberry

84

Something in their soul or in their hearts made them want to reach out and grab that product. Hopefully, it was because the net impression created by the product's advertising made them feel good about that brand. Therefore they made that instantaneous decision on an emotional level.

▷ Pepsi is surely one of the best examples of how to build a brand through emotions.

◁ With Pepsi we have gone through lots of stages in their advertising, and the two biggest stages I can think of, in a very broad sweep of memory, is music and humour.

▷ Music?

◁ Yes, music. Back in the early 60s right on through the mid 80s, music was the message for Pepsi. Pepsi was the first to ever use a singing jingle. It was a radio commercial and the song was, "Pepsi-Cola hits the spot. Twelve full ounces, that's a lot." And it caught on. It became the world's first singing jingle. So Pepsi-Cola used music in a very powerful way from the early 60s on. And that was a very emotional sell because the music made you feel good about Pepsi. Unfortunately, everybody started doing music, not only other soft drinks but insurance companies, airlines, fast foods, you name it. And so everybody was singing for their supper. And I remember someone saying to me, "Have you ever thought about doing humour for Pepsi?" And somehow it didn't really register with any of us because we were so used to having Pepsi in a musical context. And so it took us a while to really evolve into the humorous approach that we have taken ever since the mid-80s. It really came out of a shift in strategy that we wanted to refocus our efforts on young people, young-thinking people everywhere and young people love humour. They love self-deprecating humor. They love humour that comes across quickly and that's what we decided to do. In the mid-80s we started to do commercials that were less music-oriented and more humour-oriented. That's what we have been doing, evolving that since 1984.

▷ I was talking to Joe Pytka about this, and he mentioned that you also were the first to use a celebrity as part of a narrative story instead of just having them as a spokesperson for the product.

◁ Well, celebrity advertising is almost a topic unto itself. Up until the 80s, celebrity advertising was spokesperson advertising. Somebody would get up in front of you and say, you know, "I am a famous person and here is the product I think you should buy." It was a personal endorsement and it became sort of artificial. You realized these people were just being paid to hawk that product. And over time what we developed at BBDO was a way of using the celebrity. Because after all there is an edge to using

NOTHING ELSE
IS A PEPSI

Pepsi directed by Joe Pytka

celebrities. It does give you more spin. It gives a little bit more recognition, more awareness, all sorts of things. It's good in that context. But what we decided to do was to use celebrities in a different way. In the context of an idea. For example, when we created the Pepsi, "Apartment 10G" commercial where Michael J. Fox goes out the window and to the fire escape to get Pepsi for his new and attractive next-door neighbor – originally that was just going to be a non-celebrity actor. It was only when we created that idea that somebody said, "You know, it would be even more fun if we had somebody like Michael J. Fox doing this commercial." And that's what we did. He gave it much more awareness, personality and fame ... and it became a very famous piece of work. But if we had just used Michael J. Fox holding up a can of Pepsi or Diet-Pepsi, it would have fallen on its face.

▷ What if the celebrity is the product? What about political advertising?
◁ Well, there it becomes a totally different kind of product because if you're advertising a political candidate, your message is liable to change overnight, which is not true of product advertising. The reason it can change overnight is that the candidate has to react and respond to other messages being put there by his opponents. Even with that, underlying the change, there should be a thematic single solid message that represents what the candidate is all about. I think that is the greatest failing of political advertising today. It doesn't have a theme. It's all over the place. The product, in this case, a president, Mayor, governor or senator, or whatever, is not really being used in an interesting, intelligent context. You don't get the message of what that person is all about. Some time ago we did a commercial with Bob Dole for Visa credit cards. In it he came across as a warm, human, nice guy. None of that came through in his political campaign. So it's a perfect proof that advertising can make such a difference for a political candidate. And it isn't just putting that person up in front of a camera and having them speak. It's the way you use them. It's, again, putting them into the context of an idea, of what they're all about and what the message is they're trying to communicate. I think that was the success of our presidential campaign with Ronald Reagan when he was re-elected in 1984. We strategically took what was going on in America at the time, a rise in patriotism, the economy was doing well, and we decided to wrap Mr. Reagan in Red White and Blue and bring home that message again, again, and again, without faltering and without any kind of change. It was very, very consistent and that consistency went a long way to helping Mr. Reagan be re-elected.

▷ Did you create a brand there?

Phil Dusenberry

◁ We took the brand which was President Reagan and we told the truth in the way we presented him – as a very grandfatherly figure who has a staunch belief in the nation's military and patriotism and all of those things put together. We always let President Reagan be President Reagan. Never tried to make him something he wasn't. So we really took what was already a great brand and we just dramatized it in a very truthful, very honest way. If you went back and looked at the 65 commercials that were created for President Reagan in 1984, you wouldn't look at any of them and say, "This doesn't ring true." They all had a basic honesty about them and personality and that was very much it. I think if you force a candidate to be something other than he really is, the scrutiny of the camera will expose that. I think the camera tends to find the truth. It finds the truth in a performer. It finds the truth in a product that you're advertising. As a result, the camera can be very cruel in its scrutiny. It's not always very kind. It can be very cruel because it examines up closely the truth, and unless you're prepared to tell the truth, it will expose you for what you really are. It will show off your bad points, the negatives that might exist with your product or your message.

▷ In the case of Reagan you had of course an example of great communication for somebody who was naturally a great communicator.

◁ Well, you know, one thing that was very important in this campaign – and which was lacking in many other campaigns, particularly in the Bush campaign and the Dole campaign – was that President Reagan really hammered away at some very key points before he became president, while he was president, and on into his second term. So, low taxes, ending the Cold War were very basic issues ... smaller government ... everybody could understand what he was talking about. Whether you liked the man or not, disagreed with his politics are not, nobody ever had to say "Gee, I wonder what he means," or "What is he all about?" You knew exactly what he was talking about at all times and he never strayed from these issues. That's what great advertising and great communication is all about – consistency. If I tell you ten things. you'll never retain any of them. But if I say one thing and say it well and say it again and again and again, it's going to come through to you, and if you like the message then that's going to really sink in.

▷ Consistency and simplicity as the winning formula.

◁ Absolutely. And simplicity extends into the process as well. We were very fortunate in the way we got advertising approved in 1984. We simply went to President Reagan's Deputy Chief of Staff, who in effect ran the campaign for the White House. If he liked it, he would take it inside to

the Oval Office and President Reagan would approve it , that was it. Simple!

▷ Good man to good man.

◁ Simple. No procedure. No committee. No review board. No cabinet meeting.

▷ There is a famous saying: "No good advertising ever came out of a committee."

◁ Now cut to 8 years later, to 1992.

▷ The Bush campaign.

◁ Bush is now running for re-election. It was not a tough job for him to get elected in 1988. He was running against a very incompetent opponent, Michael Dukakis. Anyone could have won the election against him. But the re-election of Bush suddenly got very complicated. Suddenly, that very simple chain of command was gone and now you had to get your advertising through twenty people to get one ad approved. You had to go through a whole army of people who perhaps had the authority to say no, but not the authority to say yes. It got watered down. It took forever, and it showed in the tentative aspect of the campaign. It looked tentative. It felt hesitant.

▷ Were you involved in this campaign?

◁ I was not but I was very close to the people who were. I know what a nightmare it must have been. It was one of the reasons why I did not get involved in 1996 when Senator Dole decided to run against President Clinton because it smacked of committees, review boards, smacked of groups of people and all sorts of stuff that did not make for great advertising.

▷ I wonder how these things were handled before the invention of the camera, with presidents like Abraham Lincoln.

◁ That's interesting. Of course Lincoln didn't have the benefit of motion picture photography but he had an audience and the brilliant simplicity of the Gettysburg Address. "Four score and seven years ago, our forefathers ..., etc., etc." What we've got here is a message that took two minutes and 45 seconds to get across. I mean that was a great commercial in its own way. And imagine if it had had the benefit of film and the camera, and if that message had been disseminated quickly around the world. It would have been famous immediately.

▷ Well, cameras were there some 70 years later to cover things such as Hitler's Nuremberg Rally, with Leni Riefenstahl behind the camera. Where do you see the line between political advertising and propaganda?

◁ Well, I think the line between political advertising and propaganda is again the line of truth and honesty ... which I confess does get blurred occasionally. It becomes not a total truth or a total lie. It's somewhere in between, and I think that is where a lot of political advertising finds itself. It isn't like there's no truth at all to what they're saying. But they are finding certain aspects of truth that almost make the message a lie. They're dramatizing an aspect of this opponent that is really very negative and not totally true. I'm told that the more skilled you are at doing this, the more successful your candidate will be. But I honestly believe that dramatizing the truth in a skillful way is what is going to win you the election. With Reagan there was no blurring of the truth. He said, "I want lower taxes," and "I want to end the Cold War," and he did it. He said, "I want a smaller government" and he did that to some degree. Not to the extent that he hoped, but he did manage to make it a smaller government. It was a very honest, very straightforward kind of message which in many ways he lived up to.

▷ Why are you creative, Phil?

◁ Well, first of all, it's a lot of fun. It's a very strange business because it has incredible highs and incredible lows. Most people in advertising sort of fell into it, I think. We came from other quarters – journalism, television, the magazine business. I came from the radio. I used to be a disc jockey and I used to write radio copy in a radio station. And we all sort of came in and gravitated toward advertising because it gave us a chance to be on the national stage. A chance to show off what creative abilities we had, and to be recognized for that creativity. Also, good advertising is fun to watch. It's entertaining, in some cases more entertaining than the programs that the advertising runs in. So, all of those things put together, I think are some of the driving forces that make people like myself happy to do what we're doing.

▷ So it's the multi-faceted aspects of advertising that brings a lot of talent into this business.

◁ Yes, I think a lot of people in advertising would love to go off and write a screenplay or a movie.

▷ Which you have done.

◁ Yes, but in some ways advertising is like that. You use a lot of the same component parts, just like movies, it involves a script. It involves music. It involves editing. It involves postproduction. The difference is that you get yours on air a lot faster than when you're writing a movie. You could wait two years before you see that happen. And you don't have to wait two years to find out if you have a hit or a flop. So a lot of the same things that drive people to want to write movies also drives people to want to write and create advertising.

▷ And now you have also a lot of people who keep crossing those lines, what with commercials directors directing feature films, etc.

◁ There's a co-mingling of talent ... people like Adrian Lyne, Ridley Scott, Tony Scott, even Joe Pytka. There's this crossover because the disciplines are related. However, it doesn't mean that anyone who is good at advertising can just go off and write a successful movie or direct a successful movie. They're used to working in 30 second and 60 second increments, which can be a handicap when doing a feature film. But at least they would have the beginnings of knowing the craft, what it takes to move people. Advertising people, if they're good, they know what it takes to move people, to stir people to action. And that's really what a movie maker does. He gets people to feel something about characters and performances and events. So there are a lot of similarities and as time goes by, we're going to see more of a co-mingling of these kinds of talents.

▷ What are you personally influenced by?
◁ I think the greatest influence for me is motion pictures. And being a student of reality. It is important to be a good observer of human behaviour. Paddy Chayefsky, who was a wonderful screenwriter years ago, used to have what people call a "subway ear", meaning he could hear a dialog on a subway and write it down later on. That's why his dialogs sounded so marvelously real, so authentic. I think if you're a good observer of human beings and can get it down on paper, you're already ahead of the game.

▷ I once talked to Jeff Stark, and he said that when he goes to a restaurant he usually tends to eat alone but tries to sit next to a table where there's a conversation going on so he can pick up some of that "real dialog" floating around.
◁ Yes, you hear dialog sometimes that is totally wonderful. You couldn't possibly make it up because it is so great. The whole idea of writing good dialog, I think, is to come as close as you can to nailing the way people actually behave and the way they actually say things, but in as an interesting a way as possible. Because if you tune into most conversations of people, they're sort of dull. The whole trick for the screenwriter and the advertising writer is to make that dialog come to life, but in a much more engaging and personal way than that mundane dialog of everyday living.

▷ Final question: in what way will the Internet influence advertising?
◁ I think the Internet is a road yet unexplored although we're seeing some progress being made. It will never replace television, as we know it today, at least not in the foreseeable future. There is still a lot of work you have to do when you go on the Internet. You really have to get involved and it is very interactive. There are a lot of people in this world who don't want to be interactive. People come home in the evening after working

all day, interacting with people all day, and the most interaction they will have is clicking through the various TV channels available to them. So I don't imagine that in the foreseeable future TV will be replaced by the Internet. The Internet will at best be an augmentation of TV advertising, an additional component that's worth looking at as a potential vehicle. □

TIM DELANEY

Death in Venice was badly shot
by Visconti

In the 60's, Tim Delaney was an award winning copywriter at PKL and BMP. In the 70's he became Creative Director of BBDO London during its most creative years. Tim Delaney is the creative mastermind behind Legas Delaney, an agency he founded in 1980.

Tim has done some of the best press, posters, and radio seen in the UK. His work for Adidas, Guardian and Porsche won numerous awards around the world. His agency now has branches around the world. Tim works as hard as 3 or 4 normal people.

An ad (featuring lines that you'd never hear famous ad people say) showed Tim looking at an ad, saying "Yeah this'll do, let's go to the pub". Everyone in London got the joke.

I interviewed Tim Delaney in the office of RSA/USA where he was post-producing commercials for Telekom Italia featuring Woody Allen, Marlon Brando and Nelson Mandela.

▷ Hermann Vaske: When you gained the Adidas account you gave them a new advertising strategy.

◁ Tim Delaney: Adidas was a company that had got into trouble by not really believing in marketing. And certainly not really believing in advertising. So that our job was simply to create a relationship between Adidas the brand and a younger generation that hadn't really been addressed before. So that when Robert Louis Dreyfuss came, we had already started the process but he accelerated it, believing, quite rightly, that the brand's future was in the hands of younger people than Adidas had addressed before. And so he's in full agreement with the strategy. And, as I said, he's advanced the strategy. Spent more money on advertising. And we now have a pretty healthy relationship with young people.

▷ Is humour a valuable tool to get into people's hearts?

◁ Humour works in many cases in advertising simply because it endears the product you're talking about to the audience. It also puts perspective. One of the really bad things about advertising is when it tries to tell people what to do. Humour can depict the universal truth in a way which is sympathetic to the audience. And allow them to look at themselves and look at other people as one kind of humanity. And then say, okay, that product kind of works in that context. So humour is a way of connecting in a way that facts don't connect or selling messages simply don't connect any more.

Stills from Delaney's commercial for Pepe Jeans

▷ Where do you get your ideas from? Where do you get your stimulus from?

◁ I think most people not just in advertising but in communication swim around in a pool full of influences which can be anything from childhood influences to dreams, to films, to books, to poetry, to art. And you're never really conscious of where these things come from. I happen to believe that advertising deals mostly in regurgitated, reformulated clichés because they tend to need to make shorthand connections. So while most people in advertising think that they're pretty smart, I'm not so sure we are.

▷ Do you agree with the "Say it with a smile" philosophy? Does it sell products successfully?

◁ I think advertising that has a sense of humour works. If you sell things with a smile, people may find it more easy to part with their money. But I don't think advertising sells things. I think advertising builds relationships. Our job is to build a relationship between the product and its audience and then out of that relationship people have a predisposition and are predisposed towards that product versus another product. So if it's a car, I'd prefer an Opel to a Ford. Not for rational reasons because they've both got four wheels, a steering wheel and four seats. We build relationships which are clear and personal relationships. So it's a one-to-one relationship multiplied by millions. That's our job. Salesmen sell things.

▷ What about shocking people to sell products? Do provoking and shock tactics work?

◁ I think you can shock people into looking at an advertisement. You can do something very shocking. If you can open a magazine and show a bum. And people will say, "That's a really amazing thing. I haven't seen that before." But if it is purely just for the shock and it doesn't relate and if you're not selling knickers or you're not selling toilet paper then the bum is irrelevant. So you can shock people if it's relevant. Sometimes you need to shock people. Certainly if you're talking about charities. Rwanda or Somalia for example. Then it's absolutely appropriate to show shockin images to make people realise that people three or four or five hours away from their comfortable lives are dying. So you should shock people. If you're shocking people simply to sell detergent, then I think it's a bit stupid.

▷ What about your Pepe jeans campaign. Wasn´t one of the commercials banned?

◁ We've done two commercials for Pepe and they've both been banned. They've both been banned and MTV were fined for showing it. And the other one, MTV wouldn't show it. And the reason why we've done those

Tim Delaney   94 commercials is because our whole strategy for Pepe is teenage rebellion and the physiological fact that at a certain age teenagers have to rebel. Our two Pepe commercials both have been banned. But we've made commercials that shock for Pepe simply as part of a strategy which depicts teenage rebellion. And our desire to have a relationship with teenagers outside of their Levi's relationship or Diesel relationship is based on the fact that kids have to rebel. It's a physiological fact. So that when we are rebelling, or when we're depicting rebellion, then it means we've got to do things which are dramatically different than that which kids can get up to. So if we drop a Mercedes from a crane or if we put a kid inside a washing machine, then, yes, it's going to be pretty contentious stuff. I mean, we have a difficult time getting on air. But we have to dramatise the rebellious relationship that we're trying to engage in.

▷ What about the accusation that some people say if advertisers just have a low budget, they just sit in the boardroom and think of what they can do to get the most of PR and word of mouth out of the product. Just do something that gets banned and profit from that inbuilt PR.
◁ People often think they can create PR by having commercials or ads or posters turned into a controversy. It's not the way to do it. It's actually backfires because the amount of money it costs to make an interesting commercial or an ad won't necessarily get it banned. And also, even if it does get banned, it doesn't mean to say you'll necessarily get PR from it. We didn't get a great deal of PR from Pepe when it was banned. And we ran ads in America for Pepe which I thought would cause an absolute outcry and they never even got a mention. So it doesn't always work.

▷ Should shocking ads be censored?
◁ I don't think you should ban ads by and large unless they're gratuitously advocating violence. And if they want to advocate violence, then I think that's one thing... I think to ban advertising or indeed any communication based on a taste judgement whether you like the depiction of one image or another then I think it's pretty crazy to start getting involved in banning things, as I say, as long as it's not advocating violence or racial hatred, people can deal with images by and large much better than the courts can.

▷ Is advertising the fine art of separating people from their money?
◁ No, advertising is a mechanism by which people who make products talk to other people about those products. The selling part of it is conducted in showrooms if it's cars, in supermarkets if it's groceries, in banks if it's money. All that advertising does is try and separate brands and give them a personality so that people can differentiate. There's very little advertising that actually goes out there and sells. Unless it's a new product and you

WE STOLE THEIR LAND, THEIR BUFFALO AND THEIR WOMEN. THEN WE WENT BACK FOR THEIR SHOES.

The Red Indians were an ungrateful lot.

Far from thanking the whiteman for bringing them civilisation (guns, whisky, disease, that kind of thing), they spent years making very bad medicine.

Naturally, during the course of their disputes, the whiteman found it necessary to relieve the Red Indians of certain items.

Thousands of square miles of land, for instance, which they didn't seem to be using.

The odd buffalo, which provided some interesting culinary experiences for the folks heading West.

And of course the squaws, who were often invited along to soothe the fevered brows of conscience-stricken gun-runners and bounty hunters.

But perhaps the most lasting testament to this cultural exchange programme is the humble moccasin.

A shoe of quite ingenious construction. And remarkably comfortable to boot.

Even now, nearly two centuries after the first whiteman tried a pair on, they have yet to be bettered.

Which is why at Timberland, all of our loafers, boat shoes and walking shoes are based on the original Red Indian design.

How is this possible? Surely a shoemaker of our standing is capable of showing a clean pair of heels to a few pesky injuns?

Not really.

Although over the years, we have managed to make some modest improvements.

Rather than use any old buffalo hide, we always insist on premium full-grain leathers. And when we find a tannery that can supply them, we buy its entire output.

We then dye the leathers all the way through so you can't scuff the colour off and impregnate them with silicone oils to prevent the leather going dry.

It is at this point that we employ the wraparound construction of the moccasin to create the classic Timberland shoe.

Using a single piece of softened leather, our craftsmen mould and stretch the upper

around a specially-developed geometric last.

This has the effect of breaking the shoes in before you've even set foot in them.

It also extends the life of the shoe for many, many moons.

Our hand sewn shoes also hark back to the days before the whiteman came.

No machines. No mass production. No deadlines.

Just a pair of nimble hands making shoes in the time-honoured way.

With just a little help from the twentieth century.

Like the high-strength nylon thread, double-knotted and pearl stitched to prevent it coming undone even if it's cut or in the unlikely event that it breaks.

The two coats of latex sealant, added to stop even tiny droplets of water sneaking in through the needle holes.

And the patented process which permanently bonds the uppers to the soles.

(If the Indians had only known how to cobble soles onto their moccasins, we probably wouldn't be in business today.)

As you would expect, the result of all our

labours is a shoe which comes with a heap big price tag.

For which we make absolutely no excuses.

After all, who else uses solid brass eyelets? Or self-oiling rawhide laces? Or glove leather linings?

Come to that, what other shoemaker shows such concern for your feet when big rains come?

For example, as well as utilising all our traditional methods, our new Ultra Light range uses new technology to keep your feet dry.

They're lined with Gore-Tex to make them completely waterproof while allowing your feet to breathe. (Gore-Tex has 9 billion holes per square inch. We didn't believe it either but it works, so now we believe it.)

The soles are made from an incredibly lightweight and highly resistant, dual-density polyurethane.

And, in an uncharacteristic concession to fashion, some models even sport tightly woven waxed cotton cloth.

LEFT: TIMBERLAND LOAFERS. RIGHT: THE ORIGINAL MOCCASIN.

A far cry from the Red Indian moccasin? We certainly hope not.

Because if we ever forget our origins, or change our old-fashioned way of making boots and shoes, one thing's for sure.

A lot of people are going to be on the warpath.

Timberland Shoes and Boots, 23 Pembridge Square, London W2 4DR. Telephone 01:727 2519.

haven't seen it before and you say, "that's an interesting product and it works better than the one I've got", then it sells. But it sells via the information and the novelty, not via the ability to manipulate the mind. One of the great myths about advertising is that it manipulates. It doesn't manipulate to sell. It can manipulate, but only on the basis of personality. Not necessarily on the basis of sales.

▷ Why are you creative?

◁ Because, I suspect because my father was bright, and my mother was intuitively bright. And, they taught us to be independent thinkers. So, unlike people with a classical education, which I don't have, I'm prepared to think in a very lateral way, I have no fences about how I think. So, my upbringing, basically, allowed me to be a thinker, and then out of that came the ability to write down what I was thinking.

Why am I creative? God knows! I'm not even sure I am. I mean, I create things but I don't know whether that would be termed creative, in anybody else's terms, other than advertising terms.

▷ Somebody once said to me that everybody is creative and what separates creative people from non-creative people is the fact that creative people just do it.

◁ I fundamentally believe that everybody has a capacity to be "creative" and that being creative isn't the prerogative of a few. I think that most people have the ability to dream. And therefore if you dream, you can think up things which are different than what is in front of you. So... if creative means simply the ability to think outside the facts that confront you, then I think everyone has got that ability. And I think that if you look at creative people in advertising, by and large they are people who have happened on that career by accident and they are forced to use that creativity because they wish to make a living. So I'm like an artist or a poet that has to write or has to paint to get it out of their system, to get it off their chest, to be able to express this thing. They are driven to do that. In advertising, we are paid to do it. And therefore the demands on our creativity are paradoxically less... even though we're paid to do it but they're paradoxically less than the demands on a true or real artist.

▷ Who's influencing whom? Advertising feature film or feature film advertising?

◁ I think there are two parts of the relationship between advertising and film. One is the ideas and the concepts that you can put on film. And I think that film has influenced advertising to the extent that film continually teaches you not to be linear in the way that you show things. And not be factual. So that if you take the traditional commercial which is a woman

'A table for two? Certainly you old trout.'

Delaney's campaign for Linguaphone

in a kitchen cleaning the dishes and selling the washing-up liquid, that's traditional. Hollywood has taught everybody that not only is that not what people want to see necessarily, but also that you don't have to show the actual fact of someone doing that in order to depict that woman in that situation. You can do other things. You can be wider than that. The second part is the whole craft element to do with people like Ridley Scott, Alan Parker, Adrian Lyne. They shoot features like commercials not just in the kind of neurotic tight way that you have to show a product but they shoot them with a great deal of finesse with many more cuts. I was rewatching "Death in Venice" recently and it's a terribly rude thing to say but the film is badly shot by Visconti. It's interesting. He does dreadful shots in it which are really bad cuts, which you simply wouldn't see in a film nowadays. And it doesn't make the film worse. The film is a great film, I think. But from a point of view of how you make a film, I think that some of the craft elements that have come from British and indeed other commercials directors going to Hollywood have made the films extremely polished. From all elements of lighting, editing, music. All those things have been improved by commercial directors.

▷ What about the mutual influence of advertising and feature film? Advertising people like to adapt ideas. There are twenty rip-offs of "Blade Runner" and forty rip-offs of "Indiana Jones". And we can all be sure that there will be a lot of rip-offs of every halfway interesting new release.

◁ I think that advertising now thinks it's perfectly acceptable to take popular culture and redevelop it. So whether it's a pop song or whether it's a scene in a film, people in advertising in England, certainly believe it's acceptable to appropriate whole scenes from films and put a product in it. I think it's probably okay because the audience understands what you're doing by and large. And if they don't, then there's no point appropriating the scene. So they know it's a pastiche of another film, albeit, a film that's only just come out. Whether it's ethical, I think, is probably between the filmmaker and the advertiser. I think it's not a question of ethics. I think it's about regurgitating popular culture.

▷ Is there such a thing as ethics in advertising?

◁ I think there's a paradox here. Most principled people I've met in business are in advertising. And I think it's because the good ones try and dignify what essentially is a fairly undignified business. And therefore there are a disproportionate amount of highly principled, if not to say totally ethical, people in advertising. Where the popular conception is that advertising people are kind of sleazy and would sell their grandmother to the next-door neighbour. It's simply not that way. There are people who do stand up and say, "Look, this is not the right thing to do. We should be doing this, this and this".

▷ So what Mr. Séquéla told his mother, that he's a piano player in a bordello and that he's not working in advertising, doesn't appeal today? ◁ I think that the title of Séquéla's book was a catchy title for a book and I think it accords with what most people feel about advertising people, which is that we're below the people that work in a bordello. I don't think it's the truth.

▷ What's your favourite piece of work? ◁ It's difficult to have favourite pieces of work. You tend to relate the things that have been good experiences or where you worked with interesting people. Working with David Lynch on one Adidas commercial was exciting simply because it was working with a master filmmaker. And a very nice guy who you just stood back and watched him do things which you'd never seen before. And he did it with ease but also with a great deal of professionalism. And the music guy who he worked with, Angelo Badalamenti, was also involved in the film. And that was also an experience because he's very successful in his own right. So the two of them were incredibly accessible and approachable, but at the same time, masters of their crafts. And you had to stand back and say that was a really enjoyable experience and I like the film. Some people don't like the film. I really like the film.

▷ The surreal bits, when you go into the eye. Were they storyboarded? ◁ No, the way that we approached it was that we wanted to go from hell into heaven. And that's what we said to David Lynch. We want to create the film where a runner goes through the wall, the pain barrier, and is in hell as he goes towards the wall. And then comes out at the other side into heaven. And that's essentially all we told him.

▷ So you let him have quite a free hand... ◁ Absolutely. He's another paradox, I guess. Because on one hand, he's created the strangest images and some of the more strange films of the last twenty years. And certainly "Twin Peaks"' image is interesting. But he's a really ordinary guy. He's almost like a little cowboy.

▷ Cowboy? ◁ Yeah. He speaks like a cowboy. He comes from Idaho. And he speaks like a cowboy.

▷ From the surrealist cowboy back to your high-tech conference room. What concept is behind that? ◁ I think you can put anything in a boardroom in a place which purports to be creative. By and large, the object of an advertising agency is to say

that we can think differently than the people that come into it for help. So what we should be doing is saying we are here as an expression of the way we think. So if it's a cow in formaldehyde, if it's an object, if it's a room, it should be different from that which those people live in or can think about. We should demonstrate our ability to think outside the box as many times as we can, just to say we're different.

▷ Some years ago you did a great commercial with Emil Zatopek. Was it difficult to track down Zatopek and get him in the Adidas ad?

◁ No. It wasn't difficult to track him down. He was charmingly shy about his achievements and somewhat reticent about sort of coming forward and then he was very talkative about it and has got an incredible memory. He remembers all his big races, who was second, who was third, the dates, the medals and is completely photographic about the way he talks about his races as though they were locked into his memory. And not surprisingly if you've achieved what he achieved and on the world stage, I think you would relive that race every moment of it all your life.

▷ Do you agree with Duchamps, who said "a picture that does not shock is not worth anything?"

◁ I think a picture doesn't have to shock to be worth something. I think the picture has to be something that people can relate to and sometimes the relationship you're trying to create is one that shocks in order to make the impression or create some sort of relationship. It isn't simply that. You can show a picture of a baby to a woman and it can be the strongest image she'll see that entire week, depending on what kind of mood she's in. Or you can show a fast car to a man, that's a bit of a cliché. And he could see the most shocking pictures but the thing that he'll remember at the end of the week is the fast car because that's what he's dreaming about and craving. So I don't think it's completely about shocking. I also think that many quotations about communication really do have to be seen in the context of the time they were spoken. Communication now is moving so fast and people's sophistication about how they deal with communication is changing on an almost daily basis. We can deal with much more than we ever know and we're much more sophisticated about communication than Duchamp or anybody else of that era would have been able to understand. It's a bit like Marxism. It was fantastic as an analysis at the time. Put it into the latter part of the 20th century and while most of the principles are still interesting and could be enacted, it somehow doesn't quite fit with what we've all been brought up to believe we can achieve. It treats us as though we are always going to be peasants and therefore it was a mid-19th century analysis and it doesn't fit at the beginning of the 21st century.

▷ You have an image of the smart Tim Delaney who has a reputation to be brighter than the ordinary advertising person? How do you cope with that?

◁ I don't know whether I'm intellectually more capable than other people in advertising. There's some quite bright people in advertising. I'm interested in lots of different things and I don't have to cope with it. I'm just interested particularly in politics.

▷ What are the false images, what are the false idols in today's world?

◁ The false idols in today's world. Probably the same as they always were, money, rich people aren't happy. Sex is not a false, it's a good one. Material goods are overrated, you have to go through a period of owning them, and then you say okay, I've owned them, so they're false. I think religion is the greatest false idol of them all.

▷ Do you have Karl Marx in mind? Opium for the people?

◁ Very much so. Leadership is a false idol, the internet will stop that, I think. The more people know, the less they need leaders.

▷ Is internet the new God?

◁ Information is the new God.

▷ Why?

◁ Because the more you know, the more you need to be told what to know. Karl Marx and Lenin were right when they said it's about information. If you control the information, you control the people. So, you stop the information. The internet starts the information, so it flows, so if you stand in the middle of China, and you know about what's happening in China, and you know about what's happening in the world, you are empowered in some way.

▷ Regarding the flow of information - the internet could be a double edged sword as well?

◁ The internet could be used in any way that information can be used. The interesting thing is they, they've got to find a way, which they haven't found yet, of stopping it and encrypting it. And human being's ingenious nature will get round that way, because it's built into the technology to get round things, and to disseminate information quickly. It's the speed of the information, globally. If you think about the Middle Ages villages, village to village, superstition, Jesus Christ is based on superstition, nothing else. You know, you've got a few rocks in the ground, and some story about the crucifixion, but he was one of thousands of people that were crucified. And, if the idea is that you go from superstition to information to fast information, to intergalactic information, the more information you have, the more you will require less to be told of what to believe.

▷ What are the golden calves of the information age? What are we dancing around today?

◁ Dancing round Pamela Anderson or her equivalent. Dancing around a sports car, dancing around a Sony mini disk video recorder. Dancing around a suit of clothes or a dress designed by somebody. I mean, those are the sort of materialistic icons of the age. They're the things that people want and aspire to.

▷ Advertising is often accused of creating desires in people so that they covert things that they cannot afford. How do you cope with that?

◁ They covert things they want and the theory is that if they covert things, they'll go out and find the mechanisms, money, by work, to afford them. That's the capitalist idea, and that's the only idea that's left on the planet. So, that's what people do. Now, the ones that can't do that because of geography, if you're sitting in the middle of Chad or the Ivory Coast, you can covert a BMW, but you're not going to get one. And there lies the inequity of geography. And I think the only issue is that they're still coveting things, they just can't get them.

▷ Should all creative people use their talents to promote good causes and do charity advertising?

◁ I believe that all creative people should use their skills to try and reorder society for the good. It's difficult, because you can't just say I want to sit here and change the economic balance of power around the world, just because you can make a film or write a song. But, you have degrees of expertise, and I certainly believe that the people that communicate in the media are the most powerful people in the world now. And therefore, they can use that to effect things, you can effect something by clever use of the media. You can bring a subject to people, to the forefront of people's consciousness. And they can then act on that themselves. So we should be able to use our skills better than we're doing at the moment.

▷ What's better for creativity? Obsessive work or to take a day off once in a while?

◁ Both. Obsessive work and a day off once in a while, they're not mutually exclusive.

▷ What do you think of Toscani´s campaign for Benetton with the people on death row?

◁ I think that Benetton's advertising is largely divorced from their retail relationship. I don't think they think it's related, it's essentially publicity for a brand, and it attempts to take a moral stance. I don't think that's

MEDIA IS NOW THE DOMINANT FORCE
ON THE PLANET. IT SELLS PRESIDENTS,
DESPOTS, GOVERNMENT POLICIES,
MISSILE SYSTEMS AS WELL AS DOG
FOOD, DETERGENT AND FIZZY DRINKS.

relevant, necessarily, to people buying sweaters from them. If Luciano
Benetton and Oliviero Toscani want to talk about death or killing in their
ads, that's their prerogative, I don't think it's got much of a relationship
between what they do in business. And it may publicise the brand, but I
don't think it's pretty relevant.

▷ You certainly can accuse Benetton´s advertising for not being
relevant but you cannot accuse it for not having enough impact. In the US
there were even picket lines outside Benetton stores to demonstrate
against the "Death men advertising" campaign.

◁ I can imagine that people would take against them for it, because there
is a kind of gratuitous use of other people's misfortune to publicise, they're
still publicising their stores. I mean, it's still an ad, even though if they
want to talk about the social issues, but still at the end of the day, they
are the beneficiaries of that. And there is a morality in that, and an
immorality in that, that they don't seem to be aware of. It's as though
they can do anything in the name of the moral cause, but it's still got a
logo on the end of it.

▷ Would it have been better if they would have shown the victims as
well, like in side by side ads?

◁ They could show the murderer, and they could show the victim, but
they're still trying to get commercial gain from other people's misfortune.
And I think that's debatable, to put it mildly.

▷ On the other hand it´s nothing really new that ad campaigns are
based on creative truthstretching.

◁ I think that a lot of advertising is lying by omission, you carefully select
the things you want to say about any product. That's one level, and that

can be an old Beetle Volkswagen, where they don't tell you that because it's got the engine in the back, it moves around in the front. And they tell you to put potatoes in the front, that's what they used to do. If you come back to more serious issues, like cigarettes, it's always surprised me that people can justify it, but it's quite interesting how intelligent people are able to work in these industries, and they see no line between their corporate responsibilities and their private responsibilities. So, people that work in cigarette companies, marketing, advertising, manufacturing right the way through, all have children, and all smoke, and all understand that it's like a mass suicide. I don't know what the phenomenon is, but somewhere along the line, people were allowed to just dissociate themselves from the moral issue of what they're doing. So, as you say, hamburgers are made from certain things that people don't want to talk about, cigarettes kill people, and on and on. And, by and large, advertising people don't really want to do those things. But they find themselves in a situation where they make a choice, and it's a silent choice, it's a kind of choice of a person that acquiesces, it's an appeasement of the truth.

▷ Another problem in advertising are rip-offs. Is there a creative adultery?

◁ Yes, there is creative adultery, there's stealing of other people's goods. There is a kind of acceptance that the reinterpretation of ideas is accep-table. But it's like music in sampling, if you take modern culture, there are cross overs, and it's considered to be an interesting sort of sub art. So, if you sample music, why not sample films, why not sample books, why not sample poetry. And by sampling, it just means borrowing, reinterpreting, and then delivering it up afresh. Now, the only issue is whose is it, and in the world of music, the sampling has an author, and that's the person who decides to sample, not the original person. So, the adultery seems to be condoned in music, and it probably should be in other places. We shouldn't take it so seriously. Having said that, there is also plagiarism, and plagiarism is straightforward wrong. And that's a different thing.

▷ After we released the advertising beast from out of it´s cage. Is it o.k. to separate people from their money as long as you give them back creativity in return?

◁ Advertising is misunderstood, it's about... people create relationships, and then people, out of that relationship, people may say okay, I like that, that brand, or that product better than somebody else's. That's what we do. So, when you sit down to write something, you say "good, people will give their money over to this", that's not the issue, the issue is you're trying to get people to get closer to a particular brand, so that the subject of money and the separation of money really isn't there. You're happy that something's successful, but it's only successful, it's not really about the idea of separating people from their money.

□

NEIL FRENCH

I take my little knife and cut away everything that does not look like an elephant

Neil French was expelled from minor public school at 16. He became a rent-collector, account executive, bouncer, waiter, singer, matador, rock band manager, promoter, account executive, again, and copywriter. Then he started an agency and went spectacularly broke after seven years.
He joined the creative London hotshop Holmes Knight Ritchie in 1980. He went to Asia and joined, and left, Batey Ads in Singapore in 1986.
Then he joined Ball Partnership as Vice Chairman & Regional Creative Director. He turned the Singapore agency into an internationally recognised creative force, and got fired 1991. Nowadays French travels as Worldwide Creative Director, to motivate O & M creatives all around the world. I interviewed Neil French at Cannes.

▷ Hermann Vaske: What does art mean for you?
◁ Art. I don't know, I think art is finding a way to say something in a way that is not probably conversational, that's all. So it can either be visual or musical or a thousand other ways, maybe pictorial. But I think it's just a way of people expressing themselves without having to talk about it directly to somebody. But I don't think it has anything to do with advertising.

▷ And what does business mean for you?
◁ Business is the art of making money.

▷ Were your commercials for UBS in which actors like Ben Kingsley quote Shakespeare and Shelley poems a combination of art and business?
◁ That's a very clever question. I suppose in a way it is, but the intention of the campaign is to flatter the customer, or the prospective customer. Because if a man's got a hundred million dollars to invest, he doesn't want to be told any facts about the bank. He knows all the facts about the bank. He just wants to know that you're his kind of people. That's merely maybe making a bridge between the bank and the customer, saying, hey, we understand the way you think and your problems, and so on. And each poem is chosen specifically to relate to this guy's everyday life. That's all about standing tough, basically. Every part of it is standing tough, and don't give up, hang on in there, which is the strength of the Swiss Bank. At the end of everything, Swiss banks will always be there.

▷ From money to charity advertising. Why is there so much charity advertising around?
◁ I wish that were true. I wish that were true. I think if there were no award ceremonies, there would be a tenth of the amount of charity

advertising. And I think that's more cynical than anything anybody is doing at the moment. That really bothers me. We produced a commercial this year of the Khmer Rouge knocking the heads off Angkor Wat statues and selling them for a hundred thousand dollars a pop. And that is absolutely awful. And to try and stop people from buying those is a legitimate aim, but I think when you start to say, stop child prostitution etc, and ads like that you see around a lot... An ad is not going to stop that. It is actually a cynical effort to win an award. It is not a specific aim in a charity. And I worry about it a lot. I find it very distressing, actually. I know some are honest, 10 % may be honest, I think. I don't like them very much.

▷ Yeah, I mean, in agencies you´ll find professional cynics who only ask themselves how can I get into the limelight of awards. And there comes charity advertising-its handy. Because it´s an easy route.

◁ Certainly that's true. I mean "scam ads" as we call them these days, are a fairly legitimate way for a young team to try and prove that they can do a job, whether or not giving a brief that allows them to do their job. I think that's okay, that doesn't bother me very much, because we can all see through the crap. And a few get through because they're really good ideas and you want everybody to see the idea. But when it's done in that cynical way of, you know, I'm helping these homeless, starving, abused people. These are bad taste, I don't like them.

▷ Can you elaborate about your commercial for the temple of Angkor Wat.

◁ There's this huge temple in Cambodia, called Angkor Wat, which was the biggest Buddhist temple in the world, it still is, I suppose, in principle. But they knock the heads off the Buddhas and send them to China and Singapore and places like this and sell them on a spike to put on your mantelpiece. And a lot of people don't actually think when they buy them that it's actually a religious artefact. So we did a commercial where somebody chops the head off and uses a saw to take the head of a Christ figure and stuck that on a spike and said, hey, would you like it? And of course everybody said, this is offensive. Well, of course it is offensive. It's supposed to be offensive and I find religious bigotry even more offensive. And if people will be happy to knock a Buddha off and then find it offensive to say a Christ head knocked off, I think they have to investigate their emotions a little bit. And that's what it was intended to do. And it's working, which is the nice thing. It raised an enormous amount of awareness and we're selling many of them in the countries of the Far East. We have to stop it now, because otherwise there will be no more left. And even after the Khmer Rouge have stopped, I am pretty certain somebody else will keep going if there is a demand. You've got to stop the demand. But that is a specific ad which is measurable. Right now, you can do that. A specific ad: "Stop buying these heads." And I think it's beginning to work. And it has to work in a hurry. It's like "Save the tiger"... that's a good one, but it's not as easy to do that. Because the people who are using tiger parts probably don't watch the television very much.

▷ The... What are the tiger products used for?

◁ Sadly, tiger penis is used for... getting him hard, mostly in China. Of course it doesn't work. Why would it? But it's traditional. The bones are ground up for various medical reasons. There's nothing in those bones any different to any other bone. It´s like rhino horn. So the rhino horn has the slight benefit of being something like the Spanish Fly, and it's an irritant to the bladder. That's how that will in the end give you a boner. But tiger penis won't. So these poor buggers are being slaughtered for this. There's no point in it.

▷ Did you ever get an erection doing good work?

◁ I don't do that much good work. I hope I get an erection more often than I do a good ad.

▷ You said, you are a buddhist. Did you ever experience any Zen moments in advertising?

◁ No, no. I'm a Buddhist. So it's obviously close to my heart, the whole thing. No, I'm not really... I'm not a Zen Buddhist. I can't just really believe in nothing. Well, possibly, my brain won't get around the concept. But I think Buddhism is a way of life, not a religion. And I've worked along with Thai Buddhism, which is a sort of a softer way of going. I'm not hoping to be a monk at any point of my career, but the principle is there. In most of Asia Buddhism is a soft way of life. Don't hurt anybody. You know in your heart what is right and what is wrong, and just deal with that, you'll be okay. It's a basic principle. And it's a pretty good principle. It goes along with all the rest, without the panoply of religion.

▷ Let's talk about, the global village, I once saw an ad and it said what Caesar, what Napoleon, what Stalin, what Hitler, what Emperor Hirohito were not able to do... Then you saw this picture of a Coke bottle, Coke was able to do. Globally conquering the planet. We had incidents at Seattle, Davos and Nice... Is globalisation a good or a bad thing?

◁ I can't think of anybody who actually died from Coke, anyway. Is it a good thing? Well, it's a personal thing. I like to see the differences in people rather than the similarities. I always say that international advertising

𝕬𝖘 𝖔𝖚𝖗 𝖈𝖔𝖓𝖙𝖗𝖎𝖇𝖚𝖙𝖎𝖔𝖓 𝖙𝖔 𝖗𝖔𝖆𝖉 𝖘𝖆𝖋𝖊𝖙𝖞, 𝖒𝖆𝖞 𝖜𝖊 𝖕𝖔𝖎𝖓𝖙 𝖔𝖚𝖙 𝖙𝖍𝖆𝖙 𝖉𝖗𝖎𝖓𝖐𝖊𝖗𝖘 𝖔𝖋 𝖔𝖚𝖗 𝖇𝖊𝖊𝖗 𝖜𝖎𝖑𝖑 𝖓𝖊𝖛𝖊𝖗 𝖉𝖗𝖎𝖓𝖐 𝖆𝖓𝖉 𝖉𝖗𝖎𝖛𝖊, 𝖇𝖊𝖈𝖆𝖚𝖘𝖊 𝖆𝖋𝖙𝖊𝖗 𝖙𝖍𝖗𝖊𝖊 𝖓𝖔𝖇𝖔𝖉𝖞 𝖊𝖛𝖊𝖗 𝖗𝖊𝖒𝖊𝖒𝖇𝖊𝖗𝖘 𝖜𝖍𝖊𝖗𝖊 𝖙𝖍𝖊𝖞 𝖕𝖆𝖗𝖐𝖊𝖉 𝖙𝖍𝖊 𝖈𝖆𝖗.

17% alcohol, and available soon in selected bars with nice comfortable floors.   X.O. Beer. Take it lying down.

should celebrate people's similarities rather than underline their differences. But it's the differences that make people interesting. Men and women are different. Black people and white people are different. They're not necessarily in either way better or worse. But they're different, and that makes them interesting. If you try to flatten everything out, it's boring. So I like the differences. Especially in Asia, there's such a panoply of cultures there, which is so exciting, and people are very nationalistic in a nice way rather than in an inquisitive way.

▷ Wouldn't it be the end of civilization if you come to a mountain village in Cambodia and find McDonald's next to a Nike store? What about the much hailed cultural diversity?

◁ Yes, that does get flattened. But on the other hand, you know, you go to that village and it looks picturesque to us. But people are probably dying of beriberi and all sorts of ghastly diseases which is probably the result of poverty which causes it. Basically most diseases are caused by poverty. You know, poverty leads to bad sanitation. Sanitation leads to disease. That may look pretty to us. But to them, they have to live with it every day. And if their standard of life is increased to the fact that they can afford toilets, and then that leads to the fact that they can afford a McDonald's, I'd give them the McDonald's, actually, and save them the

Neil French

disease. I don't think it's our right to make people be picturesquely poor.

▷ So the McWorld isn't that bad, after all?

◁ No, not at all, if that's what people want. I mean, you know, McDonald's succeeds because it's a good product. That's the end of it, really, it's actually a good product. And so is Coke. So all these major brands wouldn't be there if they weren't good products. And if people with their first new, spare dollars think that the expression of their new freedom is to buy a Mac, good for them. I don't care. As I say, a picturesque poverty is for the viewer, not for the poor devil who lives there.

▷ Advertising should make a splash. What tricks and techniques are there to make a splash?

◁ Whenever we have a brief, the first thing we do is to go and get all the competitive ads. If it's a press campaign, we stick them all on the wall. If it's a TV campaign, get all of them and put them on a rail. And sit down and watch what everybody else is doing. That immediately tells you what you don't do. Now I know what not to do. And by not doing what every-body else is doing, you immediately make a difference. And I think it's as simple as that. As long as you...

▷ ... create attention.

◁ Yeah. As long as you are zigging what everybody else is zagging, then you probably got it right. And you have to cut through the clutter. Cutting through the clutter is all of it. I've seen some ads this week which are not that well produced. Not that well shot, but they stand out, cut through the zag, so they're candidates for gold. And quite right too.

▷ What about the USP. Does it still count?

◁ Well, USP is something you probably start off with. Well, this is my USP, I now know what it is and if everybody else had that same USP or a similar one, what would they do? We'll even see what they are doing. Most USPs aren't that bloody unique, actually, and the more of a generic product it is by definition, the less of a USP it has. Sometimes the USP is the packaging or the section of the market at which it's aimed, many, many things. So the USP is a useful guide to the point to where we can go. But how we get there, is what makes advertising. Not where you're going, it's how you get there. And how you get there is how you make the splash, I think.

▷ Why are you creative?

◁ I don't know that I am that creative. Do you mean, as opposed to being a suit? I think everybody is creative to an extent. Why do we choose this as a living, probably we're not good at anything else, that's my answer.

I mean, that is true. I was hopeless at anything else I tried, so I became a creative man.

▷ People were always creative, you know, the cavemen were creative, the medieval craftsmen, the Michelangelos doing jobs for the Pope, doing jobs for the kings, for the dukes, copying reality, painting landscapes, painting whatever. Now we have the camera. The photographic camera captures reality and creates real images. How did the invention of the photographic camera change reality? Did it turn craftsmen into commercial artists?

◁ I don't think so. I think the camera is merely a recording machine in its "own front", that's all it is. But you remember now that it's not a recorder of reality any more, it's that you can make reality with a camera. So the new realities are being formed by digitalisation and cameras together. So kids tomorrow won't see a camera as a recording machine, they'll see it as something like a tool, a visual tool, that's all it is.

▷ How did the digital revolution change the language of film?

◁ Isn't it funny that you see the new Jurassic Park and think, hey, that's neat. And if you go back to the old Jurassic Park you see the joints and think: hey that's corny, you see how that was done. But when we first saw it, we thought it was great. And one day we will look back at the new Jurassic Park and think: that looks corny. There will come a point when the two are absolutely indistinguishable, reality and digitalisation. It won't be very long. It will be within the next five, ten years. And I don't think that's a bad thing, it's nice to be able to create what you want rather than have to go and find it.

▷ But don´t forget that costs a little something.

◁ Well, of course it's bloody expensive. This is the one thing. Digital work is so expensive. It's probably cheaper to fly to Matchu Pitchu and shoot it than make Matchu Pitchu, this is really silly. Do you remember when we first had logos spinning round on ads? And everybody had one, everybody thought, that's was just the bee's knees, I've got to have that. Now you wouldn't dare do that. You know, I think they still do it in Djakarta, but you know, that's pretty neat in Djakarta, but in most places you say: "Hey we don't do that any more." So the fashions change almost weekly now.

▷ Let's talk about the importance of sound. Some people say it's 51 % of the picture. Do you agree?

◁ Yes, I do. I think the great thing about sound is that it gets under the radar, because while you're looking at a picture you're consciously looking at a picture. The sound isn't always that conscious. It slips under your gown, tells you what to think about what you're looking at. I always remember the wonderful film "School Exercise". Do you know the old man walking down the alley way and this little girl with the skipping rope? And, there's some skipping rope music... And the old man goes up to the little girl and talks to her and holds her hand and they go off, obviously grand-father and granddaughter, rather nice and warming. Then they play the same film in silence and as the old man goes up and... you know, here comes the trouble. It's the same picture and it's the music underneath that is making you completely change your view of exactly the same thing.

▷ How should we talk to consumers these days?

◁ This is one of my hobby horses, I'm very keen on this one. We intrude into people's homes, uninvited, because we suddenly break into what they really want to be doing, watching The Simpsons or whatever it is. And honouring your father and mother means that you actually just honour the family environment, and we do tend to forget that I think. If you could actually make sure that there are no kids watching at a certain time, then that's okay, but actually some of our work does negate what parents are telling their children, and I don't think is good for the future, and I think it's recently been proved that we've had twenty years of getting it wrong, you know, that it's getting quite dangerous out there, and it's getting dangerous largely because of the stuff that communicators put in front of the family, not just advertising men, but film makers and certainly music people. And we think: God, this is cool and they'll like that, yeah, but when father and mother tell their kid one thing and then you tell them another, the kids are going to go with the exciting option, not with the boring old dad and mama.

▷ Did you kill for an idea?

◁ Actually if an idea can be killed at all it's not that great an idea. Great ideas live, despite what people throw at them.

▷ What do you think about the current discussion about intellectual property and how do you comment on the fact that there are so many rip-offs in advertising these days?

◁ Well, I bet every advertising man likes this one, because everybody says, oh, somebody has stolen my idea, somebody has stolen my idea. Well, yes and no. I mean the first guy to have a great idea is still the first guy to have it, and the second one is never quite as good, and we all steal bits of ideas and pretend that all we're doing is bending them a little bit. There's nothing original. I think Mozart said, "I've never written anything original in my life." So stealing ideas, which is what presumably you are

French's press ad for Continental Airlines

saying, is I think, there's too much fuss about.

▷ But what about just re-shuffling the ingredients, so that something appears fresh and seemingly new?

◁ You know, if it's a way to express yourself and show how clever you are and get somebody to notice you, all those things are important, and obviously advertising isn't only for the quiet. I mean this is a terribly wrong thing to say in some ways, but actually don't forget, everybody in advertising has a career and their career is far more important to them in honesty than the sales of soap powder or whatever it happens to be. And in order to advance their career, if they have to steal some ideas or bend or reshuffle to look smarter than the next guy, that's what they do. And as I said at a meeting the other day, "this isn't the Olympics, you know, it's not the taking part that's important, it's the winning, and however you need to win you should win, whatever it takes."

I mean Picasso was not the nicest man, and you know would definitely cheat and lie to get where he wanted to be, that's cool. If you want to win you've got to win. And I'm always bothered by some cultures that say this in advertising, you have to play fair, where did that suddenly come into it? I can't believe this. You know, I understand the Olympic ideal, but this isn't the Olympics.

▷ That's a business.

◁ Yeah, sure. Well, yeah, the ideal of course has long gone in the Olympics, but the principle, it was nice when it happened, and that was amateur people, not doing it for money, just trying to be there, and joining together, it was a social thing, but now it's winning just like anything else. And soon, you know, all the rules about taking drugs, performance enhancing drugs, that will all go away because it will be too difficult to police, so if you want to screw the whole rest of your life up, to get more muscles, to win a Gold, to make some more money, fair enough. It's just not going to work. Cheaters cheat, and some of them don't get caught.

▷ Bono said to me once, "Advertising is a business of beautiful lies."

◁ Well, Bono put it very well in that case, because if it is a business of beautiful lies, I think it's also a business of really ugly ones quite a lot. You know, all products are the best, it is our job to say that they are, hence we must be lying. But that's okay, we lie for money, as do lawyers, as do doctors frequently. That's okay.

▷ Is simplicity a key to good advertising?

◁ I think if people concentrate more on what they take out after they have written the first draft, "what can I take out of this to make it better,

Neil French

to make it more pointed", then almost every script I ever see would be better. I was telling the story about the old Indian man, who was very famous for carving elephants, wooden elephants. And he had no training. But he was famous throughout India for doing the best wooden elephants. And they once said to him, how is it that without any training and with your little knife you can just produce these wonderful elephants. And he said: "Well, I take my junk of wood and I take my little knife, and cut away everything that does not look like an elephant."

▷ Your elephant analogy brings me to the question: Is advertising with animals a valuable tool to sell products?

◁ As an animal, by its nature, I rather like elephants, you know, that's why there are so many elephants used. I think that's perfectly okay. They always say, never act with children or animals, that's a very good reason to put them with your ads, I think. The problem with models I always found, is a certain proportion of the audience, is going to hate that particular person. They know somebody who looks like that. There is a famous example with the Audi ad. Do you remember the Audi ad in England, where the deeply unpleasant money trader test-drives the Audi and then he is supposed to hate it. And then he comes back and says, "No, it's not my kind of car." And throws the keys to the dealer. And then people in response, everybody hated the car dealer more than they hated the guy they were supposed to hate. So you can never be quite sure who is going to be hated.

▷ I think research found out that royalty, animals and babies work best. If you stick one of them in your ad you´re o.k.

◁ Yes, of course, exactly. I didn't think of royalty, I think that doesn't work any more, does it? Animals, yes.

▷ Did it ten years ago?

◁ Ten years ago royalty was slightly different, I think. In some parts of the world, you see... Only the Windsors seem to have gone down the tubes a bit, I think. Some royalities are still highly respected.

▷ What about the other old tricks, the Procter & Gamble method, the before and after, the side by side, the with and without.

◁ You know, I've always liked that. And I think there's absolutely nothing wrong with it. If you say before and after, then you say it with enough wit. The wit is the key. It will work and work and work again. And you see gold here. Year after year, they have exactly that technique, but with wit? Now, the problem with the P&G formulae is that you're not allowed to inject any wit into it. You know, this it not very clean, this is clean. End

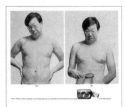

French's "Before and after" comparison for the ficticious beer X.O.

of argument. Hey, there's more we can say than that! So, you look through the old books, the old annuals, you rarely go through an award annual without seeing a lot of very nice side by side comparisons.

▷ Can you give us examples of your own ads, where you've used before/after or side by side comparisons?

◁ There's side by side, I did a campaign just a while ago for a fictitious beer which was actually campaigned the way people advertise beer in newspapers. Which in principle you should be able to do, but of course... accepted wisdom says you can only do it on television. So we produced a campaign for a beer that didn't exist. And it produced an enormous reaction, huge demand for that beer nobody could buy, very funny. And in one of the ads, which in the end got banned.. but they got it to run once, there was a naked man just cut off just above the groin... And he wasn't cut off, the photograph was just cut off at the line. And he's looking down at this with not too much pleasure about what he sees below and in the second picture, he has got a magnifying glass and he's looking down with absolute horror. And it was before this very strong beer. And it took people a little while to catch on, but it certainly did work. I mean it was ripped off, that was the strange thing. The whole campaign was ripped off by somebody in England who then produced it. And I think it won a campaign award gold with exactly the same thought. Very funny.

▷ Within your career you've won a gold in Cannes with a remarkably original film for a fish restaurant. How did that come about?

◁ Yeah, I can tell you quite a funny story about that. The commercial was for a restaurant in Singapore which had apparently the freshest fish. The idea was that the guy would go out with the restaurant man fishing on a dock. And they would suddenly look up and along comes a ship with a wok, you know, like a frying pan. And you whistle, and the fish would jump into the pan. And you walk off and you had seen, the freshest fish are at this restaurant. It doesn't take a brain surgeon to work out a script like that, but never mind. So that was it. And of course, we did it by putting the fish in the pan and then with a spring in it, and it went – bong - ... and then into the water. We shot this a few times and then the camera-man turned to me and said, I've got a problem. So I said: Well what is it? Okay, when the fish comes out of the pan it's coming out of the water head first. Yes, so. And he said, when you reverse it, it'll come out ass first. So it doesn't work, it has to come out head first. Yes. How are we going to fix this? So, it's a terrible story and I'll probably be sued by the RSPCA for this. So we couldn't figure out how to do it. So in the end we got the art director and a pile of lead fishing weights. And we spent the afternoon shoving the fish's bottom, so when it fell out, it fell bottom first into the water. And I was watching the art director shoving the lead weights into the fish's bottom, it was one of the little better moments in my life, not a big and outrageous one. But it cheered me up an awful lot, I can tell you.

▷ Well, I mean at least these fish didn't do it in vain. And it made a lot of people laugh.

◁ But it made a lot of people laugh and we ate them afterwards. So, you know. They did have a surprised look on their faces, I have to say. But... they were delicious.

▷ That's a good story. How important is word of mouth in the business?

◁ Oh, I mean if word of mouth was more reliable, we wouldn't need advertising? It's far more reliable than a mere ad, isn't it? If somebody you hardly know tells you to go to this restaurant or he just bought this and this car, you're utterly convinced. You can watch a hundred hours of ads and you'll never believe that much. That's because people believe people. Which is why talking head commercials are supposed to work. The question is: do you like the man who is telling you. That's the key.

▷ Can advertising learn from Hollywood?

◁ I tell you what, advertising copies Hollywood all the time, doesn't it? I always wish it wouldn't, every time a hit movie comes out, there are commercials that have neatly cut bits of it reshot. It's depressing that we can't be any more creative than that. But I suppose, there's an answer for it, that more people are seeing that film and relate to it than are ever going to relate to a mere ad. So, you're just borrowing the interest, that's fair enough. I think basically speaking many people denigrate Hollywood, I think it's probably a lot more creative than advertising people.

▷ And what about marketing? Marketing movies becomes more and more important.

◁ Yes, I think that's the one area where they get it wrong, don't you think? I mean, they make wonderful products and then promote it so badly. I mean, how many of these movies where you thought everybody ought to see this film. And nobody had ever heard of the damn thing. And you go around telling your friends, "You got to see this film, you got to see this film." There's a film called "Brassed Off" which is an English film which is absolutely great, it's funny, it's tragic, it has pathos, it has everything in it. Nobody has ever seen it. Nobody has ever seen it who hasn't been on a plane. I think that's the only time they ever played the thing. I keep telling people, "Go and buy the video", but I've never seen an ad for it, I've never seen a commercial for it. It probably cost a couple of million to shoot and, you know, another couple of million put behind it would have made it so, so popular. But they didn't do that.

▷ On the other hand we have big advertising campaigns for movies, that are big dumb and glossy, where literally half of the budget is spent for marketing.

◁ Yes, of course, you needn't tell me. Do they use advertising? They have their own department, I can't believe they use advertising people. What you could get for 4 million before you can get for 40 million now. I mean, you got to bear that in mind that always inflation takes care of that. You know, it always makes me laugh when they say this is the most expensive film of all times, well of course it is. Prices have gone up. They're never going to be smaller than that. It's not a fair comparison how much you spent on it and how much you're taking back. And now with video release, with cable release you get more for a film, they make money now on video and cable. I know, I've been in one. I was once persuaded to be the bad guy in a feature film. And I have to say this was probably the worst film ever made. It was one of the worst, close to Ed Wood, you know. But... I think the worst thing in it was me. But I believe it made money. Just unbelievable. It was merely because of cable and video sales. In fact, if you go to a video shop these days you can't get a copy of that film. I assume they've all been taken out. That could be the reason.

▷ Many trailers that sell movies glorify violence. Should trailers and spots be censored for that reason?

◁ Well, if you're not careful, you start to be the person who defines what is outrageous. I don't believe in any kind of censorship. What I really detest is overt violence. I think that is just disgusting these days. I can't understand why it has to get worse and worse. I have to say, I watch the films. I watched "Seven" three times, this is absolutely nauseous. And it was great. So what I'm not sure about is if it ought to be seen by kids. And the danger is with video it will be. I think that's a real thing we have to really worry about. In advertising that's never going to happen because there are so many watchdogs, busybodies who decide what we can show people.

I believe that violence is pornography. You see, I don't think sex is pornography. Sex is fun. And everybody does that, not everybody cuts somebody's head off with a chainsaw.

▷ Yeah, but kids go to video stores these movies. Not only in America but all over the world we have high school massacres.

◁ Yeah, that's my point. I mean, in the end, however old the kid is, it's going to make love to somebody. One way or the other. So it's not the end of the world if it sees people doing it, absolutely. But if it does see people cutting people's ribs with knives... You know, kids are not that smart and say: "Let's give it a try." And you see some very bad copy kids killing these days. And I'm not sure whether it's entirely due to violence or due to accidents. I think of violence on television specifically, but videos are also to blame. I think it's a problem for the developed world. A real problem. Kids copy stuff. I don't care if they go fucking each other, frankly. But I do care if they cut each other's ribs.

There's a huge difference between the east and the west. Children in the east still have great respect for their parents and for older people. In fact, luckily for me, older people still have greater respect in the east than they do here. So the culture of youth isn't quite preferable there. But respect plays an important part. In fact, when you get jostled in the street by a kid, it's a big moment. Actually speaking, nobody jostles me. But other people get a certain amount of jostling. Then they come and have to talk about it. But in L.A. or London or cities like that is the territory for that. No, kids out there are as much stranger... like all children are to older people, but they're not unpleasant, generally speaking.

I'm not young enough to know everything. And I think the Generation X is merely another group of people just like the baby boomers were, and they were also not as predictable as everybody wanted them to be. That's the fun if people were predictable, it would all be right every time and every ad would work. So all the research in the world wouldn't tell me what people are going to think tomorrow. And because by the time you've done your ad, it's of tomorrow. It's a guess every time, a gamble every time. You don't really know what these people are going to think. Probably the best way to know somebody, some single person in a group and aim the ad specifically at him, better than at an amorphous mass called Generation X. I always think of a person.

▷ Last question. Why did you pick Singapore as your home town?

◁ It picked me, actually. This is a true story. Twenty years ago I was supposed to go to Hong Kong and I stopped off in Thailand for a holiday and forgot to go to Hong Kong. And by the time I had finished my holiday in Thailand...I ought to be exact. I ran out of money, the Hong Kong job wasn't available and the guy was very very grumpy about the fact that I hadn't gone to take the job, but he said: "Oh, there's one in Singapore, do you want that one?" So, I was broke, so I said: "Yes, sure." Anyway, that's how I ended up there. But... was I a lucky boy? Oh, yes, oh, yes.

▷ Why?

◁ It's just been the best place in the world for me. Everything worked. It was the right time, the right job, the right place, it's, you know... I like almost everything about Singapore. I really adore the place, and I had never been there before. So I was so lucky that they plonked me down there just at that minute. I'll tell you, somebody out there loves me for no apparent reason.

□

TOSHIAKI NOZUE
The less you say the better

"East is east and west is west, and never the twain shall meet" Rudyard Kipling once said. In my interview Dentsu's Creative Director Toshiaki Nozue proves the old quote wrong, because the campaigns of the Japanese advertising giant, for Fuji Television, Mercedes Benz and Nissin Food won everything that could be won, from Cannes to Clio. I talked to the samurai of advertising in Cannes.

▷ Hermann Vaske: Isn't it rather unusual for a Japanese to be drinking espresso?

◁ Toshiaki Nozue: Yes, normally we drink green tea.

▷ But you drink espresso.

◁ Because I won't fall asleep if I drink espresso.

▷ That really is a good reason.

◁ For a Japanese this type of coffee is really strong.

▷ What do you do when you are not drinking coffee?

◁ I work as Dentsu's Creative Director on several accounts. I started out with copywriting. The lion's share of my work is commercials. One of my biggest clients is Matsushta Electric.

▷ What commercials have you made for Matsushta?

◁ Oh, many commercials for video recorders, for color TVs and washing machines and I did a film for the Technics electric piano for example. You might know it. You see a piano player sitting at a grand piano and playing Chopin. Suddenly a cleaning woman enters the frame, sweeping the floor. She seems to be obsessed with getting the floor as clean as possible, she never looks up. Of course she also has to sweep under the piano. When she gets close to it, she pushes it aside with her hips. She pushes the main part of the grand piano out of the frame, and only the small piano remains onstage. Thus we can see that the "small size piano" by Technics doesn't even need the big "grand piano" part. Its' sound is just as good anyway. This commercial is my creation.

▷ Excellent. Now I'd be really keen to know what you came up with for the washing machines.

◁ The outside casing of the washing machine that was to be advertised is made of "vibration-free-steel", which is, in other words, "anti-noise steel." In our film you see two musicians with cymbals. Suddenly, we hear a famous sequence from "Carmen." (Nozue starts to sing.) At a certain point in the melody, the two men are supposed to clash their cymbals. When they finally do this, one of the cymbals produces the expected clash, but the other one, which is made of "vibration-free-steel" produces just a

Campaign against illegal parking
in the city of Osaka

dull thud. This commercial is really a product demonstration.

▷ Just like the Technics film.

◁ Yes, it was very successful. By the way, I did another film for the Grand Piano. This one had Count Dracula in it. Count Dracula is playing the Technics Piano. Next to him, his servant is standing. While the count is playing, we suddenly hear a rooster crowing. So Count Dracula knows it's time to go to bed. His servant opens the top of the piano, Dracula climbs in and goes to sleep. The servant sits down at the piano and starts playing "Guten Abend, gute Nacht." While he is playing the main body of the piano disappears into the ground, into some kind of underground graveyard.

▷ Nice idea.

◁ Thanks, hahaha.

▷ Have you got more stories like this up your sleeve?

◁ Yes, one for a telephone answering machine starring the Tanaka family. Mr Tanaka is the average Japanese father, and his family is the average Japanese family. We have lots of Tanakas in Japan. So one day the Tanaka family buy an answering machine. And of course, they want to try it out at once. They immediately record a message. "Hello," Mr Tanaka says, "this is the Tanaka family." "Unfortunately, no one's here right now," Mrs Tanaka says. "Thank you for calling." The kid says. Then, as if electrified, they rush to the nearest phone booth and call home. They listen to what they have just recorded and Mr Tanaka leaves the message "It works" on his own machine. The whole family is delighted that the machine works.

▷ How do Japanese commercials differ from others?

◁ In order to answer this question, I must explain a few things about typically Japanese characteristics. Basically the Japanese speak only one language. We speak Japanese. We can communicate without using a whole lot of words. A Japanese saying goes, "The less said the better." As far as advertising is concerned, the Japanese do not want to hear so many messages. We are able to talk to each other without using so many words. This explains the fact that our advertising is visually oriented. Japanese commercials are very visual compared to those of other countries. Another important aspect is that the Japanese prefer emotional messages to rational ones. Japanese commercials must contain a lot of "feeling." As I've mentioned, the less you say the better. The advertising message must be made interesting to the man on the street. We are very good at presenting visual contents. The problem is, however, that sometimes we tend to forget the actual reason for advertising. Basically, in Japanese advertising there is nothing but images.

Toshiaki Nozue

▷ Are the Japanese more introverted than the Europeans?

◁ Sometimes, saying too much can be awful. We should try to communicate with fewer words. This is my personal opinion. In our history the politics of isolation plays an important role. In the Eido epoch we spent more than 300 years in isolation. Japan closed its door on all influences from abroad. During this time we were able to develop our own culture and remained completely unaffected by what was going on in other countries and cultures. We developed a code which made it easier to communicate.

▷ Do you sometimes meditate?

◁ Yes, sometimes.

▷ And how?

◁ Simply by closing my eyes and by not speaking to anyone. This is my style of meditation.

▷ What about Zen?

◁ No, I have my own style.

▷ Have you never studied it?

◁ When I was at university, I read a few books about it. But today I have no time for this any more.

▷ Does meditating help you in your job?

◁ As far as my day-to-day life is concerned. I owe a lot to meditation. Whether it actually helps me in my job at the agency I cannot say.

▷ So you don't settle on your desk like this (assumes Zen position).

◁ No, I know nothing whatsoever about it. If you really want to do Zen, you are not supposed to eat and drink for a month.

▷ A month?

◁ Yes, but you reduce your intake of food slowly. In the middle of your Zen exercise you are supposed to eat nothing at all for a period of 10 days. Only drink water.

▷ Cleansing from inside.

◁ Yes, yes. The old cells inside your body slowly die. Young cells develop and grow in their place. That's good for your health.

▷ Have you ever fasted for so long?

◁ No, I have no patience. I can't do this.

▷ You just close your eyes.

◁ Yes.

▷ Some time ago, I read an interview with the Austrian writer Peter Handke, in which he talked about his travels through Japan. Handke said that he had never seen such a sleepy people as the Japanese. He'd find them fast asleep everywhere, in restaurants, standing up at bus stops, in trains. Why are the Japanese so sleepy?

CHANGE COMMUNICATIONS.

◁ Sleepy? One reason why the Japanese want to sleep is because they work so very hard. Sleepy people! Haha! I don't know. I don't really think so. But more and more Japanese have to work harder and harder each day. Which is why they long for sleep, I guess.

▷ Do you sometimes sleep at your agency?

◁ Well, sleep is not the right word. Meditate is more like it.

▷ Maybe Handke got mixed up about it. Maybe he confused sleeping with meditating.

◁ Sometimes people think I'm asleep when I'm just meditating. Do you have this habit too?

▷ I wish I had.

◁ A Zen priest can go a whole month without sleep.

▷ How do you know?

◁ I have seen documentaries about it on Japanese TV. But those Zen priests have to go through a lot of exercises to be able to achieve this. In Japan we call this "stijo" – "hard work."

▷ In advertising too, the Japanese don't seem to shy away from hard work. Or how do you explain the fact that your agency, Dentsu, is so big?

◁ In our office there are more than 600 creative people at work. Lots of unique talents. Masters of various disciplines. The system of advertising in other countries differs considerably from our system. We have lots of different departments. Not just a media department, but also an events department. The events department deals with events of all kinds. From sports to music. Since Japanese agencies deal with so many different things their income is so much higher. And it keeps getting bigger.

▷ How big can it get before Newton's Law applies?

◁ Our income keeps growing and growing.

▷ But "what goes up, must come down," or something like that.

◁ Oh sure, when the recession hits Japan, Dentsu won't be spared either. But at the moment things are okay. People are the most important source of energy for the Dentsu company. This corporate philosophy has no doubt been a decisive factor in our success. Another reason is Dentsu's tradition as a corporation. Its history goes back a long way. The advertising agency Dentsu was founded in 1901. The most important for us Japanese is the relationship we have between ourselves. Since Dentsu is such a long-established company, there are a lot of good names on our client list. I don't know if I should tell you this or not, but in Japan we do not have to give up accounts simply because we have a competitive account. A Japanese agency may very well work for competing corporations from one particular industry. For example, an agency can work for Toyota, Nissan and Honda at the same time, or for Toshiba, Sony and Sanyo.

▷ No conflicts?

◁ No. Different people work on different accounts. This differs very much from the way it is handled in the West.

▷ Why do the Japanese accept this?

◁ In Japan there are just a few agencies that can create good advertising. So it's no wonder that most clients want to work with these agencies.

▷ Your agency does a lot of broadcasting in addition to its advertising. Does your agency do its own programs?

◁ Yes, but not a lot. I believe that the TV people should be personally responsible for the programs they make. We from the advertising side should not get involved in programs. We don't have a network. We can only advise the stations on how to make good programs.

▷ Why are you creative?

◁ Because I want to reflect. Reflect each day of my life. Reflection plays the most important role in my life. Creativity is what is most fun for me. Twenty years ago I worked in our TV and radio department. After five years I asked to be transferred to the creative department because I wanted to think.

▷ And how's your thinking today? Are you satisfied with it?

◁ Sometimes I meditate so I can think better, to have better ideas. Sometimes we take rather a long time to come up with a brilliant idea. But as far as I'm concerned, I always think about these things, even without a briefing. The most important thing for me is the "What to say."

Stills for Wowow
"Good TV" commercial

Only then comes the "How to say it." But in order to be able to decide what I want to say I have to reflect a lot on the product. The daily routine also is important for my thinking. Walking, sitting, smoking, etc. An excellent idea needs time.

▷ The English creative Jeff Stark believes that if you can't do a campaign in half an hour, you won't be able to do one in two weeks either.

◁ That doesn't apply in my case. I need an average of two weeks to come up with a superior campaign.

▷ You have to be pregnant with an idea before you can give birth to it. A pregnancy, after all, takes more than one day.

◁ You are right. That is a good metaphor. After all, the word "concept" somehow implies the meaning of pregnancy, doesn't it?

▷ Mr. Nozue, in your films you seem to have a certain penchant for metaphors and demonstrations. What is the reason for this?

◁ When I create advertising for a product with very good features and advantages, it is quite easy to think up a demonstration idea. But in Japan today we're creating less and less advertising for products and more and more advertising for service industries. The result is that most commercials are image-oriented and not idea-oriented. Images sell banks, insurance companies and security houses. No story, no idea. Unfortunately, more and more films produced in Japan have neither stories nor ideas.

▷ Well, if you could combine your fantastic Japanese images with some great ideas, the result would be perfect.

◁ You know, creativity always works according to the same pattern: First of all I discuss the problem freely with one or two people. We brainstorm and produce a lot of ideas. The next day we criticise our own ideas. It is of utmost importance that, during this meeting, we say exactly what we think. The third day we have to decide on a concept. It takes courage to decide on the best idea. The word "courage" is my favourite word. Courage.

▷ Why?

◁ Oh well, sometimes I try to postpone the final decision. But that is very bad. For without courage you cannot achieve anything.

▷ Let's suppose you have two equally good storyboards in front of you and are unable to give preference to either one. What happens to your courage then?

◁ The first impression is the most important one. If I have to decide between two concepts, then I make everything depend on the first impression. Intuition is of great importance, particularly in one's day-to-day work. Only then will you feel confidence and self-confidence.

▷ Have you ever made a decision that was completely off?

Toshiaki Nozue

128

◁ God alone knows that. I myself do not believe in God, but should one exist, he'd be the only one to know what the better idea was. As a humble human I have to make up my mind. And the criteria for my decision are courage, my first impression and intuition.

▷ A Jewish saying goes, "If you can't decide between two things, go for the third."

◁ Sounds like a good idea, but certainly not my style. After all, I'm responsible for our work.

▷ You say you are courageous. Are you also ambitious?

◁ No, I'm not ambitious. I think the Asian way.

▷ What do you mean?

◁ That's difficult to explain. It's an entire philosophy. You know, I could say it in Spanish: "Que sera...sera." Whatever might happen in the future, we can't understand it anyway. The Asians say, "We cannot understand what will happen in the future. Not us mortal beings. If there is a god, he might understand what will happen." The word "ambition" carries with it a certain element of "future." With the Japanese way of thinking we do not need ambition.

▷ You claim to be constantly thinking. What about your dreams?

◁ Dreams are another world. I enjoy dreaming. But for my reality dreams are of no use.

▷ They might be.

◁ If you are referring to one's inner life, you are right. But as for one's practical everyday life, dreams are useless.

▷ Let us go back once more to your thinking process. Don't you ever switch off?

◁ Not as long as I'm awake.

▷ But what about after work? The Japanese are reportedly fond of having a glass or two.

◁ I don't drink a lot. It is indeed correct that lots of Japanese are fond of alcohol, but that's nothing for me. Oh yes, sometimes I do go out with my colleagues and then I might drink a little bit.

▷ Probably just so much that it doesn't interfere with your thinking.

◁ Well, alcohol doesn't agree with me. I prefer coffee.

▷ Who is your favourite thinker?

◁ I admire Nietzsche very much. "Thus Spoke Zarathustra" is one of my favourite books. I've read it many, many times. Nietzsche is the philosopher I admire most.

▷ Does Nietzsche have any kind of influence on the advertising you create?

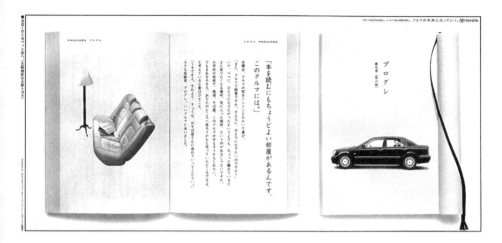

Press ad for Toyota ◁ No, he has no influence on my advertising, but he does have an influence on my private life.

▷ Does your courage have anything to do with the spirit of the old Samurai?

◁ You may be right. The samurai had the courage to do everything. The philosophy of the samurais contains courage and Zen. The most important thing for a samurai is that he'll always have the courage to kill himself should he be insulted.

▷ Is that a reason to kill yourself?

◁ Yes, it's about defending your own independence to the very end.

▷ I remember a quote from "The Seven Samurai." It goes: "Danger is always greatest when no one seriously expects it."

◁ Yes, that's right. The samurai must have constant control over his spirit and mind. The mind must be calm, the spirit must be calm, the heart must be calm. For a samurai must always be prepared for the worst. Nothing may surprise him. No matter what happens. He should not dream but confront danger.

▷ Another sentence from the samurais' code of honour is, "A samurai never looks back."

◁ That is true. A samurai may never live in the past. Each day of his life must be spent in the present, or looking to the future. He should never deal with the past.

▷ Why? Is the past boring?

◁ Yes, we should forget the past.

▷ But isn't there anything we can learn from it?

Toshiaki Nozue

◁ What happened cannot be undone. The past is the past. There is no point in living in the past.

▷ Does it bother you sometimes that you cannot step in front of your clients in a samurai's armour?

◁ I am a samurai in advertising. I may look like a normal 21th century businessman from the outside but I carry a lot of hidden weapons. Courage and the ability to control my mind. The client cannot see what I'm like on the inside.

▷ Is advertising a battle for you?

◁ Yes, there are always battles in advertising.

▷ How do you prepare for them? Where do you get your personal stimuli from?

◁ Through travelling. I have travelled Japan extensively and later also abroad. It allows me to observe a great number of different people that belong to other cultures.

▷ And how else?

◁ Through music. Music has been a decisive influence in my life. Mozart, Beethoven and Bach. Mozart is my favourite composer.

▷ Do you play an instrument?

◁ I used to take guitar lessons. But I was never good at it.

▷ But then you have injected your commercials with a considerable dose of classical music.

◁ Yes, I was the first Japanese advertising man to use this type of music for commercials. That was 20 years ago, for a stereo. I made three films for this product and one of them was about Mozart. We went to Germany, Austria, Spain and France and presented three great composers. I introduced the places where these composers were born to Japanese consumers. The films were very beautiful and won a lot of awards. Both in Japan and abroad.

▷ What advice would you give to European creatives?

◁ I believe that the Europeans tend to insist on their own philosophy too much. For example, that all culture and philosophy derive from Europe. You Europeans should be more open to other traditions and cultures. You will have to get used to adapting to other cultures, particularly Asian ones. You do have courage, you do, after all, have the spirit of the medieval knights.

▷ But we have lost calmness and stoicism unlike the Asians.

◁ Yes, it seems to me that you are constantly at war with each other. If you could incorporate a more stoical frame of mind you could achieve everything – without fighting.

Japanese lightning design by Dentsu

▷ What would the samurai Nozue have as an inscription on his tomb? ◁ That is difficult to say, though it's a good question. I think I'd choose the words "A man who was courageous dies calmly and in peace with himself." No matter what you do you always have to have the courage to make a decision. I would like to tell you a short story about when I was a child. I think I was in fourth grade when I had a fight with another pupil. I hit him, he ran away and I ran after him. Shortly before he reached his house I threw a stone at him. It missed him and smashed the window of his home. When I came home, I didn't say a word about it. Then, three or four hours later, I told myself that I should have the courage to say what happened. I told my mother that I had smashed the window pane, and then we went to this boy's family together to apologise.
□

Introduction

MARCELLO SERPA

Co-CEO and Creative Director of Almap/BBDO, Sao Paulo

My aunt once asked me:

"Cello, what do you do in the ad agency again?"

"I'm an Art Director".

"You mean, you take the pictures?"

"No. A photographer takes the pictures."

"You write copy, then?

"No. A copywriter writes the copy."

"I see... you draw illustrations..."

"No. An illustrator draws them..."

"Then... you make films... direct actors..."

"No. A film director does that..."

"You write scripts, screenplays..."

"No. Scripts and screenplays are written by the copywriter..."

"Well... You're a real artist then... You're the only one that really understands what you do."

Everyone seems to have a hard time understanding what the job of an art director is about – even ad people have some problems with it.

However, without art direction, everything that surrounds us would certainly be less charming, less beautiful.

For someone to like a movie it would suffice to read the script, and then sent it by fax to other people. Ads would be like directions set in Times and Helvetica on a medicine bottle. Classical Maoist fashion would be enough. Thank God, there are people that are able to verbalize what only the eyes hear: an image. It is no doubt – the most powerful communication tool we have. Perhaps, the only tool that breaks down all language barriers. That enters people through the retina, without any filters, and acts directly in their hearts, their souls, their sense of guilt, their desires.

Art direction can make a copy shout, whisper, seduce. It can make people in a hurry stop on the streets for a while. It can make their mouths water. It can print, on people's retinas, shapes like that of a VW beetle against a white background, a green rectangle or a piece of purple silk. As an Art Director, I am happy to have been selected to stand close to people like Helmut Krone, John Webster, Hegarty and all the others. And that is why I would like to stop speaking and be silent. I want to hear – with my eyes wide open – everything they have to teach me. Maybe then I'll be able to explain to my aunt what an art director really does.

Marcello Serpa
May 2001

LEE CLOW
Creative work is not a straight process

Along with Jay Chiat, Lee Clow must be the other most responsible person for the remarkable rise and influence of Chiat Day. Lee was the person who masterminded the torrent of creative output over the years.

Like the legendary Porsche campaign, the sensational "Apple Think Different" campaign, the energizer Bunny and the California Pistachio Nuts. But what he'll always be mainly remembered for is when Steve Jobbs of the Apple company, star director Ridley Scott, and Lee Clow himself managed to produce the "1984" commercial for the introduction of the Apple Macintosh. A film rated by advertising creatives as a milestone, and possibly the best commercial of all times. Lee Clow is a member of the One Club Hall of Fame, the Art Directors Hall of Fame and the Museum of Modern Art's Advertising Hall of Fame. Perhaps not surprisingly, he was named the 1997 Creative Executive of the Year by USA Today.

Under his leadership, TBWA Chiat/Day has become one of the most innovative agencies in America. I interviewed Lee Clow in Los Angeles, and again at Cannes.

▷ Hermann Vaske: Lee, is humour a valuable tool sell products?

◁ Lee Clow: I think humour has got to be one of the most important tools that we have in advertising. Advertising being this obnoxious business where you're interrupting people, you know, they're sitting there trying to watch television, they don't give a shit about your product, they're just trying to relax a little bit.

So if you're going to bust into their living room and interrupt them, you know, maybe doing something funny, something that makes them smile, it is a way to talk to people so they don't kind of think you're a jerk and annoying.

▷ Like your friendly Energizer bunny marching through people's living rooms?

◁ Yeah, sometimes he marches and makes people smile, other times he's annoying. And that actually is a very delicate balance about advertising, you know, sometimes he can be an annoying little shit and other times he can be very funny. Generally I think humour is probably one of the best tools that we have to work with creating advertising, because we're this obnoxious interruption to people when we butt into their living room or start talking to them in movie theatres. And if we don't entertain them somehow, make them laugh, make them like us a little bit, you're probably doing a giant disservice to whoever you're advertising for instead of doing something positive. So, I think you gotta have some fun, and you gotta make people like you; that is probably the first job.

People have more and more ways of not listening to advertising and so I think it's going to become more and more necessary for advertising to be more and more entertaining and more and more likeable and it's gotta find ways to make people laugh. I don't need to buy something from you unless I like you and if I like you, you know, I might be more inclined to buy something from you. So in one way you can say you're seducing me by being charming and likeable or the less cynical way of thinking about the same thing is hey, if I want to sell something to this guy, I'd better be pretty nice to him and treat him like somebody I like. I think humour is a critical tool and at the same time, it's a delicate tool.

▷ Why?

◁ What is funny to some people may not be funny to somebody else.

We created some advertising with people from right down here in Venice, that are pretty amusing characters for California Pistachio Nuts. We didn't have to write that humour, we just had to find those people and they're pretty funny to most people anywhere in the world and they were real you know, honest to goodness people who make you smile and make you laugh.

Conversely, you can try and invent humour or create something funny and people can say, that's not funny, that's stupid. And of course, the classic problem in our business is, you know, if you don't strike the right balance between entertainment and sell you can really turn people off.

Enjoy the ride.

And clients will always say: "Well, I think we need to see more of the car, I think we need to put a little more sell in there." And pretty soon you got this half arse that's not funny, it's not selling me anything, it's just nothing, which is why ninety per cent of the advertising in the world sucks.

Stills from Nissan commercial
"Enjoy the ride"

▷ What about ninety nine point nine?

◁ Yeah, maybe ninety nine point nine. A lot of it.

▷ The claim you were using for your nut campaign, that's a very funny one.

◁ Well, it's because I know it to be true. The best nuts come from California!

▷ That's a pun, a double meaning, which probably doesn't translate into other languages.

◁ Well, that's one of the difficulties with international humour. International advertising is the delicacy, particularly if it's language based, if it's visual based...

I happen to be an art director and think that one of the keys to international or global advertising brands is that it needs to operate much more on the

Lee Clow

visual side; and of course, a lot of humour can be very visual, as opposed to being word driven, 'cos word driven gets you into that problem that a pun or a twist on words in English doesn't mean anything to a German or Portuguese or French. So, I think you create a trap for international brands if you create a word driven advertising idea.

▷ A good example for visual humour is again your Energizer rabbit. Can you explain us the function of the rabbit as a spokesperson?

◁ Well, the Energizer rabbit, you know, had a very kind of strange birth. Once we'd created this character that's being run by Energizer batteries, then responsibility for him as a spokesman was just to show up in the most interesting, unusual, surprising ways. First it was moving from one commercial to another which the judges at Cannes decided we stole from somebody, which we didn't.

Then he's been showing up being confronted by villains who are trying to put him out of business and he's evolving some of the things now because everybody is aware of him, he's become a part of the vernacular in America.

You have politicians and athletes and people who are being indicted who get on camera every night and say: "Hey, I just keep going and going and going like that Energizer bunny." It's actually become vernacular.

▷ What is your favourite Energizer commercial?

◁ We did a couple that were fun in that genre. The one that promoted the television show for women motor cycle cops was the Hips one, which he interrupted. We also created a film called 'Dance With Your Feet', which we ran in movie theatres, which was very funny, which was a film from Marcel Marceau, a love story about two young people falling in love and it was the classic, you know, edited film trailer for this noir film and it ended up being another funny commercial. The surprise... the surprise...

▷ Nothing is sacred, isn't it ...

◁ I hope not, that's the goal. We're trying to raise the bar right now, and the challenge is how can we make him more surprising, more outrageous, more intrusive than he's been so far?

◁ Yeah. We did one Indiana Jones, which is interesting, 'cos we've now gotten licence by virtue of how long this bunny's been going and going. It's very interesting that we're now allowed to say, the bunny represents eternal life, because what happens in the commercial is the guy asks for eternal life as one of his three wishes and he turns into the Energizer bunny.

▷ Taking the piss out of Duracell.

◁ Well, that of course is the challenge. I mean, Duracell was kicking their

The Energizer campaign featuring the notorious Energizer bunny

butt for years, but I mean nobody could remember Energizer even though the two products were identical, totally identical in what they did. Duracell just opened people's minds. I always said, when our advertising can stop Duracell from doing the advertising they had been doing for ten years, it will prove to us that our advertising works. The first year that we did the Energizer bunny, in research he would come up being called the Duracell bunny, because Duracell was so defined as batteries that they were remembering the commercials totally, but they were saying, "oh that Duracell bunny". So the client had to actually be pretty ballsy to hang on for the first year until they started transferring the equity over to Energizer and giving them credit for it. We did it then for three or four years and now Duracell has been trying to invent new advertising to compete with the Energizer bunny.

▷ With regard to Energizer you mentioned film genres – in what way does feature film influence advertising these days?

◁ Well, there is an interesting crossover that's been happening. I guess it's been happening for fifteen to twenty years, where it's getting more and more of the crossover. There's probably a couple of different reasons why, you know.

On one side, the best advertising has to entertain. If it doesn't entertain people, it's probably going to be ignored and the people who work in advertising, so many of them aspire to be filmmakers, to tell stories that are longer than thirty seconds or sixty seconds, so it's kind of natural coming together.

Fifteen, almost twenty years ago now, we started working with Adrian Lyne when he first came out of the UK, who's now making feature films. And then we worked with Ridley Scott and Tony Scott, who are now making wonderful feature films. I think it's very interesting. I've watched this a few times the people that go from the advertising business and make feature films have a little bit different way of approaching the problem, 'cos somehow they've learnt how precious every foot of film is when they're doing things that are restricted to this thirty second window. So you go to a Ridley Scott two hour movie, and every scene, every picture is this wonderful painting, this wonderful presentation. And we've actually gone the other way, we've hired a few film directors to come over and work on advertising and actually I think with not very satisfying results. I'm not going to name names because it's a little embarrassing but a few feature film directors have come to advertising, worked with us on advertising projects, and they don't have the discipline to craft thirty seconds to communicate.

Lee Clow

They're so used to going in and taking a script and kind of, "all right, now, take your time", you shoot it and the actors get to kind of leisurely come up with their looks and their thoughts.

When they tried to do something that had to speak in thirty seconds, they couldn't get there. Both the film quality was not there, but also the ability to even pack the story in and make it watchable and likeable. So, that part of it I think is very interesting, but I think some of the storytellers that come out of advertising have done some very nice jobs in film-making. Phil Dusenberry very basically did "The Natural", the movie with Robert Redford in this country and he comes out of BBDO Advertising, but had the ability and the talent to translate into a longer form. I'm not sure it works going back the other way in terms of people coming from film and doing advertising. So far the experiences I've had, they haven't been... I'm sure they could do it if they spent the time to study the problem, but they come very casually to advertising, almost thinking that advertising isn't real film anyway and so they don't come to it with a "I've got to solve this problem of telling a story in thirty seconds" they very often come to it saying, "well, this is a piece of cake, you know, bang, bang, bang, I'm done." Actually, Tony Scott said something interesting to me one time.

He said: "Making a feature film is like running a marathon and making commercials is like sprinting." And he said that actually, after he's made a feature film, he loves going back and doing ads because it's so stimulating to dash through thirty seconds and it's the compressed time to produce and cast and shoot and edit and finish that is the schedule on a TV commercial, that's a whole different energy level than making a movie, where every day you show up on the set and maybe you get three minutes of a film done, and then you got to do that for a hundred days till you got a movie.

Commercials are rewarding and it's fun and there's an energy level with you. A lot of creative people in our business aspire to go over into the movie side, or writers who want to write books. I'm not sure I would have the patience for any of that, because everything from being able to work on different types of products, to do different types of commercials, to be done with something in a month and be on to something else is probably what keeps you energized in this business. You know, if I devoted two years to one thing, I don't know if I would like it.

▷ You mentioned the Scott brothers. Do you think there is a simularity in their visual language?

◁ Well, yeah there are some similarities in their vocabulary. You know,

Ridley being the older, I think Tony emulates some of the kind of lighting and the theatre that Ridley creates, but I don't know, I think Tony's getting almost a little more variety in the things that he's been able to do, where Ridley is kind of over in a kind of ultra-theatrical, dramatic kind of forceful presentation of stories. Tony's been able to go all the way over to Beverly Hills Cop and do lighter things and more fun things and do Tom Cruise... and so I think they're each finding a little bit of a different place, but I think from a visual standpoint, I can see the family resemblance, I guess you would call it.

▷ Yeah, Ridley leans a bit towards the dramatic monumental Leni Riefenstahl kind of images.

◁ Yeah, yeah. And he's very good at that.

▷ A commecial which we have to talk about in this context is "1984" the landmark commercial for Apple Macintosh. Could you tell us how you and Ridley were able to pull off this milestone in advertising history?

◁ Yeah, well, "1984" is one of those unique, wonderful moments in time. It wasn't any one thing that was special about that piece of advertising, it was a combination of all kinds of things. It was Steve Jobbs, this, you know, this Silicone Valley wunderkind who was changing the world and taking on IBM and introducing everyone to computers which back then the world was just learning that they needed computers which they now understand. It was a piece of technology that was truly special in relationship to the competitor they had, IBM. The Superbowl was an opportunity that was not as cluttered with let's take our biggest and best commercials and run them on the Superbowl then; and then we went to Ridley and created a piece of film that didn't look like advertising had ever looked. All those things together turned out to be a really good thing! So it ended up being just this incredibly unique moment in time. If the product wasn't special, if the Superbowl wasn't a little more virgin in the terms of the opportunity, if Ridley hadn't looked at our boards and said, this can look big, this can be this special, you know, all things said – it was almost like all the stars aligned properly on the day that we did that commercial, 'cos it's very, very hard to break walls, to create... break through advertising.

You know, you can have three out of four of the elements in place and still not end up with a breakthrough 'cos something... you know, the product sucks, you know.

Doing a breakthrough ad for a shitty product is not really a breakthrough, because it's like, who cares. And it was very funny after "1984", lots of people thought spending a million dollars on a commercial was the way to do breakthrough.

On January 24th,
Apple Computer will introduce
Macintosh.
And you'll see why 1984
won't be like "1984"

Lee Clow

▷ Let's talk about the idea of "1984". Is the commercial based more on Alien or Blade Runner?

Stills from "1984"
Apple Macintosh commercial,
directed by Ridley Scott

◁ Well, of course, Alien and Bladerunner were predecessors and of course we knew about Ridley before he started making feature films.
He had done Chanel, he had done a lot of wonderful advertising work, but of course that certainly helped convince us that not only does he understand advertising, that sixty seconds, we actually had a luxurious sixty seconds that time, but he could make amazing, dramatic, theatrical film à la Bladerunner, Alien. It was the perfect combination to pull off a commercial that had to look like no other commercial had ever looked.

▷ Did you ever shoot commercials with Tony?

◁ Actually Tony did some Apple, Tony did some Reebok for us, we did some Pizza Hut commercials in Italy which were very fun. Both of them are so smart, so charming to work with that they bring such positive energy to a project, you know, back to what I was saying about Tony.
When it comes to an advertising project, he truly loves doing it, you don't feel like he's, you know, doing it to fill time or make a few extra bucks. You really feel like he pours his heart and his energy into whatever the project is. So, both of them have a pretty high standard of what their responsibility is to a project.

▷ Why are you creative?

◁ Because the alternative sucks. I finally decided the alternative sucks. I mean ... I have now been in this business long enough. The people who don't want to approach, whatever their job is, creatively are just the most empty, hollow, unhappy people to me, it appears to be the most unhappy way to go through life. To not be approaching what you've got to do everyday creatively and with the idea that there's a way to do it better or smarter or different or more fun ... the alternative sucks.

▷ And the beauty is that in creativity everything goes. Maybe you write a book, maybe you write a film. And advertising really is a melting pot of the different creative disciplines.

◁ Yeah. That's one of the pleasures of advertising, you know. I still love doing a good print, a good poster. It's incredibly rewarding, which is very different from doing a television commercial. And now there's so many new mediums being thrown at us, the new challenge of our business, and I think any and all of them can be done creatively and well.

▷ Is successful advertising the small path between reason and emotion, between the left and right half of the brain?

◁ I got one of our biggest clients right now who is a very successful businessman, but I think he feels like more of his talents come from his left brain than his right brain and he's actually very frustrated about this

right now... and he's been asking me to spend time talking with him about and working on developing advertising that is much more special and much more unique for his company. And it's interesting, 'cos he started asking the questions about, well, "how do you have an idea like the Energizer bunny and where do they come from and what do you do?" And it's interesting to watch someone who's mostly left-brained try and understand how right-brained people work, 'cos it is not a process... it is not linear, first you do this, then you do this, then you do this.

Information, observation and thinking is constantly being inputted into creative people and it's the way you take all that information and turn it upside down and right side up and mix it up and spread it around, where ideas ultimately come from... "Hey! what if we put this together with this and that would be different than it's ever been done before." It would say that. But to explain this guy how you get to ideas was very difficult. They tried to write books on how and why people have ideas and I don't think it can be explained, only because it is not a definable process.

It has to do with each computer that it goes into, talking about individual creative people's brains as computers. Each person who has the ability to turn information into something creative, I think, does it in a slightly different way.

The input comes in, but how it is assimilated, adjusted and ultimately expressed in an idea or the progression of becoming an idea, I think is as different as the creative people who think.

You know, you've heard all the stories: that I thought of it in the shower, I thought it when I was driving in. I think one of the biggest keys to thinking and having ideas is to stop thinking, to disengage from trying to think and sometimes the best ideas emerge then, when there is no pressure for anything to come out and that's why you wake up in the middle of the night and you think you have an idea, 'cos you weren't trying to come up with something and all of a sudden, something's there. Sometimes you wake up in the morning and it looks like shit what you wrote down.

▷ Chiat Day has merged with TBWA and is now part of Omnicom. How do you feel about it?

◁ This Omnicom thing made so much sense, because of Nissan in Europe, because TBWA couldn't get shit going in the US and we've never been able to afford to do anything in Europe, it was just the right deal and we had to pay off our debts, 'cos it was just killing us. Jay spent too much money on things!

▷ Did that have to do anything with his vision of the Virtual Office?

◁ Jay`s typical approach to stimulation is usually shock change, speaking of shock. I don't like to shock people and change things so dramatically that everyone has to get off their arse and re-think things. I think the Virtual Office was another one of Jay's attempts to shock the agency into a kind of level of new energy, and I think there are things about how we work now that are great and better and smart, because it demands that we come together and think as teams about things.

But there are also things about virtual that ignore the human realities of how people, particularly creative people, work together. It almost tries to disown the idea that there's is the collaboration that we know there really is in our business and it denies the creative people being as insecure as we all know they are, needing each other. People cannot be just anywhere and not, at some moments in time, huddle together for warmth in our business.

◁ The creative people need to stimulate each other and challenge each other and intimidate each other, but they need to be together as opposed to always dispersed in a totally virtual way. So we're learning what's right about it and what's wrong about it and I think we're making it better as we go along.

▷ So good to know that your`re not sitting on a beach with your laptop all the time?

◁ I have got the most beautiful house and I sit there in the morning and say, I wonder if I can be virtual today? And I immediately realise I cannot, because I cannot impact other people's work and other people's thinking by phone or by computer screen. The way I work with people is I'm a human being interacting with another human being and these other modes of communication are not as powerful, as far as I'm concerned. So it's just bogus to think that I can say the exact same thing I have to say to you on E-mail as I can sitting here, talking to you in your face. It's just not true.

Jay created no rules, he just created the architecture! Actually he did try and create rules. He tried to create rules that said nobody can do anything they used to do.

They can't sit in the same place, they can't bring anything to work and some of the rules were to be frank, absurd, because it's not the way people could get the job done.

▷ Marcel Duchamps said a painting that doesn't shock isn't worth anything. Do you agree with that?

◁ No, actually I think that is one definition, but who was it? Matisse, I think, said "if art is in a place you can rest, it's not art". So, I think there's different definitions of what is art and what is the way to connect with other human beings and I think something that's soft and pleasurable can as easily be art as something that's hard and shocking. But you've got to admit that shock is a communication tool, is a communication device.

▷ A valuable tool to sell products?

◁ I'm not sure. I think getting attention, of course, is a very important part of making advertising, but ultimately, I think, once you've got my attention, I don't think I want to dislike you or be offended by you once you've got my attention and still consider buying something from you. So if you shock me in a surprising kind of way that I end up enjoying, because you were so clever, so smart, then it could work. If you shock me and ultimately I don't like you for shocking me or startling me or being in my face, then I guess you'd have to say it was a failure.

I think Benetton has been on both sides of that line, for example.

I think defining their point of view as a brand in fashion as one with a point of view in the world and one with a point of view about things political and things human, is very smart. But I'm not sure that you can totally offend me, my sensibilities to make your point and still have the same effect as being socially conscious and responsible. I guess part of that whole thing is who draws the line? Where's the line that you go over when you offend me as opposed to just shock me into thinking in a different way about something.

▷ Sometime ago in England, somebody showed me a spec-commercial based on Reservoir Dogs. The idea was to get rid of bloodstains in Mr. Pink's shirt. Would you have signed off a script like that?

◁ I'm over fifty years old. Intuitively I would say that this is not going to convince the target. But then I think maybe younger creative people, maybe talking to younger housewives, or home-makers or house husbands, maybe there is an audience that grew up with television and grew up with strong, powerful messages, who would appreciate it.

I think a message can only be defined if you first define who has it got to connect with...

□

JOHN HEGARTY

Having a great idea is the nearest thing to giving birth

Hegarty began his career in advertising as a junior Art Director in 1965 at Benton and Bowles. In 1967 he joined the Cramer Saatchi consultancy, which became Saatchi & Saatchi in 1970. One year later he was appointed Deputy Creative Director. John left Saatchi & Saatchi in 1973, to co-found TBWA as Creative Director. The agency was the first to be voted Campaign magazine's Agency of the Year in 1980.

Two years later he left to found Bartle Bogle Hegarty, one of the most successful agencies in London, winning Campaign magazine's Agency of the Year Award in 1986 and again in 1993 by winning more awards than any other agency. It also won the title again in 1994.

John's credits include "Vorsprung durch Technik" for Audi, and Levi's "Bath" and "Launderette". His honours include several D&AD Gold and Silver Awards for press and television and British Television Gold and Silver Awards. More recently, he received the D&AD President's Award for his outstanding achievement in the advertising industry.

Despite his mega success he's remained a modest, completely "unarrogant" down-to-earth kind of guy. I had the pleasure to interview John Hegarty a couple of times in London and Cannes.

▷ Hermann Vaske: What does art mean for you?

◁ John Hegarty: What does art mean for me? It usually means something I'm intrigued by, something I'm fascinated by, something that draws me into it, that has a form or a shape to it, that beguiles me in some way or another. That's what art means to me.

▷ Has the painting behind you sucked you in?

◁ It does, I mean I like the painting behind me, it's a sort of the eternal quest for a creative person, which is, fill the box, make it happen, what is in it? What are you going to wrap it in? So, I like it, it's got a kind of a sort of Zen qualitiy to it, which I like.

▷ Is there a correlation between Zen and creativity?

◁ Well I think there is. I think anybody who's read "The Inner Game of Tennis" will understand what I'm probably talking about. That actually you can only really do great creative work when you allow your outer self to fall away, and you listen to your true inner self. And I think the great creative people are the ones that are able to do that. They often do it naturally, without thinking. They don't go through a process of allowing it to happen. It just happens for them. But I think there is definitely a relationship between Zen and the art of advertising.

Press ads for
Golden Shred Orange Marmalade

▷ So did you have Zen moments in advertising or could you describe a moment where Zen and advertising have met?

◁ Yeah, I think you do. I think anybody who has ideas, who does actually have really great ideas, they are moments of pure Zen; in other words, it is where the true you, the real self, has been allowed to kind of come out to express itself. Take in a problem, understand how to deal with the problem and come up with a solution. And that's why, I think when you have a great idea, it just is, I've already said, actually, it's the nearest thing to giving birth. Because in a way you do give birth. I mean having an idea is the nearest a man will come, anyway, to giving birth, in the sense that you create something and it has a shape and a form. You know how to treat it, you know where it should go. You know what's right for it, what's wrong for it. It has an entity. It exists, it is there, it is an idea. And I think that creates in you a tremendous euphoria. A tremendous sense of excitement. And you feel, kind of all sorts of other problems just falling away.

▷ Is that a drug-like experience?

◁ It's a drug–like experience, yeah, it's a natural high. It's what runners experience when they talk about the endorphin rush and it is a high, it is a tremendous high, and I think that's what happens when you study Zen and you meditate and you get the natural kind of flow of ideas and momentum within the body occuring. And as I say, if anybody wants to understand it, they should read the tennis book on the inner game, written by Timothy Galway.

▷ What made you decide to go into the advertising business in the mid-sixties?

◁ I was at the London College of Printing doing graphic design and I felt myself very frustrated with it. Everybody was talking about typefaces and shapes, and somehow nobody was talking about ideas. And I thought surely we should talk about the idea first. And at that time there was a man teaching there called John Gillard who was a very bright man. John really introduced me to advertising, and he showed me some of the work of Doyle Dane Bernbach in the States at that time. Now I'm talking about 1963/64. It was to me like the window being opened in a darkened room with the curtains being drawn back. And I suddenly thought: "God, this is what I want to do!" And then I started looking at all their work and getting hold of old copies of the New Yorker and literally going through them tearing out every ad I thought was good. That's how I really got into advertising. It was at that moment I suddenly realized that It was actually what I wanted to do. Of course it was a very difficult thing to talk about then at design school. It was a bit like the Pope telling everyone to become Jewish. It was sort of looked down upon heavily.

▷ Today things have changed. Advertising now has a reputation as an attractive and fancy business where people travel a lot and make a lot of money in return for little work.

◁ Yes, it's got a much better image. I think that — certainly here in the UK — a lot of credit goes to CDP who, in the 70s really did start to produce on big accounts very exciting advertising. I think, from that point of view, it began to change people's perception. You know, it can be good. In a way it was the experience I went through when I was at CDP, and I thought: "My God, it can be intelligent. It can be witty and it can be charming, and it doesn't have to be deceitful and banal and clichéd. And so, from my point of view, it opened my eyes, just as, I think, in the seventies the general public's eyes were opened to the possibilities. And they suddenly said: "Gosh, this can be interesting."

▷ In those days there were lots of young and hungry people who went into advertising. People with enthusiasm. People like you.

◁ Well, in fact actually I think I was part of the first generation that came into advertising who actually wanted to be in advertising on the creative side. I'm talking now about the mid-sixties. And I was part of the first generation. A whole lot of people came in at that time. People like Robin Wright. Ron Collins ... David Abbott was working already in advertising, but people like Tony Brignull and Neil Godfrey. That whole group of people all came in around about the same time in advertising. And so we were the first generation who actually wanted to be in it and saw it as a career and had a point of view about the creative work, and because I think that we felt that we were here on a longterm basis. We're here because we wanted to change it. We weren't just angry young creative people who would fight against the system but eventually leave it. We actually wanted to change it. I think that's why, eventually, we all thought of starting our own agencies, which we realized. You know, you can't go up the chain of command. I mean you go up and you become a Creative Director. But even that wouldn't really help because you were running a creative department but you were still running it within a sort of system that was basically wrong. So eventually the only solution was to set your own agency up. And lots of those people did exactly that.

▷ Why is it impossible for you to work for other people?

◁ It became very difficult to hold a rational debate. Even with a lot of the

How many cigarettes a day does your child smoke?

When a child breathes air filled with cigarette smoke it can be as bad as if he actually smoked the cigarette himself. Don't smoke when there are children present.

creative people who were in the business. If they'd stayed in the business ... I mean, you are fighting something that you can't change. (Or you just basically disagree). I've been sort of disappointed a little bit by the last five or six years. I mean I'm not saying that we are better or different. But I think that we honestly set our agency up because we thought we can do better work. We could obviously control our destinies. And I think if you have looked at Wright Collins —even though in some ways they lost their way — I think they had a passion for advertising. I get the feeling that, in the last five or six years or so, people have been putting up agencies because they feel it's a way to get rich.

▷ Has the thrill gone a bit?

◁ I think it has a bit. It has, just a little bit.

▷ Are the creatives of today not as passionate and hungry as their colleagues of the sixties and seventies?

◁ I don't think they are as hungry as they were. There is a different kind of hunger today. I mean, I think that we sensed a great mood of change in the sixties.

▷ The walls came down and the iron curtain of boredom fell.

◁ Yes, we were tearing down the walls. And I think that when you're in that situation it is terribly exciting because you really do feel that you are storming the barricades. I mean the greatest problem of today is that it's all really been done. What we are doing now, we're playing with the formula. It doesn't mean that can't be exciting, it can be. But it's much more professional, it's much more expected of you. Good ads are expected today rather than a genuine surprise. So you got to sort of inject personally a lot more into it. And you gotta have a greater belief and faith in the business of advertising. So that it can carry you through the fact that there are lots of people out there doing good ads. That's one of the problems today. Are we doing as good ads as we were doing fifteen or twenty years ago? Actually we are. What happened is it has become more normal. You know, if I turn on the television and see a commercial break, I'll see two or three good ads. And I think "Ah, that's good. That's really good." Whereas twenty years ago it was much more of an oasis. And people talked about it: "God, look what they've done." And one forgot how appalling the other advertising was around the good advertising. Whereas today even the bad advertising is actually not bad, it's actually sort of alright. It's well shot, it's well casted ... you know, it's pretty good. You know, it's trying to be different or it's trying to be daring. Sometimes it falls flat on its face, but even that sort of bad advertising is not bad. You know, by our definition, by our standards. So, that's the problem, you really got to inject your enthusiasm into it. You are not storming any more barricades. And that does make it hard. So, it's a bit like painting or a bit like Pop music. I should think much the same really. I mean, you know, to have been a rock'n'roll star in the sort of late fifties, early sixties must have been phenomenally exciting because it really was a monumental change in music. And, you know, lots of people were debating: "Will it go on?" And now it's kind of pop music in the air everywhere. You know, it's sort of accepted. So it's much harder now to become enthused about it. You have to inject that enthusiasm yourself.

▷ Are you obsessed by your work?

◁ I think I am really. I'm desperately passionate about it. I love it dearly. I get terribly disappointed when something isn't as good as I think it could be. I get terribly depressed. It really does upset me and I think, you know, at BBH we really do feel that. But our work is still about 30 percent of what it should be. And it's got to be much, much better. We've got to kind of somehow improve standards. We've got to do that without really being compared to anybody else. I think we've got to set our own standards.

▷ One of your greatest contributions to the standards of advertising was that you introduced non-verbal storytelling to commercials.

◁ Yes, absolutely. We always felt that there were moments of drama. They weren't commercials, not in the sense that commercials were before. But I mean we kind of made our commercials stories. A story that's related to – obviously – a particular product. But definitely the story had a before and an after... And what we were trying to do always was to create

Claymation at its best: Levi's 501

bigger and bigger characters, to make the characters broader and more interesting than just simply people who exist in advertising. We tried to take the art of advertising forward. I think lots of people have not quite understood that. I think they begin to understand it when they look back. But in the midst of the battle it's always very difficult to see the game plan and see how you are doing, and to see what you are doing. But I think if you look at a lot of our work there really was this idea of dramatized moments. Trying to turn this commercial into something bigger and broader than just a piece of verbal communication. I think that's one of the things we always tried, and that I've always believed that people have often said and talked about when you asked them. You know, when you talk to advertising people, what is your favorite commercial, more often than not the commercial that comes up is the famous Volkswagen commercial "How does the man that drives the snowplow get to the

Food for Imagination:
Press ad for lego

snowplow?" And I sort of always agreed with that and said: "Yeah, great commercial." I've increasingly thought: "No, it's not! It's not a great commercial." It was very clever at the time — and one has to remember it was done in 1961 or whenever it was. But in terms of using the medium, it didn't at all. It really was a press ad on wheels as we call it.

▷ It would make a good headline.

◁ Yes, you could do it as a press ad. I said that recently. You know: "Have you ever wondered how the man who drives the snowplow gets to the snowplow?" You know, with two tracks going off into the distance and a little beetle way off in the distance. And you've done it. And I think a great commercial can't be a press ad because television is totally different to press. If they can interchange then I think you've failed somewhere along the line. I think that it seems to me that if it could work in two mediums as opposed to just one superbly it means that you are not using the one medium to its best advantage. I think that the way press works is quite different from the way television works. Especially the way film has developed at the moment. Film offers all sorts of opportunities that press doesn't. Therefore it seems to me that if you have an idea that works in both you are obviously not exploiting one of those mediums to its fullest. A commercial has to be using and developing the medium that it's in. And I think we are doing that now in the UK. I think we really are kind of playing with the medium in a way which ... I mean I sat on the jury at Cannes and I looked and listened to lots of debates about things I thought very interesting and stuff like that. But I feel with a lot of work that was being done here a lot of these judges just didn't understand what we were trying to do. And they were harking back to wanting simplicity. You know, let's get back to simple ideas. And what they don't understand is that the consumer, the person we are talking to, the general public, has moved on. And they want stimulation. They perceive, they live with pop videos, they live with commercial television, and they are visually literate people. And they know about film and they understand the technique, and they want to see how they use it. It's very important to have an idea, and technique can never replace an idea. But I think when you talk to young people today, I mean they understand advertising and they want to be stimulated not only by the idea, but by the way you've told the idea. It's just like music, you know. If you've written a melody and it's a wonderful melody, right. Now give me some great orchestration around the melody to make it really come alive and make it really feel different. I think that's what we're trying to do here.

John Hegarty

▷ What components must a great commercial made by Hegarty have?
◁ Oh, I think it's incredibly difficult to answer. I think in the end emotion is the most important component. I think that's what film or television, or call it whatever you like, can do away and above press. Press by and large and print by and large tends to be — and the consumer tends to treat it as — a piece of information.

▷ That statement would cause you some difficulties in print-oriented continental Europe.
◁ Well, of course print implies emotion, naturally it does, but it can't do it to the extent a television commercial or a piece of film can.

▷ It also works the other way round. In our snowplow commercial there is no emotion whatsoever. Even the car seems to be moved by ghosts, or do you see any people in the commercial?
◁ No, I don't think so at all. I think you see a man's footsteps. I think that's the element which I look for mostly in a television commercial. And I suppose that the other thing I look for is drama. And, again, I think that's what television can do for you. The way it can pull your emotions and the way it can take you in a certain direction, then make you change your point of view. And I think that's what I really like about it. I suppose really, you could describe our commercials as visual narratives. And I think if you look at Levis, if you look at Pretty Polly, if you look at K-Shoes, Audi in its own way, although we have a voice-over on it, but it's really more visual. The voice is almost part of the visual. It's not intended to be taken overly seriously. So, yes, visual narrative, I think, is the way I like to describe our commercials. I think it is the way film is best used, too. I actually don't think film is an intellectual medium. I think it's an emotional medium. I think that writing is a more intellectual medium. I think writing and reading are quite unnatural. Human beings had to kind of learn how to do it. Whereas they think visually. When I say "cat" to you, you don't go "c-a-t-Frankl-in gothic-48-point". You go, you know, a picture comes into your brain. I think that is kind of how we actually respond, how we see things.

▷ On a level of association.
◁ Yes, I think film is the medium that actually communicates with that, which actually sort of touches the nerve end.

▷ With your films you always managed to hit another nerve, the nerve of the age. Your films always reflect a change in society and social behavior. Can you explain how you always manage to hit the spirit of the moment?
◁ I think good advertising does capture the spirit of the moment. And

Stills from the
Levi's commercial "Creek"

that's an important facet, it's an important part of what we are trying to create. I mean, whatever you say, large messages don't really change that much. You know there aren't that many things to say. But there are new ways of saying them. And that's what really we're doing. So when we are communicating and when we are writing, we're trying to put things within the context of the moment that we are writing about. And that's very important, and that's what I guess is drama to the message you're putting across.

▷ Your Levi's commercials are a really great example of capturing zeitgeist.

◁ That's right. Also I think the other interesting thing with Levi's is, that we really capture that feeling of the man as a sexual image. I mean the launderette commercial which was the launch of the 501's was really a striptease. I mean a man comes into a launderette and takes his clothes off. It was portraying the male as a sexual image. And I think that really did touch quite a deep nerve end. And for all sorts of reasons, I mean, men were, you know, more interested in their bodies and there was a greater movement towards health ... But again I think it touches the nerve of change, you know. And the idea of the masculine body as being sort of quite visual.

▷ In your Levi's commercials you crossformed your new man with some old tunes in such a clever way that sales of the 501 went up immediately.

◁ Yes. One tries to always put layers into what you're doing. I always think about it. A film commercial is more akin to music than it is to anything else. Because even a film – you only really see a film once. I mean you might see it twice, but that's unusual. You might do it, but a commercial is like a piece of music. It get's played again and again, and again and again. And it requires a sort of certain type of content to keep it fresh. Each time you see it you must have something there that makes that person want to see it again. Just as with a piece of music. It makes you kind of, you know, I want to hear that again and again.

▷ What is it that makes you wanna see or hear it again?

◁ Well, I think it's the way in which you put the commercial together. I think it's the technique you use to tell your story. I think it's creating moments of drama in the piece. So that people wait for little bits. They know that this little piece is coming.

▷ For instance in the launderette one, when the guy takes off his hat.

◁ Yes, or when the two little boys –one comes over and looks, and then all of a sudden there's another one and they're twins. That's interesting.

John Hegarty

And, you know, the way the girls react. The way when he sits down, the big fat man who's obviously witnessed the whole thing just turns and looks at him in a very dead way and turns away. It hasn't affected, it hasn't touched him at all. He just can't understand why this bloke is sitting next to him with no clothes on. So you create little moments of kind of intrigue and drama that want to make you come back again and think about it and say to yourself: "Why is that? What was it for?" I think that's the art of great commercials. It's the desire to come back. So that they must be three-dimensional, not two-dimensional. I think I do see a lot of work that tends to be two-dimensional, it's quite flat. It's very good the first time you see it, the second time you see it, it's less good, and less good and less good. And I think you're trying to put in all those little moments. And understanding that is very important.

▷ A story about Hegarty: "If he wants to sell commercials, he acts them out in front of the client". What's the truth in that?

◁ Well, it's cheaper than doing storyboards basically.

▷ You are famous for the fact that you make jingles work. Your commercials even got old songs back in the charts again. Where does your feeling for music have its roots?

◁ Oh dear me, that's a tough one to answer. That goes back a long way. I suppose in some ways I could answer this. I was born in '44. So I was quite lucky really. By the time I was twelve rock'n'roll had begun to happen. By the time I was 14 or 15 Buddy Holly had been killed, Elvis Presley had gone into the army, and it seemed that rock'n'roll was gonna die. And then along came jazz. So we all started listening to jazz. Right through from traditional jazz with King Oliver all the way through to Miles Davis and John Coltrane. So one got a tremendous education in jazz. And then the Beatles and Blue Jazz came on the scene. And then we had the Rolling Stones, and then Bob Dylan. And then there was a real mix of popular music. Call it pop if you want; call it rock'n'roll. Call it what you like. So I then, being at college and art school, got right back into that music. So in my music I was lucky that my formative years were in the times when rock'n'roll was really sort of very, very popular.

▷ Another subject, Mr. Hegarty. How did you hit upon the idea of using Pretty Polly stockings as a fanbelt?

◁ The first thing we had was "Nine out of ten cats prefer them". There is a famous advertisement here for a cat food which, for years and years and years, said: "Nine out of ten cats prefer them." When we started working on Pretty Polly one of the things we did for them is that we just found how smooth they were. We had a cat rubbing up against a lady's

Stills from the "Polaroid" commercial

leg showing that the cat prefers the woman who was wearing Pretty Polly tights. Consequently the line: "Nine out of ten cats prefer them". When Rosie Arnold, who was the art director working on that, wanted to move the idea on she then did it to the idea of a car. And the car, naturally, was a Jaguar because that's a cat. And when the car broke down obviously the Jaguar could be fixed with Pretty Polly tights. Consequently the line: "Nine out of ten cats prefer them".

▷ We are really talking here about zeitgeist. The fact that you were always able to recognize the zeitgeist must have taken a lot of effort.

◁ Yes, that's right. I think you just have to be alert and aware to what is going on. I think that you must keep trying to be different, not for the sake of it but just to be daring. I think that we try to push the boundaries and the limits of the medium. And I think in the end people will respond to that. And if you are doing that you keep your opportunities to try things and to do things, and we keep questioning it. Why here? Why does it have to be like that? Why do you like that? Why do you keep saying that? Keep asking "Why".

▷ Why are you always able to catch the zeitgeist?

◁ I think, it's a whole range of things. It's reading. I think reading is very important. I think it's music. But I also think there's no fixed moment, or there's no fixed point, which you can get this information. I think that you are taking it in from around you. I am an antenna, a moving aerial which is receiving all the time. But I think it's also important to remember that you can in yourself influence the debate. And I think if your advertising is stimulating and it's changing, it also influences that debate. And I think we mustn't forget that. I think advertising is a mirror to society, but it can also be a product. I can also, you know, just point in certain directions. I don't think it can ever lead, because it doesn't have the resource, you know. One particular, it's too fragmented. But I think it can be a sort of catalyst for change. And I think some of the work we have done has been a catalyst for change.

▷ Society influences advertising. Does advertising also influence society?

◁ Well, you know, it's difficult to say. I mean advertising has influenced the making of films enormously. I mean if you think about it some of the directors now working in Hollywood have come from British advertising. Alan Parker, Ridley Scott, Tony Scott – they've taken the kind of the art of advertising and transferred it, or elements of it into film making. I think that you can see, you know, the sharper images, the cutting, the story-

John Hegarty

158

telling has been affected by the way advertising has compressed information. And I think they've done the same, they have taken that into films. So I think, it's certainly affecting it from that point of view.

▷ You describe yourself as an antenna. Are you afraid that the antenna Hegarty will one day lose its ability to receive?

◁ Yes, probably. But hopefully I will be rich enough for it not to worry me.

▷ The film makers you have mentioned, the Scotts and Parkers, are really global communicators. I don't know if your agency has done any successful global advertising, but it has definitively done successful pan-European advertising. Your Levi's campaign is one of the rare examples of a successful international campaign.

◁ Yes, I think it is. I think it's quite a unique product. And I think as Europeans we have a kind of combined view of America. And because it's an American product we can join in and we can all share it. I mean we will get slightly different things out of it. But I think it's a marvellous example of how Europe can think as one. I think it's a very interesting example, but I would say I think, there are a few of them. Funny enough, actually, we find the Audi advertising works around Europe.

▷ Was it very difficult to persuade the client to run a German slogan in England?

◁ Oh yes, because the research said: "Don't do it." Because the client said: "Let's research it to see what happens." And in fact the research came back saying: "Don't do it." The client, however – the client was a very brave client. And they said: "We are a German car. Why shouldn't we extol the virtues of that? It is our point of difference." And I think it was also important for Audi to establish that because it might be strange for you just to realize, but a lot of people didn't immediately associate Audi with being German because it isn't a German name. It was sort of an Euro car; could have been made in Belgium. I mean, Mercedes is German, Volkswagen is German, BMW is German. But Audi? So it was important to kind of emphasize that. So from that point of view the client said: "No, we should go with it, we should do it."

▷ In the meantime "Vorsprung durch Technik" has become a classic slogan. How did it come about?

◁ Yes, it's so simple, isn't it? I can remember it. It came about when I was down in Ingolstadt in the factory there. And we were going around and I kept seeing "Vorsprung durch Technik" and I kept saying "What was that? What does it mean?" And they said: "Well it's very difficult to translate. There's no word for "Vorsprung" in English, and I kind of liked that. It's sort of winning with technology or being ahead with technology. And it

Advertisement for
Black Levi's

WHEN THE WORLD ZIGS, ZAG

just went into the brain and I thought that's good, I like that. "Vorsprung durch Technik" — that's funny. And it's very funny actually. There was an article in one of the national newspapers. I think it was the "Guardian". They did a little thing on the famous slogans of the eighties. And "Vorsprung durch Technik" is one of them.

▷ Why are you creative?

◁ Ha, ha, ha. That's the only thing I can do really, ha,ha. I can't write a contact report. I think creative people are basically insecure. I think they have massive insecurities and they need to create something to prove their worth. And therefore kind of create things to overcome their massive insecurities. I think that's what it is.

□

John Hegarty   160

OLIVIERO TOSCANI

Provocation is a form of generosity

Oliviero Toscani was born in 1942 in Milan. He studied photography at the Kunstgewerbeschule in Zurich from 1961 to 1965, then began to work as a photographer for fashion magazines such as Elle, Vogue, Lei, Donna, GQ, Mademoiselle, and Harper's. He then switched to advertising and became the creative force behind some of the fashion industry's most famous campaigns such as those for Jesus Jeans, Prenatal, Valentino, Esprit and Fiorucci. His infamous collaboration with Benetton began in 1982 and lasted until May 2000. The campaigns he created have won him not just a place in history but numerous awards, including the Grand Prix d'Affichage, the Unesco Grand Prix and the Art Directors Club of New York's Management Medal. In 1989 he won a Lion d'Or at Cannes for a commercial he directed. Toscani and his family live in Tuscany, Italy. Oliviero Toscani is a wonderful master of the visual culture. I interviewed him in 2000 and 2001, both before and after his departure from Benetton.

▷ Hermann Vaske: So tell me why you hate advertising?

◁ Oliviero Toscani: Well, I hate advertising as it is done now. I hate traditional advertising, the one that just pushes us to consume. I hate advertising that's got no creativity. I hate advertising that is conditioned by managers and marketing and market research and all that nonsense. I think advertising is just a waste of incredible time on television, waste of space on the wall, waste of pages in magazines.

The war between creativity and the business has been lost by the creative people. Business people have been stepping on the head of creative people, by telling them that what they do is not commercial enough to be sold. I believe that even the economy needs creativity.

▷ Let's talk about your most recent project first, the "Sentenced to Death" campaign for Benetton.

◁ That's the work I have always wanted to do. You know, if you ask me, are you for the death penalty or against it? I refuse to answer that question. Because it means accepting or refusing to kill another human being. I'm against this way of thinking. I think it is outrageous that you can be in a position where you can tell somebody, "Okay, in 15 days we are going to kill you." I mean society tells that in cold blood. The State of Texas, to me, is the biggest serial killer there is. No serial killer has killed as many humans as the state. George W. Bush – one day we could go after him like we did after Pinochet. I mean this guy wakes up in the

Toscani's campaign with the people on death row

morning, and after having breakfast...two eggs and cornflakes...sentences someone to death. I mean I'm not saying that the convicted are innocent. I know they are guilty of the most horrendous murders but how can you justify condemning someone to death in cold blood? So you see it's not a question of being against it or for it. It shouldn't even get to that question. It is appalling that society still has to pose such a question.

▷ I talked to someone about the campaign who asked why you didn't bring in the victim's side as well? I am sure that you have been confronted with this point of view.

◁ Of course. If I talk to the gardener here, he will also tell me how to do my work. Everybody feels they can tell you how to do your work, especially when you take pictures. Everybody comes up all the time and says, "Why didn't you do this, why didn't you do that?" I listen to them and say to myself, "Everybody's an art director." Sometimes I think that doctors are very lucky because they put their clients to sleep before they operate, so they have to shut up. In my work this is not possible. But I'm not interested in the crime. We all know about that. We don't have to prove that these people are guilty. I accept the fact that these people are guilty of terrible crimes, I won't even discuss that. What I was interested in knowing was how it feels to be there, to be sentenced to death, to know that you will die at an appointed date. Do they sleep well at night? Do they dream? What do they dream about? Do they feel like eating?

Selling sweaters, that's ridiculous. If Coca-Cola want to build a new headquarter in Atlanta, they will call Norman Foster or Michael Graves to design it. And no one will ask Norman Foster or Michael Graves, are you designing the Coca-Cola building so Coca-Cola can sell more bottles of Coke? Nobody would approach a writer who writes for the New Yorker and say, "You've written this article for The New Yorker so The New Yorker will sell more." Probably Coca-Coca will sell more bottles of Coke and The New Yorker will sell more copies of their magazine, but that should not concern the architect or the writer or the photographer. But you know, the language of advertising has set up just such a set of values that everybody has to conform to. I refuse to conform to that. I don't do market research. I don't care. I think you can be concerned, committed to a cause, and still sell. I've heard songs about major issues by people who sold their records. Spielberg made "Schindler's List" and everything was fake, he reconstructed concentration camps with Jews being killed and Nazis and all that; and he sold a lot of cinema tickets that way. But nobody would ask him that question. And it would not be fair to ask him that question. But yes, I do hope they sell a lot of sweaters so I can go on doing what I do.

▷ You said you don't give a damn about market research. Do you feel research murders ideas, kills creativity?

◁ Well, it's all been invented by managers to cover up their mistakes, their possible mistakes. So when they make mistakes they can always say, research told me to do it that way. So I couldn't do the opposite of what they said. So it's just an excuse. Research is something to cover your ass. But all this is really the best way to make everything mediocre. Because big creativity makes big fortunes but it takes risks of course. And one thing I am sure of is that two things that are really in opposition are creativity and security. Every time you already know what the outcome will be you are just doing something that has been done before. But I am not concerned with selling. I never sell anything. Actually, I never buy anything either, there is always somebody else who does that for me. The only thing about it that interests me is that I hope the things I do will sell big so I can go on doing what I do. That is the only possibility a modern artist has, you know, exploit the system. And I don't mind exploiting this marketing machine. I don't have any other chance. When I look back at the Italian Renaissance, when you look at those painters, most of them were totally against religion and the Church, yet they worked for the Pope, they had to paint all these "madonna-and-childs" without really believing in all that. But their art, their painting, went through. They exploited the Church to do what they wanted, which was paint.

▷ How did you feel when you met these guys in prison? Did you bring some sweaters with you?

◁ It's not like they were naked, they walked in their T-shirts and red suits. I didn't want to photograph them in sweaters. I didn't even ask if that was possible. I didn't ask them to wear anything in particular, that was not the point. Actually, what I wanted to do was just the opposite. Normally, what you do in advertising is, you get a top model, say Claudia Schiffer, you dress her up, you pay for that, you put it on the wall. Everybody would like to be Claudia Schiffer, and everybody would like to then buy the product, right? I did just the opposite. I think nobody wants to be on death row. And they haven't got a thing to sell. I wanted to have as a model somebody society wants to get rid of and with no product to sell.

▷ A good formula for creativity, to do just the opposite of what is expected.

◁ It's not just the opposite. It's tragic. A tragic situation. Somebody we want to get rid of with nothing to sell. Actually the clothes they are wearing in the pictures are the ones they get on death row, the red, or brightly fluorescent orange suit which makes it easy for them to find you should you manage to escape.

▷ What do you think of the uproar, the picket line, the fact that Sears now refuse to sell Benetton in their stores?

◁ I think it's great. It's what I wanted, exactly that.

▷ You thrive on scandal?

◁ It's very strange that everybody comes to me and says, "Oh, you see what happened? They terminated their contract. There is picketing in front of the shops. They're against what you do." It seems we live in a world where everybody is afraid of being rejected. We all want to be accepted. We don't want to disturb. We want to pass through this life without disturbing. We will make our noses small the way the fashion magazines tell us to. You know, I've never seen a woman walk into a doctor's and come out with a nose like that, never. Everybody tries to conform to this stupid beauty. Everybody wants to be accepted. We live in a state of fear. And I ask myself, "Isn't it strange that everybody is so concerned about the finances of Benetton?" So they lost the Sears contract. I think it's great to lose a contract. We might get a better one tomorrow, get a better client. I think Sears is not as modern as Benetton. Sears doesn't speak the modern language, so it's a good thing we lost it. We would have had problems with them sooner or later. So it's a good way of getting rid of Sears. We don't need Sears' money. Benetton is looking for something more interesting, and I'm sure that tomorrow, the day after tomorrow, or a year from now, another company will come and say, "We want to work with you." I don't understand this fear of being rejected. The best thing is to be rejected. You can probably learn more, you can do better after that. To me, this type of rejection shows that what you have done is so strong and so good that people on the whole are just not there yet. A very interesting situation. On the other hand, when you get absorbed, when you get integrated, you are lost, you are gone. Then you are just another number.

▷ Amid all this uproar, this scandal, do you think that people still discuss the issues?

◁ Sure, they discuss the issues. In the US, as a result of my campaign, there is now a lot of discussion of whether the majority of people are really for the death penalty, or whether it is just a ruse of politicians who speculate that they can get more votes by consenting to put someone to death.

▷ The campaign also ran in Europe where there is a broad consensus against the death penalty. Nobody wants to reintroduce it, so it was less provocative here...

◁ Well, first of all, you would be surprised how many people in Europe think that the death penalty is the right way to go. I don't think there is this broad consensus. But, most importantly, I don't care if it is less provocative in Europe. The fact that the death penalty is still enforced in parts of this world is enough. It's not a question of passports or countries, you know. We have 86 countries in this world that still have the death penalty. Humanity as a whole still has this problem. That is what I am concerned about.

▷ How do you feel about the truth-stretching process in advertising? You know, cigarette advertising that doesn't tell you about lung cancer you get from consuming the product, McDonald's not telling what type of animal products they put in their meat.

◁ Well, I don't see that much difference between an animal's genitals or eyeballs and other parts of its body. We have no problem eating that, so what's the big fuss? Why shouldn't we eat everything?

▷ Yes, but the way the truth is stretched in advertising...

◁ That's not half as bad as politics or religion. Look at the lies religion has been telling us. God made the world in six days...Is that the truth? What about politicians? They all lie...

▷ Especially in Germany, where the Christian Democrats are going down lying...

◁ Especially in Germany, yes. Well, at last there is a big scandal. No one believed they could do that. But everyone can. To me this is like, "Oh, finally Germany too!" I think Kohl did us all a great service this way. Showing the world that even Germany can be corrupt. So I feel sympathy for him. Because by doing what he did he showed that corruption is a universal problem, all humanity has it. We are corrupted from the day we are born. Great. Thank you, Mr. Kohl.

▷ Did he need to be a great communicator to be able to get away with the big scam for so long the way he did?

◁ Oh, come on! Look at the Church. After 2,000 years they are still there, and people walk in and kneel and pray. Compared to the Church, Kohl is an amateur, he's a nobody.

▷ You mean they got away with a big hoax for 2,000 years?

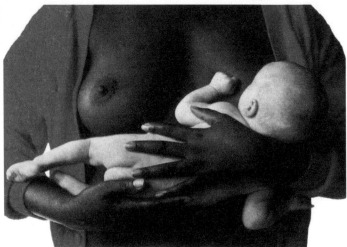

One of Toscani's posters for Benetton

◁ A huge lie, nothing else. From a personal point of view, it makes me laugh to see the Pope go around dressed like a freak. I mean not even David Bowie in his wildest years dressed more eccentrically when he went on stage. Only the Pope can get away with walking around dressed like that, and people kneel down. It's fantastic, what a glib show.

▷ You mean like an old drag queen?

◁ Well, drag queens are not that extreme. When you look at a congregation of Cardinals in Rome, it makes me laugh. You won't find a transvestite bar as extreme as that.

▷ A theatre of the absurd?

◁ No, a theatre of human behaviour.

▷ Would you like to do an advertising campaign for the Catholic Church?

◁ I think I'd better stick to what I do. I don't know if you can do better than they have done so far. They had the best artists under contract, like Michaelangelo and Leonardo, Caravaggio and Piero della Francesca. They had the most incredible ideas: They came up with the idea that the mother of God is a virgin! And these visions: life after death, resurrection – it's amazing! No one could top them in that respect. The Church is God's advertising agency, the best communication agency in the world.

▷ Mr. Toscani, who were your creative influences? Your parents?

◁ My parents? I had a father who was a photo journalist and didn't even know what school I was going to. Every once in a while he would ask me, "Which class are you in?" And I would say, "second." "Are you good at school?" he'd ask. "Yes." I would say. "Good." And that was it. I had the full responsibility for what I was doing. But, on the other hand, I have a mother, she's 90 now, very alert, very witty, very quick, who started to work when she was six years old. She was born during World War I, and because her father was a soldier she had to start to work at an early age. She had to work all her life. That's why she's still alive and so alert. And having these parents made me very independent. Nobody ever told me what to do, really.

▷ Not even the Church, or at school?

◁ No, not really. I come from a very free family, not a religious family at all. I didn't have to go to church like all of my friends who had to do all these things. But I later went to a Jesuit school, simply because it was the school that was closest. But there it wasn't so bad to have doubts, to ask questions. So I did all the things you do as a pupil at a Jesuit school, I used to serve at Mass. I was very interested in all this. The bigotry of the Church. But the Jesuits are more intelligent than that. You know, when you go to a Jesuit school, when you come out, you don't believe in anything any more.

▷ Women and creativity...Why are there still so relatively few women in the creative field?

◁ Perhaps they are more like animals or plants than men are. Perhaps they are more finished creatures. God didn't really finish humanity the way he created a finished perfect fauna and flora, so we need to be creative to finish the Genesis. So perhaps women are more finished. They can think better, they know a lot more. They can envision things. Probably women are more adult. And also in the way they are brought up, they are already more adult when they are children. When they are five, six years old they play with dolls. In other words they are already mothers at that age. Boys, on the other hand, play with hammers. They break things, they kick a ball, they punch each other. And when they grow up they are more creative, there is this inherent need to be creative. Of course, there are many women who are extremely creative, who refuse to conform to what is expected of them. But, on the whole, I really believe that women are the more perfect creatures, the ones who don't have this need for creativity.

▷ How do you feel about advertising being the fine art of separating people from their money?

◁ I don't care if people are separated from their money. I mean if you consider money such an important thing, probably...personally I have

The magazine "Colors"
created by Toscani

never walked into a bank all my life. That's a great achievement. I am very proud of that.

▷ You don't even use cash machines?

◁ I never go to the cash machine. I've always had somebody take care of that for me. Plus, you know, there are credit cards, which are fantastic. One of the best inventions ever. I can't stand those economy people who can't think of anything but money. I don't even know what they're talking about. They're ridiculous. But unfortunately, the whole world is conditioned by that.

▷ So you wouldn't consider making money an art form?

◁ No, I wouldn't. I have seen lots of very dumb people getting so rich, you know. So I don't think it's particularly difficult.

▷ Do you have any heroes, any gods?

◁ I trust in myself and I'm not embarrassed to say that. When I die, every-thing will stop existing for me. I have got no other chance than to believe in myself.

▷ No second chance?

◁ There isn't a second chance. We've got this life and that's all there is. I didn't ask to come here and I know I am going to die. So if there really is a god who created all this mess, who created the human system, if he really existed, I would take him and nail him to the cross myself. I mean I'm against the death penalty but in this case, I wouldn't think twice about it.

▷ How important is it to you to work for Benetton, not another com-pany? Could you have done the same campaign for another brand, another company that would have given you the freedom?

◁ I wish I could have done something like that for Volkswagen. I think Volkswagen is the most interesting car maker in the world today. Just to think that if Volkswagen were tomorrow to decide to have a campaign like this, that they wouldn't open any more plants in the States or in any other country that still has the death penalty...It would be a big thing if the economy got behind a thing like that. Politicians would change their minds, people would change their minds.

▷ On the other hand, why doesn't Benetton stop selling clothes in countries where they have the death penalty?

◁ No, you don't understand. I am not saying Volkswagen shouldn't sell their cars there. Benetton doesn't produce in the States.

▷ But you sell.

◁ Yeah, but that's different. There are people who can go and buy the stuff, not everyone there is for the death penalty. But I'm talking economics. I mean Volkswagen could say, we won't open plants in countries that still have the death penalty because we are European and the death penalty is against a European belief.

▷ What's the difference between building a plant and selling products?

◁ With a plant you bring to an economy, you don't just take their money. You bring work, and work is a very strong political power. So it would be very interesting if the economy got behind human ideas like that.

▷ You always stress that the great advantage of Benetton is your artistic freedom. How important to you personally is the product that is financing your work? Would you do the same campaign for an electric power station, say, this guy is going to the electric chair, but I'm doing it for electric power in Italy. How important has the product been in all this?

◁ Well, I am very happy to work for Benetton. They make sweaters, pure wool, ecologically sound. The company is very serious-minded, they provide a good quality of life for the people who work there. They are open to projects like this one. They are open to a certain kind of language. So I'm very comfortable with the company. I couldn't work with a company I'm not comfortable with. This is very important. And, on top of that, I have always worked directly with Luciano Benetton. I don't deal with managers. Probably, if Benetton were run by managers, I wouldn't work for them. They'd run it for their own interest. They wouldn't run it with a view towards the world at large. So Benetton is a very particular company, very modern, very advanced.

▷ Do you sympathise with socialist economic ideas? Are you a communist at heart?

◁ We're not civilised enough to be communist. To be communist, you need a very civilised, very developed society, and we're not at that stage yet. Perhaps in three hundred years. But the communist vision is too advanced a vision for the present level of humanity.

▷ Some people, if they look at your work, might think there is a plan behind it. What could be the next provocation? Is there a Toscani list of taboos that have to be touched upon?

◁ No, it's very natural to me. You know a scorpion doesn't bite you because it's bad, it's natural. It's not a bad animal. You put your hand there, it bites. I don't provoke you – you want to be provoked. Certainly, I want to be provoked. I go and look at a Picasso painting or a painting by Hieronymus Bosch and I find incredible provocation there. I wish that feeling would never stop. To me, provocation is a form of generosity. To provoke somebody means that you offer somebody the opportunity to see a problem from another point of view. You know, some people don't want that, they don't want to move from their perspective, don't want to move from their set of values, they don't want to move from their ethics. I think we should keep moving constantly.

▷ Do you sometimes get frustrated by reactions, like when some of your work got banned?

◁ No, I never get frustrated. There is no time to get frustrated. What we are discussing now is what I did last year. I'm already working on next year, so for me this is like looking in a rear-view mirror. It's like you're on the autobahn in your car. The future is the road ahead and you look towards the future, and occasionally you glance in the rear-view mirror, like when I talk about what I did last year. Which is why I like to go to Junior High Schools and teach and talk to young people about my work. To the young people between 12 and 16. I like the teenager category. That is where I get my gratification from because they can still judge from a future point of view. They are not set in the past, they are not looking into the rear-view mirror.

▷ But isn't it also because of the way they have been brought up, the different way in which they deal with the media?

◁ I think there is a new morality and I like to look into that. We need a new language and we need it badly. The written language is over. It doesn't tell the truth anymore. You read and read and try looking for truth but you never get there. Visual language is the new language but it is not focused yet.

▷ Where do you see it heading?

◁ First of all, we have to destroy the barriers between the categories. It's all devised by categories – this is the truth and you have to listen, this is just amusement, etc. There is no such thing as serious or funny, everything is both, serious and funny. Funny can be very serious and serious can be very ridiculous. So I think we have to destroy the different categories first.

▷ But with magazines, for instance, you can hardly tell anymore where the advertisment stops and the editorial begins.

◁ It is all advertising. It really is.

▷ Even though there might be some critical editorial?

◁ It is all advertising. You write an editorial, you write for an idea, a concept. You advertise something.

□

NEVILLE BRODY

Communication is sacred

Neville Brody studied Graphic Design at the London College of Printing. He worked with the Human League and did record covers for Cabaret Voltaire. He became the face behind The Face, the Art Director who brought the style into a lot of European style magazines. Brody created the image for Arena, did advertising for Nike, designed for Swatch and produced influential corporate identities for Japanese companies. Museums in Europe and Japan put on exhibitions of his work. His book, "The Graphic Language of Neville Brody", is the Bible of every other Art Director. I interviewed the Co-Founder of Research Studios and former Art Director of The Face in London.

▷ Hermann Vaske: Neville, your breakthrough typography and design was copied by many, many people. How do you feel now that the copiers are finally catching up with the avantgarde?

◁ Neville Brody: They are not getting equal. I think my work is accessible and I just always try to keep one step beyond. I mean the point is that people copy other people. And what you have – everything looks the same. Very similar. And then everybody can sleepwalk. So the point is, if anything is challenging, society absorbs part of the challenge into itself. And neutralizes the challenge. Happens in architecture a lot. It has always happened in art. Especially when dangerous art becomes attractive advertising. And it happens all the time in design. What we've always been doing was challenging but trying to break down traditional values. Since something we were working on became repeated we realized that was becoming a new tradition again. So immediately you have to move on. So we kept moving.

▷ You create something and immediately destroy it.

◁ Of course. If you look at Warhol's work, I feel very angry at the moment. With Warhol art history is being rewritten. With Warhol and what Warhol was doing and what he had to say. It was a big process and it changed the way of thought. And it was anti-precious. If you're using Warhol's pictures you're not allowed to crop them, you're not allowed to print anything on top of them. So the Warhol process can't continue anymore. So really someone else should take Warhol's work and retreat it again. Re-process Warhol. You can't. So in many ways the Warhol challenge has become another period in art. And it's too much even for the people close to Warhol to assume. The danger is gone.

▷ But there are new dangers and challenges.

◁ Danger is anything that you can't expect. Or anything that makes you have to struggle with something you're looking at. Advertising generally works on the basis that you don't have to struggle. Except in England. Where if you don't struggle with it that's considered bad advertising. They use intelligent advertising to flatter the consumer. And the consumers are saying: "We are intelligent – so we are going to buy the product." It's a double trick.

▷ And it works.

◁ Yeah, it works. I'm entertained by advertising. But if we see entertaining advertising it depends on how good the creative buyer is. By the buyer I mean the creative buyer, the client. There are no creative buyers left. Very few. Now you look at companies in Germany and you tell me how many have creative buyers. I mean people that really want to take risks. I mean the buyer in Germany tends to look so solid, secure and universal.

▷ That goes with the German mentality.

◁ Yeah, sometimes the German system needs some shocks.

▷ "A painting that doesn't shock isn't worth anything" is a statement by Marcel Duchamp. Would you transfer the Duchampian philosophy into advertising?

◁ Not necessarily only into advertising but just into communication... into advertising and into the design side as well. I mean in Germany, as you know, nearly all design is done by advertising agencies. The design agency is a German thing. I mean it used to be. This is the legacy of what was happening in Germany in 1920/1930. Today you have the work of Erik Spiekermann and Metadesign. He is in Berlin. And I think he is radical and experimental and a purist. I think he is the new influence of the future of design.

▷ The big break in German history took place in 1933, when a lot of creative and talented people had to leave the country. Germany was never able to overcome that loss.

◁ But there are a lot of creative people in Germany. But the system doesn't allow the opportunity to turn it into anything more than an attitude. See, I've been put into the position of being the revolutionary. But I just wanted to be creative.

▷ Why are you creative?

◁ Because I don't see any point in communicating otherwise. What's the point? Give me another reason. What other reason is there to work in design and advertising? There's money, power, greed and creativity. The creative approach is the only one. Anything else than the creative approach shouldn't be working. So I am just creative. And I refuse to stop being creative. And I think this is why people sometimes put me in a box: he's anti. It's not anti. If you want to do something well you have to be obsessed by it. I see too many things where people are not obsessed. People don't care. Well, what's important is the client being happy, the money in the bank, the friends in the industry being impressed or whatever. Well, it's a joke because the people who see this, who have to live with it, is the public. They have to live with the consequences of an advertising agency winning big clients.

▷ Well, if you make too many compromises you lose your self-respect. And if you don't, you're probably losing a client.

◁ So what. My barber said to me last week: "You must be rich. I've seen you on television." So people just assume it. But the fact is we're not. We're far from it. I am happy. We can do very creative work here. I have a number of designers plus myself. We are still quite young and sit down and discuss ideas. Not from the point of view of discussing what's best for the client, but we try to discuss ideas in a creative way. And if I feel a job we are working on isn't the best we could do then I don't let it leave the studio until we've made it good. And I think if you turn out something that you think isn't the best you can do, then you shouldn't let it out. How do you live with yourself?

▷ That's what I meant by self-respect.

◁ Exactly. Advertising, design and architecture create the environment essentially. And all the politicians create the environment. We are very responsible and it's a position of trust. And it's abused every day. I can't understand why something is not good. The excuses you always hear when you ask people why is this or that not good, are: "Well, it's not our fault. The client told us to do this." And then I say: "So why didn't you say no?" And they say: "Oh, we needed the money." Communication is sacred. It's not there to be abused. When people look at British design they think it is the best design that is happening at the moment. I mean internationally it's certainly the most successful. Eight of the ten largest design groups in the world are in London, which is crazy. The biggest have staff of 600. What can you do? It's like an invading army. This is the Third World War. This is the new Nazis.

▷ Years ago when I talked to Ted Milton from Blurt, he said: "I do art and go on stage. When I finish playing and the people are not able to applaud then I've won." Do you think that extreme in typography and design?

◁ Yes, this is dadaist. When someone applauded they felt they failed. What I discovered is you can't break a window and expect people to look at it and get something from this. But if you have, let's say, ten windows and you break each second window there is a reaction. So you have to meet the person you are communicating to halfway. You have to use a shared language in order to take someone to a further point. This is what I always tried to do. And I've never allowed things to become totally alien in understanding. Because if you do that people just can't react to it and discuss it. And the dadaist ethic that if someone applauded then they'd failed – is not quite true because they also failed because people came to see them. If people wanted to see what they were doing they also failed. I mean, it was a sort of a propagandist statement. So I accept that I am communicating. I accept the people at the other end. Their first reaction would be to like something and then applaud and maybe their second reaction is: "Oh hang on, what does that mean?"

▷ You sort of mention that in the foreword to your book, when you say: "You have to look twice."

◁ Yes, yes. If I can make a person look twice at something. I think then I have succeeded. And it's just a very simple way of putting it. Because it goes much wider. There's a famous English record cover designer called Barney Bubbles. When I went to college I went to see him. He was with Stiff and he said to me one thing which really stuck my mind. "If you want to go out there, you just can't go out there and shout. You have to take people with you bit by bit." So that's the point. You break a window and people say you break a window. Some hooligans. See, I don't think I'm being subversive in a negative sense. I'm not trying to attack things. I'm trying to push people to be constantly aware of creativity.

▷ And therefore society puts you in a box labeled "Punk and Revolutionary."

◁ That's another way society deals with challenges. Either you absorb parts or you put them in a box. So that brings us back to your first question about copying. So I've been copied a lot. There are possibly two ways to understand it. Either there was nothing else in terms of strong ideas which reflects society today, or my work was very challenging and needed to be absorbed. I don't know. I never know. I mean, people don't know why they copy. Maybe they look at my work and think this is strong, this is modern. We want to be modern too. So they don't understand why I've chosen certain typefaces.

▷ Why do you choose certain typefaces then?

◁ We need to look at communication again. The language we use to speak to each other was born 300 years ago. And we are still using the same language. We are still covering everything we say with old tradition. And typefaces are born because of the need to communicate something special about that society. And we still use the same forms. But the reasons are not relevant anymore. So it's really nostalgia in a way. It's trying to be something that we are not. And I'm trying to get to the essence of what society today is about. I'm trying to find ways to communicate that which is relevant to know.

▷ That's true. The visual communicates the spirit of the eighties. Typography got stuck in archaic forms.

◁ Yes, yes. Really, communication is the engine. It should be the engine. This isn't deliberate. Look at this page. What does this say? (Brody points to a Condor ad in a German magazine lying on his desk.)

▷ A little advertising story.

◁ And then the typography is very inhuman. I think we need to find very human forms of communication. Especially in Germany.

▷ Yeah, you're talking about a German campaign.

◁ Yes, Condor. This is pure. To me this says money and corporations. Like Daimler Benz. I must show you Erik Spiekermann's book, it's wonderful. He's done a book called "Typography Novel." On one page he has the corporate typeface of ten German companies. And it's the same typeface. It's all Helvetica. And he's the same. He feels there's the need to develop a typography which reflects different philosophical ideas. We have to find ideas now.

▷ There has always been a spirit of unity in Germany when it comes to boredom.

◁ And it's by association. It's like a big club. And it doesn't challenge anything or doesn't move anything. I'm very pure. My design is very pure. Some people still think I am a punk designer.

▷ A punk designer who is influenced by Russian constructivism.

◁ That's not true. I haven't shared some of their attitudes to communication. And I also think that the most recent period of creativity and design was in the 1930s. And I think everything else since then, with some exceptions, has been a repeat of what happened before.

▷ You, Mr. Brody, are doing the opposite. You have brought new kicks and inspiration to old typography.

◁ I hope so. What I wanted people to copy wasn't my choice of typeface. Because that was just one thing that led to the next thing. I wanted people to copy my approach to what's happening.

▷ Yes, I think you wanted to make people aware that typography is not the fifth wheel on a car, but a very important tool.

◁ Yeah, for the whole of communication. I wanted people to always be questioning. I wanted people to question what I do. But I failed because people copied me. Which led in the eighties in England to a real period of decoration. Since you've been here, you've looked around. British design is very professional. Everything is touched by it in England now. Everything is designed.

▷ Especially Covent Garden.

◁ Especially Covent Garden. But any High Street and any shopping center anywhere in England. It's got the same touch; but it's style, it's decoration, it's surface. In one year they have to change it again. Because it's very fashionable. Which is big business for the design agencies.

▷ Sure, money motivates.

◁ While money is there. Money is running out. In England we're heading towards an economic recession again. The economy is coming down again. People aren't spending money. So we are heading towards an economic recession in Europe. Especially when people don't have much money to spend. So retail places like Covent Garden won't have the money to change their designs next year. So what you are looking at is tomorrow's kitsch. I mean the Bauhaus never became kitsch. There was a spirit there. But art deco, better say art nouveau became kitsch. The seventies were very kitsch. And this is kitsch in a way. Although there is a different spirit. And I think when you come back to Covent Garden in five years it's really kitsch. Covent Garden is like Thatcher's pride. This is the Britain she dreamt of. A capitalistic park you can spend all your money in Britain's biggest industry is the media and tourism. Media is music, fashion, photography, advertising, design and television. We are really good at producing images.

▷ An image associated with your name is Neville Brody: The face behind The Face.

◁ Oh, ha. I mean The Face was just part of it. It was a vehicle. It was a really important one. Because every month I had the chance to try new ideas and take people with me. I think The Face did work. I think it influenced the way a lot of people think. But there were also a lot of negative points about the magazine. It's really difficult because the area it discussed was often an area of superficial images. On the one hand it was celebrating something I hated. It was an interesting paradox. It was very strong and I felt it was very vital. You had to see every issue. And then the paradox has gone now. I think the spirit has gone and the magazine needs to change. But there are new paradoxes. In a way Arena is the new paradox, because Arena is a shopping catalog. And I use Helvetica, which I hate. And it's supposed to be used ironically. In England Helvetica was never as popular as it was in Germany. So people don't hate it. They just copy it. It's depressing. I know in Europe I had people say to me: "He's finished. He's using Helvetica." That's the point. See, the tradition on The Face was: we changed every month. But it became a tradition. So on Arena we never change. If you fulfill expectations then in a way it's failure. That's what I mean by the Dadaists. So people went to their evenings expecting to be shocked. They were shocked. And they applauded because they were shocked. So the whole thing was a failure. I think Dadaism was more relevant through its influence beyond. I don't know. I'm getting back to these big design groups. It's like wars of the mind, wars of the eye. I can see a battle coming between the big design groups who are eating the small design groups. The point is, these big English design groups are on the stock market. Public companies with shareholders. So each year they have to increase profits. If they decrease profits people withdraw money. They have millions of clients which are the investors. So every year they have to take on more. And they have to get more design. They have to eat more countries. And in a way this is a warning to Europe. Because they are going to try and really take over. They are just exporting image. Image for money. It's turning the visual world into tourism.

▷ Only the little shops can save the creative culture. All over the world there are little shops like yours with five or six people creating excellent work.

◁ This is the battle between the big design groups and the small design groups. At the moment people are going to different sides. Some small design groups are going to big groups by being bought and we are finally

One of Brody's early works: William S. Burroughs

going to see who is on which side. And these big design groups have been growing so big, so fast. Now they sponsor colleges. Art colleges are sponsored by big design groups. They are developing things and people. It's like test-tube babies.

▷ Replicants.

◁ Absolutely. With no creative idea, but very professional. And they leave college knowing exactly the right suit to wear. Exactly how to present work. They work for two years. Then they become design managers telling a new group of college leavers what to do. I know a story here about a new design for a government agency. It cost 350.000 £ and at the end of the day the actual final design was done by someone who'd been out of college less than one year. It's incredible. What we don't have here is what we call suites. Suites of people employed by design companies to do the lunches and the selling. And then they come back and tell the designer how to present it. We don't have it. We are small and creative and the work is more important than anything. We have deliberately not created a big company. So we don't have big financial problems. That's all. It's very easy for us to cover the costs. We have to work of course. But everybody who works here is freelance. It's a freelance operation. I'm freelance. So I don't work as a company. And everybody here does their own work as well.

▷ What kind of work do you mean?

◁ Well, in the evenings and weekends. So that they can keep up their creative moral. We work as a team. We have meetings very often and discuss things. We can afford to do projects which aren't commercial projects, which is really important. And we can afford to be really creative in our work. And we might spend less on presentation. But we spend a lot more money experimenting in trying to work towards a good solution. Because we are small we can work direct. I can sit down and say to a client: "I'm not going to give you 20 ideas and you choose one. I'd rather spend a day talking to you and find out what you really want."

▷ Supposing Condor came to you and said: "We are not happy with our big international agency. Please do a campaign for us. You can do what you like." Would you do it?

◁ I'd consider it. If I felt it was right. In England I don't do advertising.

▷ Why not?

◁ Because I think that generally the standard of living is not good. And I think in England advertising creates a need that only the product can satisfy. It's not a natural part of British culture. We still feel it, which is

Neville Brody

why we can do it differently. In Japan and America advertising is part of the culture. It's an advertising culture.

▷ As Holly Johnson sings: "They know how to advertise."

◁ Yes, it's a natural thing. Selling yourself and selling things. Advertising is such a complete part of modern Japanese culture. You know, I would consider it in Japan. In Germany I would have to think about it.

▷ But if you did it, you would develop an advertising concept and not only the typography.

◁ Yes. You see, what has happened since the Pepsi Generation? The Pepsi Generation was one of the first campaigns that said: We are not selling an idea anymore; we are actually selling a lifestyle. We are selling an image. And suddenly people didn't have to have stories or ideas. They just had to have the lifestyle, the image. I mean, look at this. This Condor here is all image-based. (Brody points to the ad in the magazine in front of him.) There is no heart, there is no soul.

▷ At least the people who made it tried to find an extraordinary visual idea.

◁ It's like an advertiser's wet dream. Let's have our idea lifestyle and not take it too seriously. Let's give people a way to laugh at themselves.

▷ Self-irony sells.

◁ Yes, but it's patronizing. It's not real. You know, you're supposed to laugh at this. And you're supposed to really want to be there. It's desire-based. But it's got nothing to do with the real experiences of traveling. This has all to do with ambition. If it would just be the image I think I could forgive it, but because it's reinforced by this very fascist use of Helvetica it actually is very sinister. It's authoritive. This campaign we are talking about just because it happens to be here.

▷ We are lucky. Because examples are always more effective than abstract talk.

◁ I think that the belief that a design could be anonymous is not true. Because design is not anonymous. Because a designer is a process. The information goes through the designer and is changed into communication. So the designer does affect the information. It's inevitable. The choice of typeface changes the way you read a story. If this typeface here, if these words were done in German Black Letters – you know the medieval Gothic – I think the way you read the type would be completely different. So there is a choice. And as soon as there is a choice, and it's a human choice, then it becomes a subjective thing.

As art director Brody revolutionized editorial design

▷ It would be interesting to know what made the Condor Art Director choose that type?

◁ I don't know, but if this was handwritten it would be much more sympathetic. But you understand what I mean. It would change the way you understand the message completely. We like to use type expressively. To express the image or the idea. This ad illustrates Condor perfectly. They are a bit afraid to be human. Extremely effective. It's utopian.

▷ Germany as the European hi-tech country.

◁ Yeah, in which no human being exists. But to express Condor. I think I would approach it in a very different way. I would ... maybe this is the best way to express Condor. I don't know, it leaves you cold, but comfortable. Which is the impression you're supposed to receive.

▷ Is it true that you were the advertising inquisitor of The Face? Is it true that you gave advertisements back to the advertising agencies when you didn't like them and when they weren't stylish enough?

◁ I didn't. But advertising was rejected if we felt it was really bad.

▷ Really dull.

◁ Not dull, wrong. Wrong like an advertisement that thinks: "Ah, here's a young market. Let's try and find a way to advertise to this market. Let's try and copy the way this market lives." So we were given lots of advertising which was very fashionable.

See, what advertising does, it steals language from people that it doesn't understand, and then feeds it back. And it's saying: "We speak your language. We are your mate. We are your friend. Buy our product." And it always fails. The bad result of this is often the advertising language. It eventually replaces the real language. And it happens in Germany a lot. Thinking this is the way people speak. We can speak like this. But it's not coming from any feeling. It's very cold.

▷ And trendy.

◁ Yeah, advertisers should speak like advertisers. And should be honest about that. Then they would have a lot more respect if they did it.

▷ So it's not true at all that you're rejected advertisements for The Face because the art direction was wrong. You never rejected a double page spread by Commes des Garcons because the colors didn't go with the colors on your front page.

◁ No, that's a myth. It's a nice myth. It's a good legend. Maybe I should say "Yes." Let's change history, let's re-write it.

▷ But flipping through The Face in the old days, you could say that it got more of ...

Neville Brody

◁ ... an overall ...

▷ Yes, an overall look. It was a magazine with an overall visual concept.
◁ Sometimes we were in trouble because a lot of advertising looked like a page of the magazine. But the Face had a visual cohesion.

▷ Is the future of communication a great mix of advertising and journalism?
◁ The magazine format is the ideal format for the late 20th century, because it's a short piece of Information. Everyone thought television was the format, it's not. Television copies more and more the magazine format. Advertising starts to copy the magazine format. Little stories. The editorial format, I think, is going to be more important in the future. But to be quite honest I think the age of the magazine is over. It's not valid anymore as a cultural expression.

▷ The Gutenberg Galaxy is dying.
◁ In a way. See, music was the main expression ten years ago.

▷ But this form of expression already dealt with new forms of expression like videos. When you were at art school you did early music videos with The Human League and Cabaret Voltaire. How deeply did you get involved in film and video?
◁ I've done some television graphic design. But there is still so much to do in graphics. I don't have the time. There's still so much to do in typography. I'm trying to create new forms of language. And I think to get involved in film and television you have to become obsessed.

▷ Maybe you can do a feature with graphic structure.
◁ Anything is possible. See, what's important is in the thirties people weren't specialists. They were commercial artists. They did architecture. They did poster design, they did paintings, well, they did also films. They did everything. The advertising agency created the idea that you were a specialist. Either you were a copywriter or a typographer, or a photographer or an art director. You couldn't cross. You had to become a specialist. Now it's going the other way again.

▷ Towards a generalized approach.
◁ Yeah, communication. It has to be the future and it's really helped by this thing. MacIntosh. (Brody points to the Apple Macintosh on his desk.) This is the first time since the thirties that an individual is given total control of every part of design. From the beginning of the typesetting to the design and then to the final making of the film for printing. Everything is possible. And it's given us complete freedom. In a way it's like our weapon in the war against the big agency.

We work with it very organically. And now it's given us even more possibilities. And we can develop good ideas very quickly. And actually push experimentation. And we do things which don't look as if they are computer produced. This is like, remember the airbrush in the seventies. Everything was airbrush or Helvetica. And it was a gimmick, it becomes a tool, a real tool. It's a freedom, it's a prison, but it's freedom. And I'm using it to paint with type much more. And also to redesign type.

□

MARCELLO SERPA

There is no idea without execution

Marcello Serpa is Co-CEO and Creative Director of Almap/BBDO in Sao Paulo. He spent 7 years in Germany studying visual and graphic arts and working at the RG Wiesmeier and GGK advertising agencies. After his return to Brazil, he worked at DPZ and DM9. Marcello has won gold, silver and bronze medals at the principal Brazilian and international advertising festivals.

He is recognized as Brazil's most honoured art director. In 1993 he won Latin America's first Grand Prix at the Cannes Festival. During the last 7 years he has won an additional 40 Lions. He is the most awarded art director in the 25-year history of the Club de Criação of São Paulo and the most honoured Brazilian at the Art Directors Club of New York. He holds Latin America's only two gold medals. He is winner of two Grands Prix at the New York Festivals, of Gold and Silver statues at the Clio Awards and of three Grands Prix at the FIAP (Iberoamerican Advertising Festival). He is the first Brazilian art director to receive Gold at the One Show. In three consecutive years, he was named Best Creative Director in Latin America and Brazil at Latin Spots Magazine's 3El Ojo de Iberoamerica2 Awards; in 2000, he was Chairman at the 3rd Asia-Pacific Advertising Festival and Jury President at the Cannes Festival. And in 1998, he presided over the jury at the London Festival.

I have known Marcello since he started his advertising career in the art studio of GGK Düsseldorf. This interview was conducted in Cannes and Sao Paulo.

▷ Herman Vaske: Marcello, you are the creative guru of Brazilian advertising. Now let me ask you about humour – humour in Brazilian advertising.

◁ Marcello Serpa: We have the Portuguese heritage here and we make a lot of jokes. It's very easy to have humour in Brazil where we have forty degrees centigrade every Summer and also in Winter. And you will also find this in our advertising.

▷ A lot of humour and joy is expressed in the Brazilian Carnival. Is there a relationship between the creativity in Brazilian Advertising and the joy and creativity of the carnival?

◁ Yeah, in carnival, every samba school has a concept exactly as in advertising. The people you see here at the carnival have a different reality, they work out a concept and the reality they come up with has nothing to do with the real reality. They create their own reality, which is much more beautiful than the reality they work in. They mix up their own reality with colours, they mix up their own reality with fears and desires, and

Filtro de Co

Filtro de Ca

Embreager

Pedal da Er

Direção

Filtro de Co

Reservatóri

Stills from the award-winning VW
"Doubled Checked" commercial
by Almap/BBDO

the result is a lot of fun – it's all about colour, imagination and creation. There is humour which has nothing to do with the real reality, but is the reality that the people have in their minds and that is exactly what we do in advertising.

In advertising I think we don't work very well with the truth, we don't work very well with the reality we live in. But we create different realities, because that's what is going on now in movies, in the media, and everybody is now creating their own reality. Mixing that with their own desires, their own pictures, colours. Everybody is an artist now.

I mean in the 21st century and in the future everybody can do whatever they want and you can create your own reality about truth and vision. Truth and vision are very difficult to distinguish nowadays because we in the advertising business have a very, very difficult relationship with the truth itself. That's the problem we have.

▷ Is advertising the fine art of separating people from their money?
◁ I think it is. I think it is. But it's also more than that. It is the fine art of separating people from their fears, and it is an art itself. I think art and advertising are becoming much closer and everybody is afraid of saying it. Everybody now can be an artist, and I think art is part of life. Everybody can be an artist, everybody can make art, even for five seconds.

▷ Yes, in our contemporary culture video makers are doing commercials and copywriters are doing feature films, musicians are actors and advertising people are film makers. It's really breaking walls.
◁ I think it's breaking walls. I don't think that the advertising people should be advertising people only and I don't think movie people should be only movie people, and I don't think that the common people should only be common people.

Everybody can make advertising nowadays because it's very tough to define advertising as an art that only ad men can do. Anybody can do it. I think everyone can do it and that's what makes it all funny. Nowadays every single moment you can see a different piece of information and that's brilliant.

And it's different. And everybody can participate in the samba school, every single one can make something beautiful and I think advertising should not be only made by advertising people, I think it's more than that.

▷ Right, art and advertising superficially play with the same elements on the surface. But what distinguishes art and advertising in the final analysis is that the success of advertising in contrast to art is judged by how many products it shifts. So let me ask you about your sales tools. Does humour sell?

Marcello Serpa

◁ Only humour sells, I think. I believe in humour. I think humour is the most important part of our life and humour is one of the few words that work universally in every single language. All around the world there is humour.

▷ A lot of humour here in Brazil seems to be very visual. It's beyond the norm, it's surreal.

◁ Yes, exactly. Exactly. Surreal. As I said, advertising creativity has nothing to do with the reality. It's very colourful and that's very Brazilian and I think this trend is increasing very fast, and we are working very visually at the moment in Brazilian advertising. That was not always the case. In the past it was different. If you now look at the colours, if you see the forms, you see how bright and how surreal Brazil can be. That's why we are becoming more visual. The visuals are more important than the words and I think it works better. It's very good for Brazilian advertising.

▷ So maybe Mr. Toscani of Benetton should come here to do the real United Colours campaign?

◁ Yes, because I think that is what Benetton was lacking − a bit of humour. I think it would have been very good if they could see a different reality.

▷ Does shock stuff sell? Shock advertising?

◁ I think shock advertising shocks more than it sells. I think shock advertising is a very easy way to make advertising. Let's shock someone and that's very easy. It's easy to shock but it's more difficult to sell.

▷ Why were you awarded the Grand Prix in Cannes?

◁ Because there is no copy in the ads. Only the navels and the well-defined stomachs of a woman and a black and a white man. And on exactly the same level as the navel on the righthand side of the double-page spread there is the cap of Guaraná Antarctica Light, a diet softdrink. There is nothing else that has to be said. The benefit is clear. Here you have a slightly moist, lean stomach. There you have the bottle cap. Both of them have tiny drops of moisture on them. So you get the associations of a day at the beach, where it's very warm. Sweat, water, refreshment. But no copy whatsoever. I love this campaign.

▷ Why are you creative?

◁ Picasso was once asked by a friend, "How can you possibly draw such a perfect bull with just one line?" And Picasso said, "It took me 50 years to reduce the bull to this one line." This art of reduction is as important for the advertising creative as it is for the artist. You have to master the technique, but once you do, you can say, "Okay, now I do what I want, take away as much as I want."

▷ You have to know the rules to break them.
◁ This is just what my teacher at the Munich Fachhochschule für Graphik-Design, Gerhard Lange, said to me. He was art director at Berthold Typo and he said, "You must really know all the typographical rules before you can start playing with them." A creative's goosebumps are still the best method to measure how good an ad or commercial is. You say to yourself, "Oh, this is good." And a chill runs down on your spine. That's what we work for all the time. You know, there is this old German fairy tail of this guy who went away to learn how to be afraid. He has no idea what fear is, and at the end someone sneaks up to him and pours a bucket of cold water over his head and he goes "Oh!" People say that this is fear. For me this is good advertising.

▷ Someone said advertising isn't the Olympics. It's only about winning.
◁ Sure, advertising is about competition and all that stuff. We are just helping someone to win but I don't think we should win amongst ourselves. I think we are just helping someone to win and to win market shares and to make more profit and to make more business. So we win our client money and we make money at the same time. That's what it's all about. I think we are there to help someone to do something and that's better than to look at winning for ourselves. We are the last link in the economic chain. Advertising is the end of the process. We are just helping someone who created a product or offers a service to make money, and that's very important.

▷ Does Hollywood sell?

◁ Yes, of course. I think everybody can sell nowadays. I don't think advertising should be restricted by the advertising people. People in the movie business can sell, movie stars can sell, everybody can sell. It's difficult nowadays to make a differentiation between advertising and movies, advertising and videos, advertising and video games, and that's tough. Computer games are very creative games. So why should we say that just advertising, just ad men can sell? I don't think it is so, it's so narrow nowadays. But it's getting brighter.

▷ What about sex? When we went to the carnival we saw a lot of sexy concepts. Does sex sell?

◁ Of course sex sells. Sex is human nature like humour and we have a lot of that in Brazil too. One of the reasons maybe is the temperature.

▷ So you blame it on the climate?

◁ It is sexual. When we separate the act of undressing from sex it will be boring.

▷ How important is music in advertising?

◁ In Brazil they use too much of it... it's very easy to turn up the volume of good music and put nice pictures to it. If you don't have an idea you use music as make-up and that is not good.

▷ Pictures replace ideas?

◁ Yes, unfortunately it goes like this, pictures and music replace ideas. You take a good editor, a good musician and some nice pictures, throw them all together and then you think you have an idea.

▷ You talked about the strength of an idea. How important is the execution?

◁ There is no idea without any execution. The execution is very important. I think that's what it's all about. I think that the execution is very, very important. If you have an idea, without execution it's just a poor idea. That's what we did in Brazilian advertising a long time ago – just believed in advertising ideas and not in the execution. Now we have become world class because we improved the execution.

▷ Did the invention of the photographic camera change creativity?

◁ Something changed for sure. I think the first thing that a human being tried to do as an artist – before he became an artist, because the conception of art is something new – was just wanting to draw; to make a clone of reality. And as people had a lot of time, they used to spend a lot of it trying to get reality on a piece of paper or canvas.

So the energy that you need to learn how to draw reality took a lot of time. There was no place for anything conceptual because they were trying

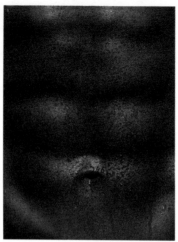

to make reality look like something beautiful. This was the goal for the first artist. And the craftsmanship, or should I say technique of drawing, became much more developed late in the century.

And then came photography, and photographed reality was there in 30 seconds. You didn't need to paint a painting or make a drawing for an hour, days, months, years – you had a picture of reality in 30 seconds.

So the technique of drawing, the technique of putting reality on paper, was not so necessary any more. So people use the emotion. How to put emotion on a canvas? How to put emotions or lights or some impression on paper or canvas while the reality was on the photography?

The same phenomenon happened in the cinema with the quality of colours. So there was a lot of space for someone to think more about emotions and how to express them. Also you used intellect, you used taste, feelings, and it was much more important to be placed in the art than to put reality on a piece of paper. So I think it's changed a lot.

▷ How would you define an artist?

◁ I think the human being has to think in layers, they have to put different etiquettes, different things on everything, so that everybody knows where something belongs. But it's hard to tell what an artist used to be. I really don't see clear limits between artists, conceptualists and political propaganda. I don't see the limits any more, the limits are just finished. I can see a lot of art in a piece of cinema, I can see a lot of Picasso in a drawing, anybody can draw Picasso today, because it's not so complicated, so I don't see the limits any more and that's very difficult for many people – to feel comfortable in a world of communication where there is

Press ad for
Liz stockings

no limit. People want to be artists, but an artist today is some kind of a showbusiness man, more than an artist. I can make a drawing and hire a PR guy in a media and I will be an artist, and will be called an artist by the media. So that's how you handle the media that makes you an artist, or an advertising man or a businessman or a singer.

▷ There was a title story in the Sunday Times Magazine about Damien Hirst and there was not a single photograph about a piece of art of his, but four or five beautiful photographs of Damien Hirst himself.
◁ That's what I say, the artist has become a piece of art himself. Because the work that he is doing is less important than his signature. He's a media happening. A media happening happened there in the Sunday Times. I see it all over the place. What the media sees is much more important than the fact itself.

▷ What about truth in that respect?
◁ Actually I don't see truth in advertising at all. I don't see truth at all. And I think there is no big deal about it, because if people are on the sofa watching TV, there is a relationship between propaganda or advertising and the consumer. It is a secret code to let the people know what they have seen is advertising. And advertising has simply a goal to sell something to someone, and to make it appealing – much more appealing than the product itself. It's something that the consumer knows. But it's very open and nobody's expecting the truth from advertising. They are expecting truth from the politician, they are expecting the truth from the media. People are still expecting to see in the newspaper the truth and I think this is much more important to see the truth in a newspaper than see it in an

195

ad. People think 'this is an advertisement, someone is paying for that to sell me something.' And if something is not true in advertising you can still complain. Journalism should be the truth, because the people buying the newspaper believe exactly the lines they read. So the responsibility of the media is much more, it's much bigger than from advertising. That's what we thought when we developed these campaigns for Folia De Sao Paulo, the newspaper of Sao Paulo. It is very well known for politics and having a very sharp eye on the truth.

▷ What was your briefing for the campaign for the Sao Paulo newspaper?

◁ The briefing was not exactly 'truth seeking people.' The briefing was to bring across that the newspaper was a very sincere newspaper that is not aligned to politicians.

The briefing for the Sao Paulo campaign was not that they were looking for the truth, the Sao Paulo was very well known for being not aligned with any political parties, and no political philosophies, and everybody knows that here. They had become a little bit of a pain in the ass to institutions, society, advertising people and businessmen – always looking for the truth, hidden somewhere.

We heard the word 'sincerity', that was the key word for the journalists that were working on the newspaper.

So we talked about how to make an unusual newspaper commercial, very dramatic sounding, independent sounding, and we looked for the truth in a very nice speech. They wanted an exciting commercial.

▷ Could you give me an example of the content of those commercials?

◁ Yes, the first commercial is with a presenter, he's an advertising presenter and he has a new product he's just launched on the market. And he's launching a microwave and just saying that if you want to buy this microwave, fine, fine for you, but I don't like this microwave, actually I hate microwaves, so that's the kind of relationship with someone who is a misplacement.

The other commercials we showed a lawyer who is saying that his client is not telling the truth, that his client is guilty and he's not in a position of 'let me go out of the jail'. He's the lawyer and he's saying "I'm just pissed off with my client because he's guilty and told me and I want to knock his face off".

And another commercial is the boy with the girlfriend and the father comes and asks 'what is your intention with my daughter, just to fuck her?' And that's the truth, that's what it's all about. Looking for the truth is sometimes not quite the thing to do.

But for someone who's working for the Folia de Sao Paulo, that's the only thing they know, that's exactly what it is.

▷ What do you think about political advertising?

◁ I respect people who are doing that. I myself actually never, never do political advertising. I tell you why. Because first in a country like Brazil if I'm doing political advertising, as in other countries, they have a lot of things that are not so clean. I think political campaigns are not clean, and in Brazil the situation is really not that good. And I think if I'm selling someone, if I'm selling a product, something I can understand, like a man or a proposition, or a philosophy, I have to be 100% behind it. And it's sometimes very tough to find a political candidate that you really trust and you would do it for. And I don't think I could make a political campaign for any client or product, so I won't do it, I don't like it.

▷ Talking about political advertising. What's the difference between the Leni Riefenstahl sort of propaganda and packaged goods advertising?

◁ The difference between Heinz Beans and political parties is that Heinz Beans don't kill 6,000,000 Jews. And that makes a difference. And that's why it's so difficult to be behind a political party because you never know what's behind it. And that's the difference – beans don't kill Jews.

▷ Another topic. Do you find that public service advertising in brazil has a double morality?

◁ Yes. Public service is like the stuff with Leni Riefenstahl. You should not forget what we are doing and that's very important. And I think public service advertising has a little bit of a problem in regard to conscience when that advertising at the end of the day is not helping anybody. And I think it is quite good to help someone, and to use the power of the communication, the power of advertising, to move people, to do something good.

And I think it is the basics of advertising – communicate and move people. Move people to do something different, something good, or buy something, or do something good. And I think that's quite fantastic to do that.

But I am noticing that the ego of the advertising industry is becoming bigger and bigger and bigger. I've seen lots of public service campaigns that weren't produced to help someone, but to help the people who created them win awards. And I think that is a misjudgement and it's not right to do that. I see in England thousands and thousands of ads trying to save dogs, kids and foreigners and so on and I think 'that is good', those issues are important, but I saw a lot of awards that these ads won. They decided to do public service, to enter the ad or commercial in an award show, but not to do a public service. It was simply for the creative person's ego. I don't think that is quite fair, I don't think it is ethical.

And so I do a lot of public service campaigns. I'm doing at least three at the moment, just to help, it is free, we don't have any money for that. We just ask some friends to do it. But I always tell all our friends, photographers and cinema directors, that I'm doing it to help people, not to win awards. Once, when I was in Australia I saw a wonderful ad written by Bob Fishlock, who made an ad for the Art Directors Club in Australia.

It was a hand that was holding a dead dog and the headline said, "HERE IS MY DEAD DOG. WHERE IS MY AWARD?" So that's a very funny ad and reflects what happens at the moment in advertising. I think this is a pity. They're looking for media, they're looking to shine, everybody wants to shine, everybody wants to be creative, everybody wants to have their fifteen minutes of fame. If you use a dead dog or hungry kid in Brazil to do Public Service. That I don't think is fair. It should help the kids. We should do the advertising, but not so that our egos are benefiting of this, but for the kids or the dog.

And some of the drugs campaigns I really don't like. Because I see that drugs campaigns are much more to help the people win awards than to stop drugs. I saw a commercial, I think it's from London, I think from Tony Kaye, and they're just talking to the camera. If you see the commercial you understand that.

There's no creative trick behind it. I don't like the creative tricks for public service, I think saying the truth is hard enough.

▷ How far can you go?

◁ How far can you go? It's tough for me to say. Someone did a commercial here in Brazil and it was from a former agency, and it was there that I saw a commercial with a lot of Jewish people in Auschwitz, dead corpses and someone put the song, "Unforgettable, that's what you are", and you see Hitler making Heil Hitler salutes or something like this. It was a commercial … nice creative idea, the only problem is the commercial was made in Brazil for the Anti-Nazi movement and there is no Nazi movement in Brazil at all. So this commercial was made just to win something in Cannes, and I think that's bullshit. I actually don't like this commercial, I think they don't help anything, actually they don't help anybody.

If you want to help somebody you have to think about the problem itself, not think only about being creative.

I was a jury member on the Brazilian ad show two years ago and I saw a commercial, an ad for this number that you call when you are trying to commit suicide. You call someone to help you in the last minutes, just for some help, and it was a wonderful ad. The only problem with the ad was that there is no telephone number on it, so the creative guy just forgot to put the number. So I think this is not ethical at all.

▷ Is good selling always an emotional sell?

◁ I think there are a lot of different ways to sell a product and there has to be always an element of truth involved, maybe you just have to put the truth in front of the consumer and they see the truth and say, "OK that's a truth that I didn't know, so it's important for me." And sometimes the truth is not that important because you already know it, but you have to create an emotion, a relationship to the consumer so he can reconnect with his own emotions.

So once a good friend of mine gave me a book about an Italian photographer from Napoli and I saw two pictures that illustrated very well what I thought.

And I once used this in a workshop. The first picture was a night picture and you see two prostitutes and there was a problem in Napoli because there were a lot of transvestites, and the prostitutes were having a lot of problems in selling themselves because the people didn't know who was a transvestite and who was a prostitute. So there were two prostitutes who just wrote on a very big piece of paper – 'WHORE'. So that's advertising, and you say – that's the information, that's a differentiation between a whore and a transvestite. So if you go there you know exactly what you're buying and that's advertising in a primitive, very simple form. That's hard selling.

And the second one is about using emotion and was a picture of someone lying on the stairs of a big street in Napol. The guy was in a bad shape, and if you passed by he wanted some money from you, and you had to put a coin in a hat.

But there were a lot of people like this in Napoli and to differentiate himself from all the people lying on the streets, he just put a small, small piece of paper near the hat which said "I am in this situation because of my brother in law."

Everybody in Italy can remember a brother in law who was a real pain in the ass, and so they could relate to the brother in law, and could design and draw the whole picture, the whole life. The problem of this guy lying there had become an emotional relationship and so it was much easier to put in money, put your hand in your pocket, and put some coins in the hat. And I think this uses advertising as an emotional link and I think it's another very good example how to differentiate yourself.

□

PAUL ARDEN
It's right to be wrong

Paul Arden was creative director of Saatchi and Saatchi in their most creative years, in the eighties.
Before Arden went there, Saatchis was famous for its print, but not for its TV. During Arden's years it became the hottest TV agency in London. Having won just about everything there was to win, for TV and posters, Arden left to open his own production company. As a director he has won nearly as many awards as he did as a creative director.
In its first year in business Arden Sutherland-Dodd was named Campaign's Production Company of the year, and has since become a hot-house for exciting young talent from all over Europe.
I interviewed Paul during a break in shooting a commercial, at Shepperton studios in the UK.

▷ Hermann Vaske: Why is it wrong to be right?
◁ Paul Arden: Being right is based upon knowledge and experience and is often provable. Knowledge comes from the past, so it's safe. It's also out of date. It's the opposite of originality.
Experience is built from solutions to old situations and problems. Experience is the opposite of being creative. And if you can prove you're right, you're set in concrete. You cannot move, with the times or with other people.
Being right is also boring. Your mind is closed. You are not open to new ideas. You are rooted in your own rightness, which is arrogant. Arrogance is a very valuable tool, but only if used very sparingly.
Worst of all, being right has a tone of morality about it. To be anything else sounds weak or fallible, and people who are right would hate to be thought fallible.
So it's wrong to be right. Because people who are right are rooted in the past; rigid-minded; dull and smug. There's no talking to them.

▷ And why is it right to be wrong?
◁ Start being wrong and suddenly anything is possible.
The future opens up. Ideas are allowed back in. You are no longer trying to be infallible. Safety is out, excitement in.
You are in the unknown.
You're pushing the frontiers out, extending the imagination into places it's never been. There's no way of knowing what can happen, but there's more chance of it being amazing than if you try to be right.

Stills from Arden's Kellogg's
Cornflakes commercial

No one can be blamed if it doesn't work. Blame belongs to moral situations, and being wrong steps outside morality. Also, blame is an attempt to back out of responsibility, and what else is responsibility but the ability to respond? People respond much faster to temptation and excitement and other aspects of wrongness, than they do to people being right.

Of course, being wrong is a risk. Risks are a measure of people. People who won't take them are trying to preserve what they have. People who do take them often end up by having more.

Being wrong isn't in the future, or in the past. Being wrong isn't anywhere but being here. Now. Best place to be, eh?

▷ Did you always know what you wanted to do?

◁ Yes, I always knew what I wanted to do. I wanted a job in advertising. My father was in advertising. He was a commercial artist. He was different from other boys' fathers and I was very proud that he was different. I had no idea if I was any good, I just wanted to be in advertising. I was quite good at art but I couldn't draw. My first job was as an assistant to a commercial artist, and I remember spending a miserable year lettering on cardboard boxes and sacks. It was horrible work. I was unhappy.

▷ What did this unhappiness drive you to?

◁ I don't know, but you know when things aren't right. I wanted something better. When you're young you go into advertising because you think you can change things. I wanted to work in the best agency. Colman Prentis and Varley was the best agency. My boss was Colin Millward. The great Colin Millward who became the creative director and a founder of CDP.

▷ Is dissatisfaction crucial for your work?

◁ In the last 8–10 years I have become more satisfied with my work, and that worries me. Because I always considered people who say they know what they're doing to know what they're doing. If you work from knowledge you are not going anywhere new. So when I get to the stage of being satisfied I worry that it is not right. But I have to admit I'm a bit more confident about going into a job than I used to be.

▷ What made you confident all of a sudden?

◁ Tim Mellors was always a glamorous, a very charismatic person. And I got fired from Doyle Dane Bernbach and he left DDB to work with me. I found that very complimentary. I didn't have confidence at all, and that gave me quite a lot. It was the first time I realized I might have something. I became the creative director of a small agency when I was 31 and was fired after a year. But we did do good work in that year. Peugeot cars. Stanley tools. Dutch fruit & vegetables. I thought I had made this agency good. I then went to an other small agency called The London Advertising Partnership, which for obvious reasons we changed, naming it the Colmans. And I made it good. And then I realized I probably was a good creative director.

▷ You finally found that one thing you always wanted to do.

◁ I had a fantasy when I was 16. I thought if ever I became a creative director in a medium-sized agency that would be a success. I never thought about being a creative director in a big agency. That was beyond my wildest dreams!

▷ Did it frighten you?

◁ I was terrified. A creative director. I was terrified.

▷ Nevertheless, you became the creative director of the biggest and most creative agency in the world. Saatchi & Saatchi in London.

◁ It's a gradual thing. Everyone told me that an agency of Saatchis size would be very different from a small agency but it's not really very different, quite honestly. It's the risk, it's your attitude, it's your will to do whatever you want to do. In my case I wanted to sell goods, that's what drives me. But in a way which pleases. Possibly the most disenchanting aspect of advertising is the way agencies are always trying to please the client. Creative people are always working for the public. How will the public react to my advertising? How will they feel about it? What will they think about it? Will it work? Will it sell? We spend so many sleepless nights thinking about solutions to those questions. And it's almost irrelevant. It's not what a client wants from US. All he wants is superficial studio work, a little bit of decoration to his own quite often rather bland and light corporate thinking.

▷ Do creative people whose work does not frighten them anymore not produce good work?

◁ Absolutely. They stop producing good work. Every time I sit down to solve a problem I fear that I can't do it. I just can't. And then somehow, but dont ask me how, one does. However, I'm rather spoilt in that I work with some very clever people, it takes away some of the pressure. If Simon Dicketts, James Lowther, Jeif Stark, Jeremy Sinclair or Charles Saatchi have an idea I've got to make it good enough for them, I must make them happy. Do you see what I mean? At the end of the day, the writer takes the responsibility for the way the words are written and the art director takes the responsibility for the way it looks. The art director may have the idea. The writer may decide on the visual aspect of it. But each of you in the end have to take your own responsibility. Otherwise, change your job title or change your job.

Nivea art directed
by Paul Arden

▷ That would support what you once told me. You said, Hermann, everyone has to specialise.

◁ Yes, yes. If you decide you are going to be the best of what you want to do, you will be the best of what you want to do. If you decide that you will be the best writer in the world, you will be the best writer in the world. Or at least pretty close to it. But you can't be the best painter and the best film director and the best writer at the same time. You can't do all that. If you want to do that you are trying to be famous. You can't do all these things. You can't do all those things and be brilliant in all of them. You just want to be successful, make money, be rich and be famous. And being famous is very nice. I would like to be famous, but not at the expense of not doing something incredibly well. Too many people don't give a damn about quality, all they want is glamour and riches. They quite like to latch onto a bit of quality but it's not what drives them. They want money first and then glamour or fame. I want quality first, money second, and fame third, ha, ha, ha.

▷ Do you respect people who want glamour first?

◁ Frankly, no. They have a role. If you have to have a regular relationship with a client, it has to be sweet. You do need account people. You do need charming people. That's a good point I just made.

▷ Very good.

◁ Hahaha.

▷ It was the first point you ever made to me.

Paul Arden

204

◁ Was it? So I'm boring you. Can we talk about global?

▷ Sure. Wasn't it Saatchis, together with Professor Levitt, who created global advertising?

◁ Global advertising was inevitable in a shrinking world. The theory of global advertising is fine. The problem with it is the people. I'm sure we all know that when you're dealing with one person, say a client with a small account, you can deal with it very straightforwardly. There is nobody in between trying to give their opinion. The bigger the client gets, the more money he spends, the more levels of hierarchy there are in between. The client may have good people working for him and the agency may have good people working for them but the process is not at all straightforward or truthful. "What will the boss think?" It rules corporate life. It's the death of good advertising. Take any megaclient. There you are dealing with corporate people who don't really want to make decisions because it might be the wrong decision. And even the man at the top is not an entrepreneur – he too is a corporate man, because he went through the same system. However, when the chairman of a major client deals directly with the chairman of an advertising agency and they decide to make something really good, the advertising has every chance of being wonderful.

▷ You were certainly able to create a couple of extraordinary long-running campaigns, for instance Silk Cut. How were you able to sell a campaign of that mileage?

◁ Well, it's a case of top man dealing with top man.

▷ One of those rare examples.

◁ Yes, one of those rare examples. It's also an example of trust.

▷ How did you sell it?

◁ Charles Saatchi sold it directly to the chairman of Gallagher. The chairman was a very great man. It was good man to good man. When we did the campaign we didn't know if it was going to work, it was too new, too different, it couldn't possibly be researched. You do your very best and your gut does the rest but you don't actually know. And it is that not knowing which is everything. It is the whole, and that is why I work. When you say you know you're just rerecording old tunes. But usually the things that you do that are different don't go through, and one can get to the state where one doesn't attempt the impossible. And that's serious. That is serious.

▷ Is there a way of reducing the fear of clients?

◁ Trust.

▷ Do you think there is such a thing as new?

◁ 10 years ago, a man I really respected said to me that we don't have ideas, ideas are out there, floating by in the wether. What we have to do is to put ourselves in a state of mind to pick them out of the ether. I couldn't quite get it, I heard it, but I couldn't quite get it. I understand it now – at least I think I understand it now.

▷ Are there new ideas?

◁ There are new orchestrations. Take Stravinsky. Not that I like his music, what I like is what he said. He said, I don't compose music. I invent it. Yes, dreams are inventions.

▷ How do you approach a campaign? How do you get the idea?

◁ There are two questions there. The answer to the first is logic. The answer to the second is illogic. Let's talk about the second part. I have a couple of tricks, which when up against it, I do employ, though I'm usually pretty desperate at this stage. One: look out of the window. Let your eyes rest on the first thing you see. Let's say it's a chimney, make a campaign using the chimney. Two: do the exact opposite of what is required and expected. Let me give you an example. What is the one thing you wouldn't do if you advertise elegant jewelery? You wouldn't think of dustbins, tires, spanners. So start putting rings in the treads of tires and bracelets around drainpipes – just where you wouldn't put them and immediately you have the same kind of presence. If you put the broach or bracelet on a ladys arm or by her throat, it's ordinary. It's safe, and it's not going to hurt anyone. If you do what you shouldn't do, it will create attention and gives what marketing people call a brand image. It's brave, it's risky, it can be wrong. The higher the risk, the greater the rewards. But you've got to gamble, most great entrepreneurs gamble.

When Jean Genet was interviewed by the BBC he said: "Do we have to do this interview face to face? Me here, you there, camera over there? Can't we do something different?" The interviewer said: "What do you mean?" He said "Can't we stand on our heads or let our hands talk?"

▷ Who are your creative influences? What about Pina Bausch?

◁ She moved armchairs around on stage, so that the armchairs could dance. Well, that was aware that there was something going on, suddenly dance was different. It changed dance. I'm not even sure whether I saw it right, but I think the armchairs were dancing.

Arden's Levi's 501 commercial

▷ Could you explain your fascination when you saw the Pina Bausch performance in Brooklyn?

◁ I think it was probably the best theater moment I ever had. I was at the Brooklyn Academy of Arts to see the Wuppertal Dance Company. It was a very big stage and the curtains opened up. Across the stage was a wall about 10 foot high at the front of the stage right behind the curtains. It was so strong, immensely strong. It was unexpected. It was marvelous. What happened was that the wall collapsed backward and the dancers danced amongst the rubble. I thought it was a pity they collapsed the wall so early, a great pity. It was so strong. I could have stayed a long time with that wall. Maybe with a little fly walking on the top. Just like Warhol's "Empire State Building." Nothing happening. However, she did it. Marvelous. Thank you, Pina.

▷ Are you influenced by other German artists?

◁ Well, I haven't read Schiller or Goethe. I quite like Fassbinder. Blossfeldt. Karl Blossfeldt. Every time I see a flower photographed, I think Blossfeldt did it better.

▷ Better than Penn, better than Mapplethorpe?

◁ Oh, yes. I adore Dürer's logo. The idea of Berlin is exciting, Berlin's nightlife.

▷ Did you ever dive into Berlin's nightlife?

◁ No, but I like the idea of it.

▷ What about George Grosz?

◁ Im not mad about George Grosz. I like Bauhaus. Bauhaus was the strongest thing to come out of Germany.

▷ Who's your favorite film director?

◁ John Webster once said: "A director is someone who comes between me and my idea. I know exactly what it means. A director, he wants to interpret the film his way, he wants to appear creative. He wants to take your idea and make it his own. You've been working on it for 6 months and you know what you want. What you want is someone to help you execute your idea and express what you want, that is what a director is for. The answer to your question is Carl Dreyer. (Well, this week.)

▷ Who is your favorite art director?

◁ Jeff Koons.

▷ Isn't he an artist?

◁ Is he? He has an idea. He takes a kitsch item, has it copied by a master craftsman and signs it. That's art directing, isn't it? It's the same with Damien Hirst. He has an idea, has someone make it for him, or has someone photograph it. That's what I do.

Silk Cut art directed and photographed by Paul Arden. Model made by artist Ron Muik

7mg TAR 0·7mg NICOTINE
SMOKING WHEN PREGNANT HARMS YOUR BABY
Health Departments' Chief Medical Officers

▷ Let me tell you something. I think it was about an agency football match. Saatchi were playing. Somebody asked if Paul Arden was there. And he said: "Ha, he wouldn't play, the colour of the grass isn't the right green."

◁ Heheheheh. Hahahahaha.

▷ Would that be true, Paul?

◁ I like the quote. Put it in.

▷ Are you good with people?

◁ I wouldn't describe myself as popular. People won't say ‚very nice chap' … I don't know. People respect my point of view. Leave it, leave it. Ask other people to answer that one. You answer whatever you want on that question. You were there.

▷ What is your biggest wish?

◁ I would like to make uncommercials.

□

GEORGE LOIS

Advertising should be poison gas

George Lois is one of the original Bernbach disciples, and has many disciples of his own. He is also the original enfant terrible of advertising; he was getting into trouble with his first ads at Doyle Dane in the fifties and sixties. He opened Papert Koenig Lois, which did great advertising that also got him into trouble. Then he opened Lois Holland Callaway, which did even more great advertising, and got him into even more trouble. And while he was fomenting a creative revolution in advertising, he was doing the same in graphic design, and editorial design.

'Seminal' is an over-used word, but his covers for Esquire over nearly 3 decades are still being copied today. He created campaigns for Robert Kennedy and Ed Koch. He developed ads with Salvador Dali and Andy Warhol for Braniff Airlines.

His campaign with Mick Jagger made MTV famous. He has written 3 books: George Be Careful (1972, Saturday Review Press, New York), the Art of Advertising (1977, Abrams, New York) and Covering the 60's, The Esquire Era (Monacelli 1996). A lot of people nowadays, call themselves creative, but very few deserve to breathe the same air as Lois. I interviewed him at Lois/GGK in the eighties and at Lois/USA in the nineties.

▷ Hermann Vaske: What does advertising mean for you, George?
◁ George Lois: Once I was doing a television interview with David Susstein many years ago and I was there with heads of two big giant marketing agencies and somebody said, "gentleman, can we start by asking what is advertising?" – the chairman of the board of Foote, Cone & Belding, whatever it was, went into this five minute thing about marketing and what are you going to do with research etc... and finally he came to the conclusion on air that advertising says; "here are the facts, please buy me." And the other guy, J. Walter Thompson, said, "that's terrific, that's very well put." Then someone saw that I was making faces and said, "George what are you making faces for, don't you agree with these people?"
"Well, I don't know," I said, "I don't think these gentlemen and me are in the same business," and he said " well what do you think advertising is?" And I said "I think advertising is poison gas and, you know, advertising should attack your eyeballs, should attack your throat, you know, should stun, your head should jolt back a little back and hopefully should knock you down. Advertising should try to do that."

▷ Mr. Lois, how would you characterize your advertising?
◁ We're very different from any other agency in this country. All this agency cares about is doing great work. And there are very few agencies in America like that. We have 20 accounts. We have 18 incredible success

APRIL 1968
PRICE $:

Esquire

THE MAGAZINE FOR M

stories ... I mean where we generated business, saved the newspaper, created the product. You know, from three stores to a thousand stores. So, we're sort of known as a miracle agency.

▷ Miracle agency? Isn't that biblical metaphor a bit strong?

◁ MTV got on television because of what we did. So we're known as the agency that creates advertising miracles. We create great, giant successes for our clients. And when clients come to us, we promise them that kind of success. No other agency in the world has the balls to say what I say to our clients.

▷ Is there a direct correlation between winning awards and selling the goods?

◁ Winning creative awards? To win awards today, you have to be a f---ing fool.

▷ Why?

◁ Because there are 200 award shows. They're all stupid, foolish. I haven't sent anything in to an award show in 18 years. Anybody who does is an asshole, because all they do is put on their tuxes and collect these awards. J. Walter Thompson said, "We won 400 awards last year". And Ogilvy said, "We won 324". I won zero awards last year. The only time they meant something was when there were only one or two shows. They depend on the greed and stupidity of ad agencies that want to say to their clients, "Look at all the awards you got".

▷ It's a bloody business.

◁ And the idea that we feed their faces, because they're taking advantage of the avarice and greed of the ad agencies, is beyond belief. If you have the least bit of talent and intelligence, you don't enter award shows.

▷ It's ego feeding.

◁ Yes, but it's beyond ego. It's to make your clients believe that you are a creative agency. We show our clients we're creative by the results the advertising gets. USA Today, the newspaper, comes to me ... they're going out of business. They're selling like three pages a day. I start doing advertising for them and three months later the average is nine pages a day. The guy who runs the paper wrote a book and he said, "That agency saved my life". Another example. Nobody in America wanted to go to Greece. The President said, "Don't go to Greece". He hated the Greeks. So I did a campaign with famous people saying "My parents came to this country from England. And finally I'm going home. To Greece." They're going home to Greece, because we were all born there. Our civilization was born in Greece. That campaign filled their airplanes. Pauline Trigere came to me with a problem. She'd lost a lot of business. She said people

George Lois and the Esquire era

thought she was dead. Because she had had big problems with John Fairchild, the guy who runs the fashion business in America. So I did the ad ... "Dear John", written by Paulin Trigere. The letter said, "After all these years and so many terrific collections –is it still over between us? You don't call, you don't write. I still love you. Pauline." America's fashion business went crazy they said Pauline Trigere was telling John Fairchild to go f--- himself. She went on TV and received dozens of stories in the New York Times, Time Magazine, Manhattan inc. writing about the woman who was fighting back. She got all her customers back, and she didn't have to run another ad for ten years. The point is that we do miracle advertising here. Advertising that – WHAAAMMM!!!! (he imitates an explosion) – creates an effect.

▷ And impact.

◁ Impact the next day. Impact with publicity.

▷ Yes, it's impact through incredible PR.

◁ I do advertising that's beyond advertising. I make a million dollars look like 20 million dollars. Most people make 20 million look like nothing. Before we run advertising, we make the product famous – we design it that way. Let me show you something else. They wanted 712 Fifth Avenue to be the most snobbish address in the world. So we ran this ad. What ad? Everybody in New York went crazy: What? Where? Who? What was going on? Everybody in the business was calling. The Wall Street Journal got 700 phone calls; what's going on at 712 Fifth Avenue? I don't think that's advertising, I think it's poison gas. Shhhhhhh. It's like a grenade that explodes.

▷ If your gas explosions are able to create big successes with small budgets - great.

◁ I started my first agency in 1960. I did the first advertising for Xerox. They had 20,000 dollars the first year. I did commercials with chimpanzees making copies. Everybody in America was talking about it. What I figured out when I was a little kid was to do advertising that seemed outrageous. So everybody else in the business is in advertising. I'm in something else. I'm in poison gas, they're in advertising. They think advertising is an ad, to look at and react to. I think advertising is an explosion.

▷ An explosion that is sometimes controversial.

◁ Yeah, it's controversial, it's unusual, it's shocking, it's surprising. You know "I love my mug"? A mug is a sign. And a mug in America is a face too. We made a commercial using the guy who was "Jaws" in James Bond. He said, "I love my nose, I love my toes, I love to pose. But most of all I love my mug." We sold the root beer and the face as well when this ran.... ZAK (Lois hits the table with his fist).

▷ Let's talk about MTV. How did you make Americans love MTV?

◁ MTV was at Ogilvy's for 12 years. They had a couple hundred thousand viewers. The people who decided what goes on cable said it was for kids, stupid. And the music business said, if that works it will hurt the business. MTV came to me and I did a commercial with Mick Jagger. I did "I want my MTV", kind of a funky commercial with the logo. We ran it on cable in San Francisco. At the end a voiceover said, "If you don't get MTV where you live (and nobody did), pick up the phone, dial your local operator and say what Mick Jagger says: "I want my MTV". It took maybe two days and the cable operator in that town would call up MTV and said, "Get it off the air, I hate it", because he was getting thousands of phone calls: "I want my MTV ... click. I want my MTV ... click. I want my MTV ... click." Not just kids, but thirty and forty year old people. And that's how MTV got on television. That forced them into it. It was a success and the cable stations said, "Fine, I want it." Then the business people said, "Oh my god, I'm selling a hell of a lot of records." When I work for a client, I say, "How do I kill him?"

▷ Why are you creative?

◁ I understood when I was very, very young that I wanted something to happen, that I wanted to do graphics. But I found out that it wasn't just visual excitement. I wanted communication. Communication makes people do something. Did you ever see my Esquire covers? That cover with Mohammed Ali as Saint Sebastian with the arrows? Congress went crazy when they saw that. Because they understood that I was saying he was a martyr. When I did Lieutnant Kelly, an American GI who killed Vietnamese children, I showed him with Vietnamese children. Good advertising makes you say "Ahhh" or "Wow". Makes you either want to buy something or to be for something or to be against something. Advertising that doesn't do that is a lousy piece of advertising. In my opinion, 99.9 percent of advertising sucks, because it doesn't get you to do anything.

It's a challenge to crack problems, that's why I love them. I love accounts that are in trouble. I love accounts where their business hasn't been doing too well. I find that most clients will allow you to do the best work you know how, when they're in the deepest trouble. They can accept a strong piece of advertising because they think, what the hell.

▷ You wrote 'George, be careful' and 'The Art of Advertising.' People who write books are considered dangerous. Are you?

◁ The only thing that's dangerous about my book is that it makes all other books written about advertising look stupid. I've tried to read most of them. I think Ogilvy's book, Confessions of an Advertising Man, is a

"Dear John Letter" for Pauline Trigère by George Lois

disgrace, because he lists his rules of what you should and should not do in advertising. There are no rules in advertising. The only rule is that there are no rules. And a book like Jerry della Femina's is a cynical book about what a silly business it is. I take advertising very seriously. People come to me and they need help. I'm very lucky, because a certain kind of client comes to me, that's predisposed to exciting answers. Somebody comes to me who has already accepted in his mind that he's only going to get something unusual. But people who want exciting, thrilling work, when you give it to them say, "Oh my god, that's a little too strong for me". That's OK. The point is, I'm lucky because I do get a lot of people who say, "George, save me".

▷ Assuming that there are seven basic jokes and seven basic patterns in advertising, wouldn't there be a chance to find solutions systematically?
◁ No, I don't think there is a system. In The Art of Advertising, I talk about the market power, I talk about what happened, I talk about how I solved it. But if I thought it could be solved systematically, then anybody who's bright could do it. I mean, Norman Mailer couldn't do advertising. A great writer can't do advertising. And Robert Rauschenberg or Jasper Johns can't do advertising. It takes a different kind of talent. It takes someone who understands language and understands visual and understands that one and one could be three.

▷ It's interesting that you mention the language first.
◁ Always. And street communication. I am very direct with my advertising, I always punch them right in the face (Lois demonstrates it with his right fist). You don't look at my advertising and say, I wonder what he's talking about.

▷ Street communication versus intellectual bullshit.
◁ Right to you. In your face. (Lois demonstrates it again with his left fist).

. ▷ I remember reading an interesting article of yours in the New York Times about street talk.
◁ I've done that since I was a child. And I think when you really communicate with people by using exciting and colorful language, which I do all the time, people are more apt to listen to you and be surprised by it. Because most language in advertising is so dull. So I think I know how to talk to people, not only in making a presentation and selling my work, but I know how to talk to people on television or in print ads. And when I talk to them, I try to convince them of something, that a product I'm selling is better than a product someone else is selling. I think I try to sell a product that's better than another product. Because I believe that great

advertising in and of itself becomes a benefit of the product. In other words, great advertising can make a product look better, go faster and taste better. That's what advertising is all about. People who don't understand that don't understand advertising.

▷ You use a lot of puns. Aren't you afraid that people don't get what you say?

◁ No, I think people are very, very smart. I think in our culture, the American culture, that vast majority of people understand puns and double meanings. I think they're grateful for them. I think those nuances are fun for people to react to and play with when they see a commercial or an ad.

▷ I suppose you know Visual Thinking, the new book by Henry Wolf. He seems to have another view. He believes in approaching things systematically.

◁ I think it was a silly book. And by the way, Henry is a wonderful photographer. He was a great magazine art director. Not good, great. But he drew on things that he had done and tried to show some systematic way to visualize things, and I think that was foolish. If you look at The Art of Advertising, there is no system to how you do it. Because I always say there's an answer in the problem. At the end of every year, people ask, what's going to happen next year in the business? What style, what fashion and what kind of advertising will there be? And I always say, "Hey, I don't know until I see what the problems are".

▷ Who cares?

◁ Well, aside from "who cares". The problem dictates the answer in my mind.

▷ Anyway, to jump on trends is the dumbest thing you can do.

◁ Of course. When people go one way, I go the other way. When people start copying me, I do something else. One of the things you can do systematically, if you must do something systematically when you're in advertising, is to look at what everybody else is doing and make sure that you're not doing anything like it.

▷ That sounds like some kind of system.

◁ Yeah, systematically I do it differently. He,he. That's the only thing I do systematically. If it were systematic, any intelligent college graduate could sit down and figure it out. But there's a magic to advertising, a lunacy. There shouldbe some craziness.

▷ "George Lois, the crazy Greek of advertising". Did you call yourself that?

◁ I didn't, but I was called that by other people.

▷ Cracking a joke that was on you.

◁ When I started in advertising in the early fifties, being Greek was very unusual, and still is. Anything ethnic is. I mean, the business was run by WASPs. So the fact that I was ethnic, Greek, was very unusual. And because I was an enfant terrible and I didn't take any bullshit I was considered a lunatic. Except by my clients and people who knew my work. They say I'm crazy like a fox. Because my advertising is pumping with life. My clients, everyone who knows my work, understands what I'm doing is advertising that's going to work.

▷ What are the benefits and what are the dangers of ethnic advertising?

◁ Well, Doyle, Dane started in '49. And the accounts were Levy's Bread and a lot of New York accounts. So there was ethnic built in. Then we got Volkswagen and we sold a Nazi car in a Jewish town. We sold a Nazi car in a country that hated the Nazis. It was unbelievable. I was the first ethnic art director and I trained a lot of Italian guys ... everybody called them my graphic mafia. I trained Sam Scali and a whole bunch of guys. Yes, the early advertising of Doyle Dane was ethnic. It was Ohrbachs. It was New York. I've done hundreds of campaigns and dozens and dozens of New York campaigns.

When I do a New York campaign, I make it very New York. And when I do a campaign out of New York, I make it very New York. You know why? Because New York humour is understood by everybody in this country. For 25 years you could listen to the Johnny Carson Show. Johnny Carson told a lot of ethnic Jewish jokes. Everybody in America understood them. It's part of our culture. So much of my work has a chutzpah to it. It's wise guy and has an attitude. Everybody understands that kind of humour. I would never run a piece of advertising across the country that I didn't think people would understand. I'm not even sure what "too New York" means, but I pretend there's something that is just too New York. I mean, you instinctively don't run it everywhere. You run what's right. You run what people are going to react to. When I did "When you got it, flaunt it" for Braniff Airlines, you could say it was very New York. It says, when you think you're terrific, show off.

That's not nice to hear. But when you hear "When you got it, flaunt it", that's very funny. So when I did the campaign, I had Andy Warhol sitting next to Sonny Liston. And Andy's talking about this and that. And Liston says, "What is he talking about?" Finally he looks at him, and looks into the camera, and Andy's saying, "When you got it, flaunt it". Then there's a baseball pitcher, a very famous New Yorker baseball pitcher and he's talking to Salvador Dali. And he asks Dali a question about baseball. And Dali starts to explain it to him. It's idiocy, except it's wonderful idiocy. It says, if you're flying an airline from here to Dallas, instead of flying on American Airlines fly Braniff. Because it's a very sharp airline. It's got colored airplanes. Sit next to famous people, sit on leather. And their business exploded.You hear the expression, "When you got it, flaunt it" in America every day. It's part of our language. I try to do things that take from the language or add to the language. I insist on doing things in advertising where there is a slogan on your lips or a picture in your head. And one and one is three. But I always try to do something where I put words in your mouth. I don't want you to think a certain way about it. I want you to say something about it. "I love my mug". On HBO for instance. HBO is a big movie channel. And I wanted to tell the world that HBO knows more about comedy than any other channel in the country. The campaign that was running on the air had a famous line, "We are talking serious comedy here".

▷ The paradox obviously helps to make the joke successfully.

◁ It says, here we are serious about comedy. And in fact, in the last couple of weeks, Robin Williams, Whoopi Goldberg and others have been raising a lot of money for the homeless. And they've said, "We are talking serious comedy" a million times. The point is, I want to put words on your lips. Very important.

▷ Do you agree that advertising today is better than advertising in the sixties?

◁ No, not even close. You've got to understand that 99.9 percent of all advertising is still garbage. It was garbage in the sixties, it's garbage in the eighties. But there was some advertising in the sixties that was more brilliant than the best advertising of the eighties. An incredible percentage of advertising is still dull, half-witted and untalented. On the other hand, the fact is that in the sixties advertising was seen in a whole new way. There was a lot of brilliant advertising that took you by surprise, because it was so refreshingly different and it was so unusual. That was pioneer work. And in the eighties there were people just trying to do terrific advertising. And as such, if I had to analyse the 20 best things I know that were done in the sixties and the 20 best things that were done in the eighties – I think the things from the sixties would be better in terms of outrageousness and brilliance. I believe that, but you'd have to research it. In the eighties you expect or try to see surprising and interesting advertising. In the sixties it was like a cyclone, it came out of nowhere.

▷ Are you always thinking in terms of campaigns or are you sometimes thinking of one shot ads as well?

◁ Always campaigns. And if you do it right, you get so much publicity from it.

▷ Public Service advertising, for instance the AIDS problem, is often controversial. What do you think about approaching such serious themes with humour?

◁ I used humour for my commercials for Lifestyle Condoms. You see the Phantom of the Opera walking into a store with flowers. The salesgirl says, "Oh, Phantom, you're taking a date to the opera?". And he says, "Yes, and I'd like some Lifestyle Condoms". "Oh, good for you", she says, "but you didn't have to wear that mask to ask for them". Meaning, don't be ashamed. At the end it says: Lifestyle condoms, a matter of condom sense.
Crazy commercial. They wouldn't run it on TV, but they did run it on cable. For instance, MTV wouldn't run it, but it ran a hundred times on cable news. And again there was tremendous publicity. USA Today, every newspaper in America had stories. And it was new, because it used humour. Every commercial that's ever run about AIDS talks about how you can get AIDS, you can die. And this thing said, don't be ashamed, go in and buy condoms. So that kind of humour broke through and got tremendous publicity.

▷ You can say things with humour that you can't say any other way.

◁ I can get away with murder with humour.

▷ Mr. Lois, you are known as a fantastic presenter who puts a certain magic in his presentation. May I ask the magician of advertising if there were times when his magic formula failed?

◁ I don't believe a great campaign sells itself. The more seemingly outrageous an idea, the more problems you may have selling it. Some people say, well just do the campaign, put it in front of people and it will sell itself. I don't believe that at all. When I do a presentation for a client, I explain to them what they're going to see. Then I show it to them. Then I explain what I just showed to them. I go through three processes. Sometimes I'll talk for half an hour or more about a campaign and about the positioning before I actually show it. I don't care how intelligent the client is, I don't care how smart the client is. I go through that process and actually make sure they understand every reason why I did something. I almost give them a travelogue of what I went through, and it's amazingly exciting because you review your own thought process. And in most cases they are very excited by going through your mind, by going through the process that you went through. I'm very literal sometimes. I tell them I did this and then this happened. And I didn't understand how this ... and I found something else. I did it ... and then I got the big idea. I literally almost give them a blow by blow.

George Lois

▷ How much of your presentation is magic, myth and hypnosis, and how much of it is the quality of the work?

◁ I've always said that 90 percent of my work is justification. Which means 90 percent of my time is spent selling my work and protecting it. From clients, from fellow workers, from people around me. The important part of your job, besides doing great work, is selling and protecting it. Every art director/writer and creative person must understand that.

▷ Do you believe in the drama of presentation?

◁ Sure, everybody has his own style. I usually make the presentation very humorous. It's usually very dramatic. The important thing to understand, however, is no matter how well you sell it, if the work isn't really a great idea I wouldn't know how to sell it. If I didn't have a great idea, I'd be the worst salesman in the world. I could sell a great product, but I couldn't sell a lousy product. You could tell my own feelings about that campaign by the look in my eyes. I must have something great to sell. If I do, I think I do a great presentation. If I don't, I think I'm pretty bad. And indeed, I try never, never to sell anything that I don't think is great.

▷ In your personal work you tend to quote art history. Mohammed Ali as Saint Sebastian and Andy Warhol's Campbell's soup. Your Bob Dylan music video visualizes art history from 4000 B.C. to today. Do all these quotations mean that you have difficulty finding original visual ideas?

◁ It depends on the situation. I create new lines and slogans. But I also try to take advantage of historical perspective and popular culture. And again, I do both things depending on the situation. I never sit down and say, "Gee, I think I'll try to do something historical today, or I think I'll do something new today". So to me there's no clear answer other than the fact that the more you know about things – the more you read, the more you understand art history, the more well rounded you are, the more education you have – I believe the better chance you have to do advertising that has relevance and power. That sounds a bit mystical, but I've told young people they should go to a museum once a week, they should read a book a week, they have to read the New York Times every morning. The more you know, the more tools you can use from the corners of your mind, the better prepared you are to solve problems.

▷ How do you get your personal stimulation?

◁ I do sports. I'm very involved. I still play full court basketball at my age. And when I'm home, there's always a ball game on television, whether it's basketball, football or baseball. I keep up with every detail of sports, because I love it.

▷ Picasso once said, there is no rule against bad art. Is there a rule against bad advertising?

◁ No, I don't think so. I think he's right. There are many instances where professionals in New York reacted and said, that's terrible advertising, when I knew that it was maybe in bad taste but probably terrific advertising. That happens a lot. I think once you look at something, whether it's art, advertising, architecture or film and say, that's in bad taste, it doesn't mean much. Because the bad taste of today is the good taste of tomorrow. I think if a person is truly open minded, then nothing can really shock you. I mean, burning the American flag isn't shocking, spitting on a crucifix isn't shocking. It's just an act, somebody playing a game. You don't shoot someone for burning a flag or spitting on a crucifix. They're obviously disrespectful in the sense that they're trying to get somebody mad about it. But that shouldn't shock anybody, and you shouldn't care about it. It's just someone venting their spleen. That's OK with me.

▷ Do you have to be egoistical to be a good creative?

◁ Sure, in the sense that you say, I will get hold of the problem and I'll solve it. And I will carry it through to the end, nobody will interfere with it, nobody will water it down. I'll make sure that the vision and idea I have is carried through. That needs somebody with confidence in themselves and a strong sense of ego. It's important that you make sure that you do the kind of work you want to do, and don't let anybody stop you. And in not letting anybody stop me, sometimes I'm as tough as I know anybody could be. I'm not known to eat shit, as we say in America.

▷ How do you approach work inside Lois/GGK? How do you work with your creative people to get the best results? Do you say, "Well, that's interesting, but what about other solutions?" Or do you say, "It's garbage, throw it in the trash!"

◁ I'm pretty direct. I don't pussyfoot around much. If I don't see the answer in a storyboard or an ad, I immediately attack the problem and say, what are you trying to solve here? What are you trying to say? They usually find out in the middle of it, that what they've shown me isn't really right. You get people back to the basics and try to get them to refigure what they're trying to do. It's not criticizing, because they criticize it themselves, and you force them into that kind of thinking. There's a lot of instinct involved in advertising, but it's still basically an intellectual sport.

▷ Mr. Lois, what would you write on your tombstone?

◁ "When you got it, flaunt it."

□

HELMUT KRONE
I'm only interested in the new

Visually, Helmut Krone was Bill Bernbach's earthly representative. Both of them started the creative revolution. With ads like "Think small" and "Lemon" Krone invented the new page. His Volkswagen "Snowplough" commercial is in all Top 100 reels of Best Commercials of the World. The tallest of his milestones include ads for Avis and Polaroid, Porsche and Audi. I interviewed Helmut Krone at DDB in New York, and a couple of times after he retired, in his loft in Soho, and in his country house in Long Island, and in Berlin.

▷ Hermann Vaske: Helmut, you're one of the kings. How did you rule?
◁ Helmut Krone: I thrust DDB into the mainstream of American advertising. I broke the look. My writer, Bill Casey, helped me a lot. Writer? Art director? I don't know what that means. Creative person would be a better word.

▷ It's interesting that you replace the words "writer" and "art-director" with "creative person."
◁ Bernbach was a creative person. An adman. He thought in pictures and supplied the copy later. He would say, "What if we make the whole page black?" I would ask, "Why, Bill, why?" And he'd answer, "I don't know. Let me think about it" He started out as a speech-writer, writing political speeches. But in advertising he thought mostly in pictures. He called the pictures images and from them he just intuitively knew how to break up a page in a totally new way. That was the biggest thing that anybody had ever seen before. He was crazy about new formats. People thought he was a writer; I'd say he was whatever he needed to be. I know because he spent a lot of time in my office, and he started every assignment visually.

▷ Good copywriters are visually strong anyway.
◁ There isn't much copy anymore, certainly with the increase of TV, which is basically a visual medium. Let me show you my Chanel layout. Chanel does about five ads in five years. And then they run and run and run. You do a lot of ads for them, but you don't sell a lot of ads. I'd say to them, "This ad is good. We'll run it for five years."

▷ Very economical.
◁ Oh, that's not the reason. There was a time in America when there were two forces at work. Rosser Reeves and Bill Bernbach. And Rosser Reeves said, "I don't care who the writer is; it's the positioning and how many

Or buy a Volkswagen.

Think it over, New York, Chicago, San Francisco.

'1.02 a pound.

In search for the new page.
Helmut Krone for Volkswagen.

times you run it." Bernbach said, "I can run it once and create a revolution." I'm with Reeves. I mean, I hated his ads; I didn't want to work for him. He used to tell a story about a man and a mule. The mule wouldn't pull the cart, so the man took a sledgehammer and cracked him over the head with it, almost broke his skull, but not quite. Another man came by and said, "Why did you do that?" He replied, "Because he's not pulling the cart." "I know, but you almost killed him." "First I had to attract his attention."

▷ How far can you go in attracting attention?

◁ What he meant was, I have to keep hitting them over the head seven nights a week on television, and I don't care if they hate me or not, as long as they go out and buy the product. It's terrible, and everybody hated Rosser Reeves ... but I think he was right.

▷ Why didn't you go to work for him?

◁ Because it wouldn't have been fun. Why didn't I work for Ogilvy?

▷ Probably too many rules.

◁ That and a lot of other things. The big thing about Bernbach is, he did something I could never in my life do. He took little people and elevated them. He made them bigger, because I can't believe that everybody in this agency was talented. But he gave them enough rope, enough space.

▷ He was good with people.

◁ I think he was a little lazy, which is good, because if you are like me or Ed McCabe or somebody like that, you tend to do everything yourself. "Gimme, gimme, gimme. I'll do it".

▷ That's also a question of self-confidence, and trusting other people.

◁ I don't know how he did it. I can't imagine. I could never do that, trust somebody else.

▷ Why not?

◁ Because something in me says, if it can go wrong, it will. My wife has said to me, "Why don't you get some kids to stretch your canvases?" I'd say, "Because they just wouldn't be square".

▷ If you don't handle every single step of your campaign, you'll get something completely different than you started out with.

◁ Not Bernbach. He looked at it when it was finished. And you could see his reaction in his face. You'd read the numbers in his face from 1 to 10.

▷ His score?

◁ Yes, and if you only got a 5, you thought you'd die.

▷ Did you ever get a 5?

◁ That happened once or twice. It was terribly important for me not to lose anything, so I had some screaming sessions with him. Then once, Doyle came in and shut me up, told me to get out.

▷ And did the screaming help?

◁ I don't think so. I couldn't help it anyway. I remember doing a full page New York Times ad. The picture covered the entire page, and across the bottom, hugging the picture like a caption was one II pt. line of copy running clear across the page. No headline.

▷ Very innovative.

◁ That's the least you could say about it. It was for the first VW dealer in the United States. And it showed a well dressed man sitting in an Eames chair. There was a big glass window, and he was watching his car being serviced. This was an idea they got from a dealer in Berlin. – "The beautiful part is when they fix your car." The point is that this was a new way to break up space. And Bernbach said, "You can't do that. Blow all that type up and then you can do it in five lines across". Which I did, you know. He thought that was hot stuff. That wasn't hot stuff for me anymore. We had arguments about things like that.

▷ Could you tell me more about your work on Volkswagen?

◁ We went to Germany, to Volkswagen, and we accepted the account. Doyle, Bernbach, an account man named Ed Russell and I visited the factory and saw how they put the cars together. On the plane ride back, Russell wrote out proposals for six ads ... they were the USPs, the unique selling points of the car. That's Rosser Reeves; we didn't call them that, but that's what they were. And they included non-obsolesence, because the car never changed from year to year, and the engine in the back. Every ad we did had to hit one of these six USPs for as long as I worked on the account, and in fact they'd try to tell you how many of each. Russell would say: we need three, non-obsolescence, and four, engine in the back. The inspection system was number four ... more inspectors than workers.

▷ Really?

◁ No, but we said so. You know, Bernbach once told me, our mission isn't to tell the truth. It's to appear as if we were telling the truth. If you can tell the truth, that's fine. But he wasn't a big believer in looking for it ...

Lemon.

This Volkswagen missed the boat.

The chrome strip on the glove compartment is blemished and must be replaced. Chances are you wouldn't have noticed it; Inspector Kurt Kroner did.

There are 3,389 men at our Wolfsburg factory with only one job: to inspect Volkswagens at each stage of production. (3000 Volkswagens are produced daily; there are more inspectors than cars.)

Every shock absorber is tested (spot checking won't do), every windshield is scanned. VWs have been rejected for surface scratches barely visible to the eye.

Final inspection is really something! VW inspectors run each car off the line onto the Funktionsprüfstand (car test stand), tote up 189 check points, gun ahead to the automatic brake stand, and say "no" to one VW out of fifty.

This preoccupation with detail means the VW lasts longer and requires less maintenance, by and large, than other cars. (It also means a used VW depreciates less than any other car.)

We pluck the lemons; you get the plums.

looking for fun in one's life was more like it. He wasn't sure what the truth was. I don't know either. Only children know what the truth is. As you get older, you know less and less about it.

▷ A lot of great movies, for instance, don't sell reality. Did you like doing TV commercials?

◁ It was the worry of my life. It frightened me to death. I don't care about film. I like things that sit still.

▷ Like a painting?

◁ Yes. You can study it.

▷ Would you have liked to become a painter instead of going into advertising?

◁ No, I wanted to be an architect.
My greatest influence, and one of the greatest men of the twentieth century, was Mies van der Rohe. So I wanted to be an architect like him. But I didn't, and I'm glad, because they are really boring. Architects are really dull, compared to advertising people. They're like graphic designers.

▷ How did you get into advertising?

◁ I had two interviews. After World War II, I put together a portfolio and it was half industrial design and half advertising design. I had an appointment with a Bauhaus guy here in New York to do product design. And I had an appointment with a small fashion agency. The fashion agency interview came first. They said: 'We'll pay you $ 50 a week.' I said: "Good, I'll take it." I never went to the other interview. And I've never been sorry. In fact, I'm happy that I didn't spend my life designing flashlights.

▷ So you went into advertising via fashion.

◁ You didn't go into advertising in those days if you had any integrity. There were about six of us, and we all knew each other. We were Bauhaus orientated designers. Gene Federico was one. Before Bernbach opened his agency, there were fashion agencies and there were pharmaceutical agencies. They weren't big, but you could do good work. There was a German typographer named Tschichold; we all wanted to do typography like Tschichold.

▷ Doesn't David Ogilvy mention him in one of his books?

◁ He may have mentioned him in a negative way, because he would have rejected Tschichold. Ogilvy also said that Bernbach worshipped at the altar of creativity. They were arch-enemies.

Helmut Krone's snowplough –
one of the best commercials
of all time

▷ What, for you, are the components of a good ad?

◁ There is no answer. I don't even know if it needs components. I have spent most of my life dealing with a headline, body copy, picture and signature; trying to make a page look like it doesn't contain all four of those elements.

▷ Did it ever get boring?

◁ The only thing I can remember was being scared all the time.

▷ Why?

◁ That I couldn't do it again. I have no guts, no inner integrity. I blamed it on having German parents.

▷ Could you explain that?

◁ Because my mother was a North German, and she was not a lot of fun. She said that I would amount to nothing. And I believed, as a result, that German boys are considered wrong until they prove themselves otherwise. A goddamn thing. I've been trying to prove something to my mother ever since. I was always afraid. Bernbach would come in and say, "Guess what? We got a new account and you're on it" I'd say, "Bill, I can't. I'm already doing something else". And he'd say, "You can do it."

▷ Did that give you confidence?

◁ No, not confidence. A sense of importance, plus fear.

▷ Why are you creative?

◁ Well, I don't think that I am. I've always been able to fool everybody. I have borrowed a lot from people, I've stolen a lot. I really have. I don't think anybody is totally creative. What you do is take something you remember and then you give it a twist. I'm not interested in beauty, I'm not interested in craftsmanship. The only thing I'm interested in is new.

▷ New? Is there such a thing?

◁ Of course there is ... because new is a relative term.

▷ That's what I meant. In advertising and other art forms there are only a limited number of basic patterns.

◁ But the variety within is infinitive. I mean what Paul Klee said, when he said new. He said, "I don't care how small it is. I want to do one thing that's new in my life." Well, he did it a few times. A picture made of horizontal lines; small things like that.

▷ Do you think that the real artists of today work in advertising and not in the arts?

No. 2ism.
The Avis Manifesto.

We are in the rent a car business, playing second fiddle to a giant.

Above all, we've had to learn how to stay alive.

In the struggle, we've also learned the basic difference between the No.1's and No. 2's of the world.

The No.1 attitude is: "Don't do the wrong thing. Don't make mistakes and you'll be O.K."

The No. 2 attitude is: "Do the right thing. Look for new ways. Try harder."

No. 2ism is the Avis doctrine. And it works.

The Avis customer rents a clean, new Opel Rekord, with wipers wiping, ashtrays empty, gas tank full, from an Avis girl with smile firmly in place.

And Avis itself has come out of the red into the black.

Avis didn't invent No. 2ism. Anyone is free to use it.

No. 2's of the world, arise!

◁ Well, that's been a question for a long time. I don't think that advertising is an art form. I did for a long time. Bernbach said, "Advertising is the most vital art form of our time". And I said, "I believe, Bill. I believe." I'm not so sure anymore. First of all, I think advertising has gotten out of hand. It's so self-conscious. We were pretty innocent back then. We didn't know we were causing the creative revolution. And when you think, you're part of the second or third wave of the creative revolution, then you've got a problem, because you're thinking about the wrong thing. We were just trying to make it stand up so that it wouldn't fall down.

▷ You were avantgarde. Isn't it disappointing that time and copycats are always catching up with the avantgarde?

◁ It's flattering. You know the Avis page ... it's the most copied in the world. I liked doing new pages like Avis and having people copy them.

▷ How important is humour as a tool?

◁ I don't know. That's like asking, do you like yellow better than black? We only had one rule: dominate the book! Whatever magazine you go into, you have to be the best. That was Bernbach: dominate the book!

▷ A tough act to follow.

◁ I think advertising today is screwed up. This word 'creativity' has gotten totally out of hand, and I feel sorry for the clients. They're not getting a fair share. The name of the game today seems to be: Make nonsense commercials. If they mean something, they're not creative enough. I think we can blame that on the English; they're the ones who are really good at that. We're going to have to swing back to some solidity and some genuine concepts and ideas. Go through a magazine like Vogue, or watch an evening of television ... if it makes any sense at all, it seems too old-fashioned. I'm glad I'm not doing it.

▷ You don't like British advertising?

◁ Well, I don't see a lot of it. I've seen the British Airways Manhattan and I have seen the seat and the bird. They're beautiful but very cool. They're not as good as Chicago at its best. It's like what a critic in New York said about Andrew Lloyd Webber's 'Phantom of the Opera': "My Gal Salit it ain't" That's an old Gershwin musical. You know what I mean. That's really something you can chew on.

▷ That's interesting, because the English accuse the Americans of producing crap.

◁ It may very well be crap. But it's always been largely crap.

Avis can't afford dirty ashtrays.

Or to start you out without a full gas tank, a new car like a lively, super-torque Ford, a smile.

Why?

When you're not the biggest in rent a cars, you have to try harder.

We do.

We're only No. 2.

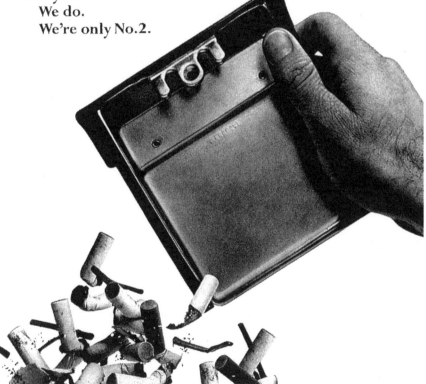

Porsche as seen
by Helmut Krone

▷ Will advertising swing back to storytelling?

◁ Oh no, no, no. I'm not going to say it has to, because it depends on how it's done. I'm just saying that the general trend in advertising right now is going off the deep end. Jesus, it's only advertising, It's not art. All we try to do is solve the problem. The other thing is that there isn't very much that could be done in New York today. It's such a client orientated business now.

▷ Hasn't it always been?

◁ No. In the sixties, when we went to the clients with our portfolio, they rolled out the red carpet and said, "Here they come. It's gonna be a great show." (Claps his hands.) Now they don't do that. They don't really look at the ads; they look at the scores and they say, "Number 20 looks OK. Let's see number 20."

▷ That's right. Do you remember the DDB ad with the headline: Starting today, you can fly from Tel Aviv to Cairo. On El Al. The picture showed a drawing of a pyramid, and this pyramid was combined with an upside-down pyramid so that it became the Star of David.

◁ In this country, that would be considered too cerebral, too much from the brain and not from the heart. I don't know if Americans get such a kick out of graphic devices.

▷ That's why New York welcomes German and Swiss art directors as valuable assets.

◁ Ha, ha, ha. I think there's an awful lot of bullshit connected with so called creative advertising. It's too introspective. Rather than reaching out like Mother Teresa, a lot of advertising today is not finding its mark. Saatchi and Saatchi, for example, do fancy advertising, but often they are not reaching the people. It's like pissing into the wind. On one hand, you have the Saatchis', and on the other, Mother Teresa.

▷ That's an interesting thought.

◁ There have been a lot of agencies that do some remarkable work in New York that have never suffered from this stigma of creativity. And they never had to carry the torch. This goddamn torch, which really becomes like a monkey on your back.

▷ Did you ever feel the pressure?

◁ I have felt it terribly. And I've said to myself, what would Helmut Krone do next? And that's when you start dying.

When you're only No.2, you try harder. Or else.

Avis can't afford to relax.

Little fish have to keep moving all of the time. The big ones never stop picking on them.

Avis knows all about the problems of little fish.

We're only No.2 in rent a cars. We'd be swallowed up if we didn't try harder. There's no rest for us.

We're always emptying ashtrays. Making sure gas tanks are full before we rent our cars. Seeing that the batteries are full of life. Checking our windshield wipers.

And the cars we rent out can't be anything less than lively new super-torque Fords.

And since we're not the big fish, you won't feel like a sardine when you come to our counter.

We're not jammed with customers.

Press ad for Polaroid

▷ That seems to be the fate of mega-stars.

◁ Unless you have some basic simplicity to begin with. I did have a lot of that. When you don't keep it simple and basic, for the people, you're in trouble.

▷ Were you ever scared of running out of ideas?

◁ Yes, every Monday morning.

▷ How did you overcome your fears? How did you hit upon your ideas?

◁ I wish I knew. Mostly when I wasn't working, when I was doing something else. Driving, shovelling snow, things like that. But very seldom in a room. Especially with a writer.

▷ If you could start over, would you go into advertising?

◁ I wouldn't go into advertising. It's too scientific now. The kids don't know this, they just know what they see in the annuals. They don't know the problems today. And their instructors don't tell them. The instructors are mostly my age. I feel sorry for the kids in a way. They all go into advertising wanting to 'think small'. But the research people shoot everything down.

□

JOHN WEBSTER
The human mind is like a car engine. It needs fuel.

Sony, Hofmeister, Quaker Sugar Puffs, Smash, Volkswagen, John Smith Bitter, The Guardian, Courage Best Bitter – no one has done as many extraordinary campaigns as John Webster. He has won Gold awards for commercials simultaneously as copywriter, art director and director. On his own he has regularly won more awards than the best creative departments of other agencies.

John Webster was Creative Director of BMP for a couple of decades, in the eighties and nineties. We met for several interviews in their office at Bishops Bridge Road. And even in the new Millennium, Webster still comes in to the agency a couple of days a week with his extraordinary ideas.

▷ Hermann Vaske: What works better, John? The hard sell or the soft sell?

◁ John Webster: I don't know too much about the rest of the world. In England there's a kind of distrust for the hard sell, you know – and therefore we have to get into people's psyches by other means. And there is a huge lot of humour in this country. People in Britain hate those who take themselves too seriously and therefore humour is very, very potent I think.

▷ Your agency is quite heavy on marketing and planning. Concepts are checked very carefully. How is an agency that produces such extraordinary creative work so strong in planning and marketing at the same time?

◁ Well, from the time the agency was formed, planning and research and creative have been side by side. They work together. Normally in agencies, they're enemies. They fight each other. Good creative work comes from getting good creative people. Accurate marketing comes from making sure you're saying the right thing. Historically, creative people have been suspicious of planners, since they tend to turn down good ideas. But here, we take a different approach to planning. Planning goes out with animatics, rough versions of the TV commercials, posters and press to the target audience, and they have group discussions about them. They try to figure out what's good about the ad and what's bad. If it's wrong, why? They like good advertising, they don't want boring advertising. So you're o.k. if you can marry creative and marketing.

A tough act
to follow.

John Smith Bitter TV-campaign

▷ It's obviously a successful marriage at BMP/DDB. Is there a direct correlation between winning awards and selling products?

◁ I don't think it's very difficult to write an award winning commercial. It's very much more difficult to write an award winning commercial that actually sells the product. But it's the only thing worth doing. You know, we are told to sell goods. We are paid to sell goods, we are not paid to win awards. So in my view, my job is to sell.

▷ You seem to be an animal lover. In fact, in quite a number of your commercials, you've used them. Do you love animals?

◁ Yes, I do like animals. You're quite right. England is a nation of animal lovers. It's a quick way to an Englishman's heart. I think a lot of it is coincidence. That is, because we did certain animal campaigns we attracted clients who also wanted similar campaigns. Then a beer came in and they had a bear as their symbol. It was the Hofmeister bear. One thing follows another.

▷ So you agree with Ogilvy, who said consumers love babies and animals best.

◁ Absolutely. There's a women's magazine that did an analysis about the importance of graphics on their cover. First is royalty − if royalty is on the cover, they sell more magazines. Second is babies.

▷ Are the animals in your commercials just substitutes for humans, except easier to handle and you have more fun playing with them?

◁ They are all metamorphosed human beings. Metamorphosed into animals. But more than that. I would say that I probably made my reputation through inventing characters − not always animals − characters to represent the clients. A lot of ads use famous people. I have always seen that as a disadvantage, because very often the famous people take over. Whereas if you can design a Hofmeister Bear, you become famous. And your product gets enormous benefit. It's a big advantage when people invent their own character and make it famous through the advertising. It's more branding. So over the years, I've invented a lot of characters.

▷ Humour is definitely one of the tools you've used. Is there one specific tool, or is the only rule that there's no rule?

◁ There's no rule. There is no formula. That's one thing I've learned being in the business. Humour, I think, is a very useful tool in England, because English people tend to mistrust the hard sell. So you have to be more

John Webster

subtle. To sell something to an English person, they have to love you first. Unlike Americans, I think, who have a different attitude toward a salesman. I think in England you have to be much softer to get people to like you. Humour sells here.

▷ What influences your work?
◁ Difficult question. Nothing specific. Jacques Tati films, Laurel and Hardy. I don't know ... a million things. I would say that I try not to be influenced by other advertising. I think that's a mistake. A lot of people, when they can think of an idea, go back to the advertising books.

▷ Where do you get your ideas from?
◁ Listen to a piece of music. Get it from outside. Otherwise you're just copying. Everyone goes through a block. And the worst thing a creative person can do is just sit there. Get out, get your mind moving and talk to someone, listen to them. Go and see a painting. If you keep trying to push it, push it, push it, nothing will come out. I think the mind is like a car engine. It needs fuel. Any creative person needs that. In fact, when I hear anything, when I see a painting, I keep it, just lock it away.

▷ For most of your commercials you are both, the art director and the copywriter. Do you prefer to fly solo?

Stills from Quaker Smash-
"Robots" commercial

◁ Most of the time, yes. When you run a creative department, you don't have a lot of time to sort things out with other people. So a lot of work is done in the evenings or away from work. But sometimes I work with other people. It varies. Very often you get stuck, and it's nice if you can bounce ideas off someone else.

▷ What about commercials?

◁ The less people there are involved, the less you have to compromise. If you have a single vision and you bring someone else in, they put something in, and someone else puts something in, and your vision has changed. The swan has changed into an ostrich. It's purity to have the idea, write it, art direct it, sell it, go to the production company, see it through the filming process, and go to the client with it. When you've written something, nobody is going to care as much about that idea as you do.

▷ Too many cooks spoil the broth.

◁ Absolutely. You don't know what's going to come out when people compromise.

▷ Do you think the real craftsmen of today work in advertising?

◁ Not exclusively, no! There are craftsmen in every field. I think most of the craftsmanship in advertising is in production. I think there is a certain lack of craftsmanship on the writing side, compared with the sixties.

▷ We are living in the so called age of nonverbal communication. Is that the reason?

◁ Partly that, and also we're living with a generation that has been raised with television. There has been an explosion of video techniques and computer graphics. Which I think, funnily enough, we're now seeing a reaction against. There is a movement back towards storytelling, away from all that flashy stuff, which I think is good.

▷ High touch instead of high tech. Stories instead of flashy visuals.

Webster´s Guardian commercial

◁ Yeah, that's right.

▷ Are stories the secret of your success in getting to consumers?

◁ I think so. Consumers have to be involved. I don't think high tech or special effects are enough; they have to be used in conjunction with something a bit more meaningful.

▷ Can you imagine using rational tools instead of emotions?

◁ Yes, but it depends on the product. If you have a product that is logically and rationally and obviously a good product, fine. But if you have a product like beer, one beer is the same as any other. Petrol is the same as any other petrol. You can't sell petrol logically. It's like air. People take it for granted. There is no way you can sell that rationally; you have to sell it emotionally. There has to be an image. Whereas, if someone has a cure for baldness, then you sell it rationally.

▷ A cure for baldness — could you sell that emotionally as well?

◁ I don't think you'd have to, unless there were 20 different cures for baldness. Then you'd have to find an emotional way to put yourself above the others.

▷ You tend to prefer the emotional side.

◁ Yes, because most of the products I work on have no particular benefit. Take a brand of paint. They all paint the wall white. How can you sell that rationally?

▷ Do you think advertising is an art form? Or does it just play with art?

◁ It's not an art form. Advertising is a business. It happens to use some of the techniques that are used in other art forms, but it's not an art form in itself. If pieces of advertising happen to also be pieces of art, that's merely a coincidence. I would add that just because it's a business, it doesn't have to be ugly. I mean, a piece of architecture doesn't have to be ugly. You can make it attractive, interesting and let people enjoy it. Why not? I'd rather do that than do something that people hate.

▷ Do you think some of the work that's done here in England is art?

◁ I don't see it that way. I see it as answering a problem. Maybe that's unusual. I do have to say, we have two commercials in the Museum of Modern Art: The Guardian, and John Smith Yorkshire Bitter. I still wouldn't call them art. Nevertheless, I'm quite proud of them.

▷ The Guardian commercial is a very interesting piece of communication. How did you come up with the idea?

◁ Well, start with the client. Nice, very intelligent people. The strategy was that they were independently owned. In the period when we were doing that advertising, all the newspapers were being taken over by powerful people. Rupert Murdoch, Robert Maxwell etc. And they were pushing their own policies through their papers. The Guardian is owned by a trust. The writers there are free to write what they want. So the brief was to convey that message. The problem was, how. So we'd imagine writing various types of stories. For example, reports of accidents. If you ask one witness about what happened, his report might be totally different from another witness. It's only when you ask two or three people that you begin to get the true story. We started with that ... the first script was a black youth on the ground, being beaten up. The next cut was a policeman beating. So, you naturally assume he's beating up the black. Then in the third shot you see that there's a skinhead on top of the black guy, beating him. And the policeman is trying to get the skinhead off the black. It's only when you see the whole picture that you know the truth. But the Guardian felt it was too racist, that it might cause a lot of problems. So we had to think of another example using the same idea. We ended up modifying it to show the skinhead racing toward a businessman, who clutches his briefcase in panic. The next cut reveals that the skinhead is pushing him against a wall so that he won't be hit by bricks falling from a construction site above him.

▷ It's a didactic piece of film, demonstrating that there is no objectivity in film, not even in documentaries.

◁ There is a nice story about that. We got a phone call from a chap one day, asking if he could borrow the film. I asked why, and he said, "Well, I've been accused by the police of doing something." He was going to court, and a policeman had seen him doing something which was mistaken for something else. And he wanted to use our film as evidence that it could be other. We agreed and sent it to him. He used it in his defense. But I never heard if he got off.

▷ That advertising was a new concept. Hadn't you done something with celebrities like Peter Ustinov before?

◁ Yes. When we inherited the account, we had to continue a campaign that had already been started at Thompson's, which was people being interviewed in the street.

▷ Picasso once said, "There is no rule against bad art." Is there a rule against bad advertising?

◁ There is no rule. Bad advertising inflicts itself on millions of people. I've been embarrassed if I've done an ad that's bad and people haven't liked it. So I've made my own rule against bad advertising. I don't want to do it. I'd rather not do it at all than do bad advertising.

□

PHILIPPE STARCK
Advertising is a parasite of society

Philippe Starck gives the impression that he is always on the way to the airport. He is a marathon man. His designs have improved taste and style of our times. His lamps, toothbrushes and chairs are not the privilege of a few, but are accessible to far wider audiences. Starck's ubiquitous orange juicers are as likely to be found in homes in London as they are in Milan, Tokyo or Sydney. His restaurant and hotel designs are today considered to be temples of post-modernity. The Paramount in New York, The Delano in Miami, The Mondrian in Los Angeles and St. Martin's Lane in London are places of pilgrimage for the illuminati of the worlds of fashion, advertising, music, art, film and those who want to be seen to be seen. In short, Starck is a modern day phenomenon.
I met the High Priest of the avantgarde in his Paris home to talk to him about art direction, design and why advertising is a parasite of society.

▷ Hermann Vaske: Philippe, why are you creative?
◁ Philippe Starck: Why am I creative? Well it's always the same thing. I am creative to be loved. Apart from that, I had a special problem when I was young. I was a real sweet kid, almost dumb. But strangely enough, I wasn't rejected by society because I was different, but I was invisible. And if one is invisible, you really get sick after a while and you do everything possible to exist. The one thing, that came to my mind to exist was remembering the invisible man. You know the invisible man from the movie, that only exists when he's robed in some clothes. The invisible man was the first parameter in my creativity.
I asked myself next, how I could become visible? How could I put on these clothes? And then all of a sudden, I remembered that my father was an inventor who created airplanes and other things and that he always said to me: "In order to make a living, the only profession in the world is to look for ideas from your inner self." These kind of thoughts I got at the very beginning when I started out. And then you create further to survive. After a while one got the duty to work not only to survive, but to work for your fellow human beings. Then one has to follow your intuition and generosity and to devote yourself to ideas and assignments and a society which helps your fellow human being to have a better life. Your work then takes on another dimension, a more modest one, a more honest one and a more respectable one. Although the discipline of survival is already a respectable assignment, one should, and I repeat, not work for yourself, but should work and create for others.

▷ Does your creativity thrive in chaos or discipline?

◁ I believe, discipline is an over dramatized word, but I believe in an organization. Because organization is totally liberating. On average I work on 250 projects simultaneously, which means that I have an inbuilt computer that runs pretty well. Although this computer has a limited life expectancy and it is working on a couple of projects simultaneously. You know, I have learned to live with that paradox. My creativity is a kind of magma which continously is in motion. Because with the projects you see here I'm pregnant between 5 and 40 years. I work very fast and at the end of my pregnancy the magma equals the end result. And it is my spiritual work to see in there a hologram and a three dimensional creation. If it is an object, I let it run from all sides in front of my very eye; if it is a location I fly and move in this location and look at everything. After that I am only the printer of the hologram, that was evolved out of my magma. One has to be very flexible in this magma and should avoid giving birth too early. At the same time one has to divide the magma into claims and parts and also into single fields, so that it is accessible and readable when one needs it.

That is the economy of the brain, which is followed by the economy of the time. Because every creation develops out of the economy of a time when one is able to concentrate. That's why time has an enormous meaning for me and that's why I have timings that are worked out to a single second like this one. These things are updated 3, 4, 5 times a day so that every second is very efficient. For example to talk to you, or to concentrate or to sleep. That's absolutely necessary for life. I don't understand those people at all who call themselves creative and live in a chaos. I don't understand that because it is such a loss of time. It is better, and I repeat myself, to get organized to liberate oneself.

▷ Do you think that creativity can help solve the problems in the world?

◁ Can creativity save the world? That is not the question. Our species differentiates itself from other animals through creativity and the ability to dream. It is the creativity of our species which led to the development and existence of our civilization. It is our romanticism, our poetry and our joi de vivre. So creativity by itself can't naturally save the world. But because we are extremely creative individuals we do something good for mankind through our unique creativity.

▷ How do you personally approach your creative problems?

◁ How do I solve my own creative problems? I don't have any creative problems. Because I'm not doing anything if it doesn't come to me naturally. I don't force anything and I'm not searching for anything. You know, the old joke: there are people that search and there are people that find. I devote my time exclusively to the finding.

And if it doesn't work, it doesn't work. I don't look to the right and I don't look to the left. I live in a complete physical autocracy, in a complete cultural autocracy and also in a spiritual autocracy. For me creativity is only gymnastics of the brain and of concentration. And my bed is my fitness studio. That's why I have a bed in my office. Basically I never go to the office and if I have to think about something – what rarely happens – I just go to bed. I lay down and spend my time dreaming and waiting until my software has downloaded the programme. That's why I have a table standing right next to my bed, so that only a minimum of seconds get lost between my bed and my table. And if it's ready and accomplished I'll sit down at my table and print.

▷ Can you elaborate on that?

◁ When I think about objects or projects, whether it is an airplane or a ship, or a car, or a toothbrush or a building or something else, I ask myself if they are really useful and how I can make them more useful. If I create an airplane I ask myself: is it really useful and how I can make it more useful? I'll ask myself how I'll be able to contribute to the product or the project, or whether it deserves its existence. And you know at the end of the day it's pretty simple because it's all a question of parameters. There are 1, 2, 3, 4, 5, 6 parameters and one could say that out of 6 parameters at least 4 are needed, so that your creativity can be differentiated, so that the results are different. Because, for a building, and you could say, even a city, I use different parameters. For an airplane or a car I use different parameters still. For a piece of furniture I use other parameters and for a piece of electronics or a pair of glasses I again use other parameters. Actually there is nothing else and the idea always stays the same. The idea is driven by the wish to be useful and is based on global generosity which is – at least I hope – present in me. Then the idea is executed with a precise intuition which is part of my education.

▷ Is it better to communicate with words or pictures these days?

◁ You ask me if it is better to communicate with words or with pictures. For me it is not a question of what is better, because there are numerous other ways of communication. If it's communication with words you could be approached directly. Good. But words often come out of the conscious and the conscious is often easy to read and is always lying. Therefore words are not the ideal channel to communicate.

Within pictures the communication goes via a vector which can be manipulated a lot. That's why a portion of... distrust is absolutely necessary.

I personally do believe that one of these days working and communicating will be on an unconscious level, sending micro-signals, vibrations and messages of love. The communication between people on a subconscious level would be more easy to read and would lie less. And that would be the only true communication.

A message can work without words and via objects, it can be communicated between the lines of an article or through the dots of a TV screen. Let me give you an example. When we speak now, perhaps the melody of our voices is more important than what I say. That means before you read the sub-titles you are receiving the music and the melody of the voice, which either is liked or disliked. I do what I can and I am only what I am; but I believe more in the unspoken word than in the spoken word.

We should remember what the French philosopher Lacan said: "That what's been said, kills." In other words, when one says something one kills it instantly at the same time. That's why I only talk in the most extreme emergency situations. I don't have another choice.

▷ How important is art direction for you these days?

◁ For me art direction is very important. I do it and will do more and more of it. These days I try to create more and more and produce less and less. I try to give up production and only create concepts in regard to the big social goals and creative solutions. Those are the assignments that I find exciting.

I am not interested in art direction or aesthetic or cultural work, I am only interested in art direction as a political means to an end to change the production and the orientation of the great societies of the planet. Because I am working in the creative arena of form and visuals I use them for doing politics. As far as I'm concerned it's mainly politics. If I am the art director of a railway company I don't just try to design a nicer compartment wagon, rather I try to influence the thinking of the people that ride on that compartment wagon. If I would be the art director of a cosmetic company, I would not try to create better smelling products, I would rather try to tell the people who use that product a story about themselves – about how we can slow down death, and living very consciously and things that do not have a connection to the product as well.

▷ Are you involved in any advertising campaigns at all?

◁ No, I never, never do advertising. I don't like advertising as a social phenomenon. I mean advertising is a parasitical thing. Advertising is the parasite of society. But within this useless product, within this useless concept of advertising is an extraordinary eruption of creativity and a melting pot of creative talent. Because it incorporates everything I love.

Thinking in cross connections, fast work, the use of symbols, the way things are expressed without words. There are many talents in advertising amongst the commercial directors, amongst the advertising music composers, amongst the art directors, amongst the copywriters and conceptual people. It's a pity that all of it is useful for nothing.

▷ How do you regard the difference between art and advertising?

◁ If it was the same thing, it would have the same name. It is very interesting to see, just to read, all the different names. Architecture, decoration, art, design, advertising and things like that. That means, there is strictly no relation. It's always something about creativity, but after all, the parameters are different. We must remember that advertising is there just to help people to steal the money out of other people's pockets. And because some of these people have a lot of money, they can rent people with a lot of talent to steal a lot of money out of a lot of people's pockets.

▷ That's very well put. Now if we go back to what we talked about: the profession of an art director. What do you reckon the difference is between an art director and a designer?

◁ One more time, it is not the same thing. If we take the classical idea of a designer, like it was expressed by Raymond Loewy, one of the first designers in the 50s, Loewy said: "Le laid vends mal"; "Ugliness sells badly". The contrary idea is that beauty sells better. This was the idea of a designer – a designer was somebody who tried to make sexy objects to help a company to sell more products ... which is the material way of advertising. When design is like that, advertising and design are the same thing. Advertising is conceptual and immaterial, we can say, whereas design is material, but at the end it is always to make a proposal more sexy and to sell more. I never agreed with that.

And definitely I think the idea is obsolete, dangerous, dishonest and an old way of thinking. Today a designer must have enough honesty, respect, vision and tenderness not to make more sexy objects and to produce more for the customers – we have enough objects amongst us – but to invent new services which can really help people to have a better life and to bring happiness and to send a message of love.

Now the designer is not obliged through the material to express himself. He can just create a concept, just speak, just fight, just work with people from mathematics like I do now, work with people from biogenetics and biotechnology like I do now. He can do a lot of different things. So a designer is no longer somebody who just produces other objects to make money. That I think was the old concept.

Advertising is still just to sell. There is very, very, very little advertising which offers a political statement, something interesting enough to balance a little of the venality of the process.

There was a lot of criticism about Benetton. We all know that it was to sell more T-shirts, but something was interesting. At the same time, they tried to shake things up a little and to use every dollar spent in advertising for a double language. A language which says: "Look, this is a rebel, this guy is dying of AIDS, this guy is killed by government next week, and at the same time: Look, we are so beautiful, we are so smart, buy our T-shirts, they are better than the others."

Benetton is almost the maximum advertising has done in commercial advertising, not political advertising, like Amnesty International. That is interesting as a matter by itself. But that's why we can repeat: All advertising and design are not the same. New ways to do design, to think design, as an aid to give people a better life, I think is really different from advertising... because advertising is definitely, structurally, just to make money.

▷ What could you advise young people that go into the creative disciplines of design and advertising? Are there any kind of rules they should follow?

◁ Definitely. Young people in any creative work must have a rich life, must have a lot of experience, good and bad, must be generous, must have a vision, must first work for themselves to survive, it's normal. But after they must very quickly understand that they have a duty to inform society, a duty to help people to have a better life. And they must be completely open and confront issues like that and do them.

▷ When you get a briefing or a problem on the table, how do you usually go about a project?

◁ We are very special. First, we have some rules. Very strict rules. We never work for weapons, hard alcohol, tobacco, gambling, religion and anything which could come from dirty money. In our contracts, all our customers must prove the source of their money. If there is any doubt, that they have anything to do with dirty money, Mafia or anything like that, we don't take the risk and we don't do it.

That's the first thing. Then if we meet the person, we first try to see if this person wants to do this project to bring something honest to people, or just to make money. If they just want to rent us to make money, we don't do it. I think to say "no" today is a very positive parameter. We must be courageous enough to be suspicious and say "no" if we think there is a doubt. That's why we say "no" to 85 percent or more. If we think the person is honest, is positive, we check that the project merits to exist and

Cattle Hot Bertaa and shoe prototype

is a project that can bring something else, can bring a political statement, a love-statement, an ecological statement, a subversive statement - any statement. If this is the case, we start to think about it, and finally come to the human relationship with the person. The person, the customer, must become a friend, we must be completely in tune and it must be a love affair between him and us. It's very important. When we think the project is good, when we love the person, that becomes a real love affair, and if the two parents are in love, they make beautiful children. Because in the end the only goal is to bring love and happiness. And to bring love and happiness, it's like fresh fish, you must always protect it. It must always stay fresh. From the first meeting to the final result all the aspects of the process must be elegant, harmonious and with love and things like that. If it's not made like that, you never reach the goal to bring love and happiness.

▷ So good work comes out of harmony.

◁ Harmony and elegance. One of our main rules is elegance. I don't say elegance of the product – we make what we can – but definitely elegance in the way we do it.

▷ How would you define the future of the visual culture?

◁ I don't know exactly. I never think about that. But I'm not anxious for visual culture, because everything now goes through a screen. There are screens today for televisions, computers, mobile phones and watches, and definitely, all these four screens will become the same. That's why at the end, ninety percent of the communication will be two-dimensional and visual. After we must wait 15 to 20 years to have a neuronic connection, that means a direct connection with the brain, so that we need no more audio or visual – but cortex-communication. But we must wait a little, not a lot.

▷ Is that why you are talking to biogenetic guys?

◁ Absolutely.

▷ That sounds fascinating.

◁ We have worked on it for a long time. But now we're reaching the goal and I think in one year...one year and half, we shall produce one of the first mass market bionic objects, which will be a polyvalent platform of intelligence, which will be under the skin. We have announced the product one month ago in Switzerland, in Basel, at the watch fair, and we think that it will be finished in one year or one and a half.

▷ Can you elaborate a bit more about that product?

◁ It's a polyvalent platform. It's a small piece of metal you will slide under the skin. It is an implant under your skin that will give you all the services you need depending on what you will download on it. It will

Philippe Starck

start with all the services of a watch, and very quickly it will become a healthcare unit, an information board, a telephone, a computer...everything.

▷ Please put me on the waiting list for that one.

◁ OK, no problem. My pleasure!

□

Introduction
BY JOE PYTKA
Director, PYTKA, Venice California

Advice doesn't do anyone any good; we must learn from experience. (Ezra Pound)

The (ART?) of filmmaking will not grow unless the filmmakers learn from experience. The golden age of film was created by men (and lamentably few women, mostly actresses) who had lived real lives.

They were refugees from Hitler's Germany, cowboys from the real west, roustabouts-survivors. The actors, writers, cameramen, producers, and directors had experienced life firsthand and through their work gave true insight into the life experience. That's why their films have such long lives and continue to give pleasure and rank with the best literature and painting. This is message that must be remembered and heeded.

There have been advances in technology that have made the craft of film more accessible and more convincing and more practical and less of a black art but has not made films better. The craft has overtaken the art. The technical moment has replaced the moment of truth. The French New Wave which freed actors to perform in the absolute has given way to the Technological Wave which binds actors to marks on a greenscreen, marks for the Louma, the Steadicam.

The future lies in using the newfound technology to
bring beauty and truth and honor to the work. To tell
stories that couldn't have been told in such a way before
but staying true to honest observation of the human
condition, to resisting the abuse of this wonderful and
powerful medium for pure profit and exploitation,
to use these new tools not for destruction but for growth,
to tell the stories of mankind in a new and honest way.

Joe Pytka
May 2001

TARSEM
Originality is the art
of concealing your source

If it had been up to his mother, Tarsem would have stayed in India and married a girl his parents had selected for him. But since Tarsem respects his parents, yet doesn't listen to them, everything turned out quite differently. With his legendary commercials for Levi's, Nike, Coca-Cola and Superga, Tarsem has become a superstar among commercials directors. His first feature film, "The Cell" with Jennifer Lopez and Vincent d'Onofrio was a visually striking thriller. The film was not only a great success at the box office it also got critical acclaim in the newspapers. In addition it brought Michèle Burke and Edouard Henriques an Academy Award Nomination in the "Makeup Category".

▷ Hermann Vaske: Tarsem, how important is the idea of an ad as opposed to the execution of that idea?
◁ Tarsem: I think the idea is practically everything. If the idea doesn't work, no amount of fluff will change that, unless, you know , it's an ad for perfume or something like that.
▷ But you are known for bringing an incredible amount of style to your commercials...
◁ The execution is important, of course, and I'd love to say that this is what counts but it's not true. Most of the work, the conceptual stuff for the commercials I make, is done by the agencies. Of course the visual is important because the media is so competitive. If you look at television, there is so much strong stuff around. And most people nowadays have the attention span of a remote control. You know they're going to start zapping the moment the visuals aren't interesting enough. But if there is no idea, the visuals alone won't be able to do the job, people just won't remember it. And I say this even though it is my job to bring the visuals to an idea. But it's the idea that attracts me to the project in the first place.
▷ But there is a sense that, in terms of ideas, everything has been done before. That ideas are basically just recycled.
◁ ... stolen, yes. Ideas are stolen all the time. But, you know, originality is the art of concealing your source. As long as you can mix it up enough, and bring enough of yourself to it, it's not really stealing.
▷ Do you think there is a correlation between creativity and spirituality?
◁ I don't know. I wouldn't say that I am a spiritual person. And a lot of people might say that I'm not a particularly creative person either, so I don't know if there is a relationship between the two things.

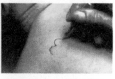

Stills from
Centraal Beheer commercial

▷ Is advertising the fine art of separating people from their money?
◁ In the best of cases it is a fine art, hopefully. But it's about informing people about the product. In some instances it might create some false demand, of course, but then it might not. It might just provide information about a product.

▷ You mean as long as you give something back to people in terms of extraordinary creativity it is okay even if there's no substance to the advertsing?
◁ No, I don't think that creativity is all you need to give to people in an ad. I think your product has to be something that people hopefully can use.

▷ But if the product is crap?
◁ Of course, if the product is crap, creativity, a cool ad, might sell it initially but later on people will catch on, everything catches on through word of mouth...

▷ But would you want to work on it?
◁ When I get a script, I just look at the product as something that needs to be sold to these people, and it'll do the client x amount of stuff. I think it's kind of selfish of me but I don't see beyond my nose. I think, by the time they come to me, a lot of money has been spent by the people who are doing what they do. So I think if they haven't done their research right, they will just lose at lot of money and that might just evolve them out of the market, but that's really their problem. By the time they come to me I'm not judgmental about it. Provided I like the idea, I just trust their judgment and the research they have done. On the other hand, I don't think I'd be able to do a cigarette ad. I just have a problem sitting around people who smoke but with most other stuff – beer, all kinds of booze – I'm just not judgmental about it. I think if they have come this far....I don't drink but I don't really like people who don't drink. All my friends drink. So I would do an ad for mostly everything if the idea works, if it is my kind of thing. Hey, I'd do an ad for tampons, for biscuits. It wouldn't matter as long as the idea was great.

▷ Would you have done an ad for Hitler?
◁ No. I would do an ad for practically everything as long as it's a material thing. If I did an ad for Hitler, I would be selling a philosophy. I am in the business of selling material things, not philosophies. Not that I am a very material person myself. I never had any money in my life until now. And, you know, now I could have any car I wanted – and I don't even own one! I have two scooters instead. So I don't think I'm a material person even though I sell material things. But never philosophies. So I wouldn't do religious ads either. I wouldn't do ads for Hitler or the Pope.

Tarsem

▷ Do you think there is any religion with a stronger emphasis on creativity, a religion that produces more creativity?

◁ Religion has outlived its usefulness to mankind. Religion and patriotism: I think they are both a bloody big problem nowadays. For me the only big benefit of religion is the art that was produced as a result of it in the past. With the Pope using people to produce art for the church – people he knew were gay, for example, even though he wouldn't agree with their outlook on life, and vice versa, but he still employed them for producing art for churches, which were, of course, advertisements for the institution. So the art itself is really the only good thing that came out of that. But for me that's really it.

▷ Do you think that if religious faith were revitalised there would be more creativity too?

◁ I don't know if it needs to be revitalised. I'm glad it is going away. I wish it would go away even more. Religious faith doesn't need to make a comeback. For me, that would be going backwards.

▷ Why are you creative?

◁ I don't know if I am. It's just part of my job. My work appears in magazines such as "Creative Review", so I guess that's what makes me creative. I would never call myself creative. I am analytical, I believe in statistics and I believe in graphs and I work from that. It always depends what I am working for, sometimes if it's a perfume ad it will just need to have a girl walking around looking beautiful but if it's an ad for a car or for shoes, it will have to be different. What kind of audience is it going towards? So I think that a lot more of my work is rather analytical than creative. I think it's best to first figure out the graphs and then try to make work that will shine and stand out from the other guys' work – and if that's creative, I guess I am.

▷ Who would you say, has had the greatest influence on you?

◁ I think my career was made by my ex-girlfriend. Before I met her, as she likes to claim, I used to be an Iranian with no taste, that's what she always said. Of course I'm not really Iranian, and I don't know whether I have taste or not, but she always called me that. It was she who was really responsible for opening my eyes, for showing me a lot of stuff that I couldn't see before I met her. She taught me everything. And, about four years ago, when we split up, I think for a whole year I did absolute garbage. My selfconfidence was completely shattered. For a year I shot crap, and only when I started to do the Levi's commercial with the blind guy in the washroom, and the Nike commercial that's set in the Colisseum, did I get back on track, regained my confidence and started to think, maybe I can

Stills from Superga commercial

Stills from Diet Coke commercial

function again. But without this woman I really wouldn't have a career.

▷ Didn't your parents have any influence on you when you were younger?

◁ If my dad could have helped it, he would have made sure that I'd gone into business. He absolutely hated me having anything to do with media or advertising or film. Just hated it. Now he has kind of come to terms with it. Or maybe not really come to terms with it. He's had to re-evaluate his world because of what I do. You see he's worked all his life to just get by. And I know he thinks I get a lot more money than I deserve. He might be right there. But I never listened to him. Just as I never listened to my mother. She still doesn't have a clue what I do. She'd rather have me be a successful businessperson, get married to a girl she chooses, etc. But I don't think anybody should listen to their parents, and most people don't. Otherwise we'd be still back in those caves. You know our genes are a little bit different from one parent, there are two parents mixed in. Your environment is different from theirs and all this makes up progress, I would say, evolution.

▷ So life is competition?

◁ Life is competition. Life is evolution and evolution is competition.

▷ And sex is an important factor in all this?

◁ It is. I'm pretty committed and pretty faithful to my girlfriend, so I'm okay in that respect but, hey, guys who like to fuck around... hats off to them.

▷ Nobody's a saint and everybody has a dark side?

◁ Nobody's a saint and, you know, there never was. I have problems with people like Mother Teresa. I think the last thing my country India needed was another saint. God knows we have billions of them. The biggest problem India has is its overpopulation, and here is a person who has a really beautiful philosophy on every other subject, about being nice to each other, but the one thing that really makes a material difference in India is the number of people. And she refused to have the people educated in this respect, was, as an ideologue of the Roman Catholic Church, an enemy of population control. So, in the final instance, she probably did a lot more harm than good.

▷ Lady Di was for birth control, I believe.

◁ If she was, I would put her way ahead of Mother Teresa. I mean in an ideal world I would put Mother Teresa above everyone else but this isn't an ideal world, and it's criminal to ignore that. So a lot of harm can be done by these so-called saints.

▷ Would you call your visual style original?

Tarsem

264

◁ I guess I influenced a lot of work but I don't know if that makes my own work original. It's just that my background is very different from most people in advertising and, as I said earlier, creativity is mostly the art of concealing one's source. And my background... the fact that I grew up in India, who I slept with and who I didn't sleep with ; what school I went to, and where I ended up... all that comes to bear when I look at a script that has been sent in. You know the old story of Picasso, who was asked how he could charge so much money for a painting that perhaps took him three hours to make. And he said, you're not paying for three hours. He said that it didn't take him three hours to do this painting, it took him thirty years. It's your whole life that comes into it. I feel the same is true in advertising. When a script arrives, I don't just look at it and say, okay, this will happen, and then this and then that. I look at it and I just have a slightly different perspective on it than most people out here. Like I'm sure that if some of the guys from, let's say, London went to India and did some advertising there it would be bloody different from the advertising they're used to there: It would be hard to get in at first, perhaps, but once you were in you would be treasured for your different perspective on things. But on the other hand it's not really me that's different, it's the people who employ me who are different. They want something different and so they come to me. By employing an Indian director who lives in L.A. and Italy, and then having him do a car commercial for Germany, that's really different and original. I just do it how I see it.

▷ So these people are breaking walls, boundaries, in a way...
◁ That's exactly where it's going. The world is getting smaller and smaller but hopefully not at the expense of diversity. I love diversity.

▷ Good. So you won't want any part in creating a McWorld?
◁ It's getting there, I'm afraid. I would hate that. You mean McWorld as in McDonald's or MacWorld as in laptop?

▷ Well, uh...
◁ Could be both, I think... This brings to mind a wonderful square outside the Pantheon, I used to shoot there. I really love the place. There used to be a café that was really, really beautiful and now you go there and there is a McDonald's in its place, and hey, I'm not one to bitch about it, but there it is... But then people like McDonald's, so what can you do?

▷ Yeah, people like McDonald's, and people also like Coke. One of your most popular ads was the one with the swimming elephant for Diet Coke.
◁ Oh yeah, the elephant ad. That was fun to do. That was really special. One of the few things where I worked with the agency on the original

Stills from Smirnoff commercial

Stills from Levi's commercial

idea. The idea that I loved about it was that nobody knows that elephants can swim. Actually, I had to learn to swim for this commercial. I wasn't able to before but the guy who was supposed to get the shots of the elephant swimming screwed up and shot really terrible stuff and then went off because he got an offer to do a Speedo commercial in London. The stuff he shot was really garbage, useless, very bad visibility. You couldn't really see that elephant swimming. Unfortunately, the agency liked him and they said, oh well, you know, that elephant is coming mysteriously out of the mist, so it doesn't really matter if you can't see it that clearly. And I thought to myself, what a shame, the amazing thing is the swimming elephant and if you can't see him well, what's the point of the whole thing? So I decided to go back to Thailand to get some better footage. The agency didn't want to pay for any more trips to Thailand where those elephants are, they were satisfied with the crummy footage they had. So I paid for it myself and flew down there, to those islands where all these swimming elephants are. They sometimes swim from island to island. So I learned to swim and then what was supposed to be a one-day shoot turned into ten days because we got hit by a cyclone the moment we landed. It was really difficult and, of course, I still couldn't swim very well. They had to put a belt around me so I could float. And in between I went underwater in a tank from where we shot the elephant. Unfortunately, we discovered something else too. Elephants swim like submarines, they swim underneath, submerged in the water and they keep their trunk above the water. The water pressure to their sides makes them shit every four seconds or so. So this elephant kept shitting these basketballs that would come out of its ass and we were shooting from the back and the visibility got very bad everytime the elephant started shitting. The only solution was to catch these basketballs of shit before they deteriorated in the water. So we kind of caught them and put them on the boat so they wouldn't muddy up the water... My editor cut a swath out of it that's actually more interesting than that commercial. He made a compilation of scenes where you see these basketballs of shit coming out of the elephant's ass like those cannon shots in that piece by Tchaikovsky.

▷ How important are awards to you?

◁ I've only gone to one of these awards ceremonies. That was when I got that award for the Smirnoff commercial. After that, I decided that I wouldn't go to any more of them. I'm not the kind of guy who's cut out for something like that. I never know what to say, I don't know what to do. Plus I don't even have a single award anymore. I don't know where they all went.

I must have lost all of them. I guess they are important for advertising because people see these commercials all over the world, they get international exposure, and then they say, oh, you've won this award or that, and it gives them confidence to choose you. Internationally, I seem so be doing a lot better than many other commercials directors. So perhaps if you're looking for the bigger picture, if you're trying to talk to a lot of nationalities, you can do worse than hiring a gypsy to do the director's job. I got famous for doing things like the Levi's "Swimmer," which was the first commercial I ever made, where it's all about the visuals, this was not something that works on dialogue or subtlety. That may be great for a regional audience but when you have to speak to the whole of Europe, you won't have any luck with that kind of approach. Telling a story through dialogue cannot really work if you're trying to speak to a lot of different countries. You need to tell something visually. And since I am very visually oriented, I got very lucky because great visuals are international.

▷ Your mentioned the Smirnoff commercial, which is surely one of the great surreal advertisements of all time...

◁ That was good fun to do, because, originally, when they came in, they had an idea which was very strong, but it was kind of getting lost between things... They had an idea where there is supposed to be a party, in Los Angeles, contemporary party... they said a very hip, contemporary party in Los Angeles, where a waiter goes through with a bottle in his hand. And through the bottle you see, uh... you know, like an alternate universe. And I just said, I love the idea that you've got an alternate universe in a bottle; I don't know how the fuck you sold that to a client that's for alcohol, but I don't like the setting. I just thought, LA? First of all, I said, I've never been to a hip party in LA, so forget about it being hip. I said I want to change the surroundings. And they were very open, they said, fine, what would you like to do? And I just asked my production designer, and I said, what was it that you would like to build. And he said, oh, I'd like to build something like an old-fashioned ship, and I said great. So we said, boat, okay? They said, fine, and then we just wrote these scenarios, and they said, this is okay, this is too much. Then, of course, you have to give and take from the client, you know, I'm coming up with dark images, they want light images; I'm saying the necklace can turn into a snake, and they're saying, can the steps turn into a piano? I'm saying, can we turn the cat into a tiger, or a panther, and they're saying, can a jack-in-the-box come out of the box? So you find the right mix that you think you can compromise on, and then we made that ad. And, of course, the piece of music that I wanted for that, we had to fight very hard, because, you

Stills from Tarsem's
Nike commercial "Good vs. Evil"

know, that's the music Stanley Kubrick had used in "The Shining." So I went for that, and of course the client loved the film, and then they just said, we want to change the music. But the agency really backed me on that. The client wanted something contemporary and hip, it was a bit disappointing, but in the end, the client agreed that it worked best with that piece of music.

▷ You've also done a lot of car ads. Which were your favorite ones?
◁ Most car ads I've done were for Audi. I like the simplest one of the lot best. The German one of the guy who has his wife drive him to the airport and she asks him where the gas tank is and he can't remember because the car uses so little gas. I think this ad is so strong conceptually. If you look at it from the point of visuals, it's nothing. You don't care who the director is. This is quite unimportant. But the idea is strong. I love stuff like that, it makes my job so much easier. On the other hand, there's a commercial for Audi I did for a French agency, and that was very visual and actually got into a lot of trouble in France since it was very, very sexist. It said something like: This man has money, he has power, he has an Audi and he will get the woman. And then we see the car pulling up and the woman's voice-over says: "People think that we judge men by their wallets. We don't. We look at their souls." And then we see the guy braking when a kid's ball rolls in front of the car and he gets out and gives the ball back to the kid, etc. And then the woman gets into the car. When I read this, I thought, "This is bloody sexist." I called a few friends of mine and they said, it's okay. They didn't really understand because they aren't in advertising. I did the ad, which was written by a woman, by the way. It was very successful and it is one of those commercials where the look is so much more important than the idea. It was very beautiful-looking. But I kept saying, this is really sexist stuff. So when it came out, it was criticised like hell. I got outraged responses from all over. But I had told them that I thought the idea was sexist ten times. And everyone kept saying, no, no, no, don't worry, in France this is different, this is okay. So, you never know. I just don't judge anymore, I leave that to the church.
□

RIDLEY SCOTT

I've been shooting for nine weeks with nine cameras and I'm 4 hours over schedule

Ridley Scott was raised in London, Cumbria, Wales and Germany. He studied graphic design and painting at the West Hartlepool College of Art.
He shot his first short film at the Royal College of Art in London. After a travelling scholarship to the United States he joined the BBC as a production designer and became a director within a year. Three years later he formed RSA, one of the most successful production companies in the world, with offices in London, New York and Los Angeles. His "1984" commercial for Apple Macintosh is valued by many professionals as the best commercial of all time. His first feature was "The Duellists", which won him the Jury Prize at Cannes Film Festival in 1978.
His next film "Alien" won an Academy Award for Special Effects. In the following years he directed the milestones "Blade Runner", "Legend", "Black Rain" and the academy award winning "Thelma and Louise".
More recently he directed "Gladiator", which won five Oscars including "Best Picture" and "Best Actor" and was the most successful movie at the 2001 academy awards.
2001 saw the premiere of "Hannibal", starring Sir Anthony Hopkins, another blockbuster he directed for Dino De Laurentis. The musical score was by Acadamy Award winning composer Hans Zimmer.
I spoke to Ridley Scott in Morocco while he was directing his new monumental epic "Black Hawk Down", a thriller about an American Special Forces mission in Somalia, starring Josh Hartnett and Sam Shepard.

▷ Hermann Vaske: What is the difference between working with ad people and working with people in feature films?
◁ Ridley Scott: At the end of the day there is no difference. Because you are using the same crews in feature film as well as in commercials.

▷ From crews to the format. What is the difference between commercials and feature films. Your brother Tony once described commercials as sprints and feature films as marathons.
◁ It's a very good comparison because a feature film is the very, very long form, not just in terms of the end result, but the process of getting there. You know – after a schedule like mine right now – I'm half way through – and I've still got nine weeks to go, and it's all day, every day, into the evening. So it's very long, it's a matter of pacing yourself.

▷ What do you do first when a script lands on your desk?
◁ The first thing I do when I get a script in is to draw a storyboard. I can draw well because I spent seven years at art college. I always compare it with the blank piece of paper a writer starts with... not knowing what to

Stills from the
Apple "1984" commercial

do. So when I begin to doodle with an empty piece of paper, somewhere in the back of my mind there is the vision, and judging the vision is the deciding factor: whether to do it or not.

▷ Lee Clow once described your collaboration on "1984" as a magic moment in time. He said to me "If Ridley would not have seen the story-board and had not said 'This can look big, this can be special', that commercial would not have been possible."

◁ Yeah, I take ideas on from advertising for the same reason I take on a film. The nut, the idea, the incapsulation, whether it's a film or a commercial, is very important. And very often my interest will be got simply by a phrase in terms of what the film is about. Like someone said to me "well, this is gonna take place in the Roman Empire at the German front and ending up in Rome." That was enough. I was immediately very interested in that arena. And what came second was "Oh, what's the story ?". But it doesn't always happen that way. Normally it's all about story, story, story. And at the end of the day it has to be about story... well great stories and great characters.

▷ One of your actors from "Gladiator", Richard Harris, told me a while ago "You don't have to read the scripts and meditations of Marcus Aurelius to play the role of Marcus Aurelius".

◁ Yeah, he was great to work with.

▷ Why are you creative?

◁ Why am I creative? You mean as opposed to who isn't ? Hahaha.

▷ Yeah, what drives you, what motivates you?

◁ I think it goes way back when. I mean, it's part what you're made of.

Ridley Scott

272

Initially your mind leads you down certain directions with a certain kind of curiosity. Your own eye was one that got very obsessed with detail when I started out and I was functioning as a painter painting students. I think that probably made me decide to expand and, going down, the root of expanding into a painter was the obsession with detail. I was always critizised for that. Then the obsession with detail really paid of when I started to do advertising because I probably brought something new to the arena. First of all — it may sound very simplistic — but I started to light things differently, and that was an observation of the performance of light really. And at that particular time there tended to be very high key chromatic commercials and unrealistic interiors that never looked like they were real. And my attention to detail really got me work immediately in a very big way, I started to make that look very real.

▷ So you think God is in the detail.

◁ Ah, not necessarily. I mean depending what you are, if you are a writer, God isn't necessarily in the detail, or maybe it is. You may argue "No, God is in the story", but then the story usually is the detail. And all those details add up to a final result which theoretically is a story. Everyone works in a different way. In the early days I had to work very much on camera, and in fact, I preferred that. It gave me more control, so that during my years in advertising I would do my own operating. Then, in feature films, I did my own operating on the first three. That was also an extension of what's in my mind, which is that detail. And therefore it's simpler to stand up, walk across the room, and adjust something that you need to have in a certain way, simply because you see it that way. Now we've moved into an era which, in the business they call video assist, which ironically now every director simply looks through the viewfinder, because he's staring at a TV-Set which is channeled through a viewfinder. I mean for instance, I'm using nine cameras at the moment so I've got nine monitors and walkie talkies in direct communication with the operators. So every shot I usually talk into a position exactly where I want it: either the size of the lense or I want the dressing adjusted in a certain way. So it's an extension of where I was 20 years ago.

▷ Yeah, but that's obviously what you and your contemporaries, the so called Famous Five , were able to bring to Hollywood – was the attention to the detail and the attention to every second.

◁ Yeah, I think advertising, particulary in the UK — because the advertising that obviously led us was from the United States in the fifties and early sixties — started to take off in a larger and more important form in the UK, from around the sixties onwards. That was a very creative period, the

sixties and seventies, where advertising agencies still had the aesthetic excitement of treating every commercial like a little film. And because it was thought of as being a film – particulary in frame as well – everything was about detail and light and, of course, the idea.

I think things have shifted from that now. Because we moved away from having written dialogue, because now advertising is very "pan". It's very international and of course languages don't travel. So commercials ironically become more and more and more visual.

▷ Because puns don't cross borders.

◁ Yeah, yeah, which is a pity in a way because at my particular peak in advertising, I used to do only visual commercials, and Alan Parker tended to get all the dialogue commercials. And I was always very frustrated because I wanted to be able to get more dialogue and I was only getting visuals. And ironically now the whole business has shifted in a visual direction.

▷ The visual commercials you did from Mazola Corn Oil to "1984" were very ahead of their time.

◁ Yeah, I mean, you don't think of that at the time. You're just in a very competitive avenue. You know, in the late sixties and early seventies I'd just started my company and I had about 2 or 3 really serious competitors in those days. The rest were, I'm able to say, low weight competitors for us.

▷ Does your creativity thrive more on chaos or on discipline?

◁ Well, I think I'm so experienced that I am automatically now disciplined in a rather large way. We're doing a film now which is logistically a nightmare. But here I am nine weeks in and, I think, about 4 hours over schedule... I've been shooting for nine weeks with nine cameras and I'm 4 hours over schedule.

▷ Every second is very precious.

◁ Yeah, my point being – gradually you build together personnel who you trust and you build a very great team actually.

▷ What's this movie all about?

◁ It's based on a book called "Black Hawk Down". Black Hawk is an American attack helicopter. American Special Forces were sent in by Clinton into Somalia in '92 to arrest a General Hadid who was essentially practising genocide in the hundreds of thousands.
And it's one event which went wrong. It was meant to take a 39 man experienced team into a 22 hour nightmare. And in that process 2 Black Hawks got shot down. And it was an entire under-estimation of the circumstances, and the capability of the Somalian troops, who were essentially half civilian, but from a community that is probably one of the most overarmed civilian communities in the world. The Russians left behind them almost a billion dollars worth of arms, shells and bullets.

▷ You have a great bunch of guys down here. Could you tell us a little bit about your cast?

◁ I have a new guy who's gonna be very interesting called Josh Hartnett who actually is one of the leads in the film "Pearl Harbour" by Michael Bay. I got Sam Shepard, I got Ewan McGregor. A whole bunch, it's a real ensemble. The cast of actual characters was about seventy, but there are about 35 speaking so it's quite complex.

▷ It's definitely not something you shoot in a studio.

◁ No, no. I discovered that this town near Rabat, resembles Mogadishu very closely. And, it seemed the coast like Mogadishu is on the Indian Ocean, Rabat is on the Atlantic. So it's a very very stressful movie.

▷ Now talking about problems like genocide in Somalia, do you think that creativity can help solve the problems of the world?

◁ I think it can illuminate the problems definitely. I mean that's exactly what I'm trying to do, but at the end of it I can't come up with answers. You only come up with questions. In this instance the question would be the right of an international group, which is the United Nations, particulary the US, having the rights to step into a country to intercede. Should they do that, or should they not do that? And I think at the end of it all the answer is very clear. But you can only present questions at the end and not answers.

▷ Yeah, but it's great if you make the viewers discuss that current debate.

◁ The ideal thing is if they're still arguing in the car park after they've seen the movie.

▷ You bought Shepperton Studios in London. What is the difference between London and LA creatively?

◁ First of all Shepperton is purely and entirely a service industry. It's supplies no creativity whatsoever, other than creativity within a group of artisans, plasterers, painters, setbuilders, etc. But, other than that, it's really a factory. It doesn't develop material at all, unlike an American studio of course, which does.

▷ Many people say that the British creativity is more creative than American creativity. Would you agree with that?

◁ No, there are good ones, and bad ones and medium ones wherever you go. I think there is still a layer and level of craftsmanship that still exists in the UK which probably parallels the craftsmanship in Italy and in Spain. Those three countries,in terms of film craft, are probably the best.

▷ Do you fear that the craft, reality and truth in storytelling gets lost within the whole digitalization of filmmaking? That the truth in the performances is lost.

◁ I think there is a danger in perceiving digital capabilities as a new form of filmmaking. It isn't! All it means theoretically is that the video is cheaper. Eventually, in the long run, it will be cheaper and quicker. But it's just a tool, it's a device for capturing an image. The fact that we're relying on silvered plastic as a way of getting an image into today's world of technology is kind of primitive. But us, as filmmakers, we still love the plastic and the silver.

Stills from "Gladiator", the film that won more Oscars than any other movie of the 2001 Academy Awards

□

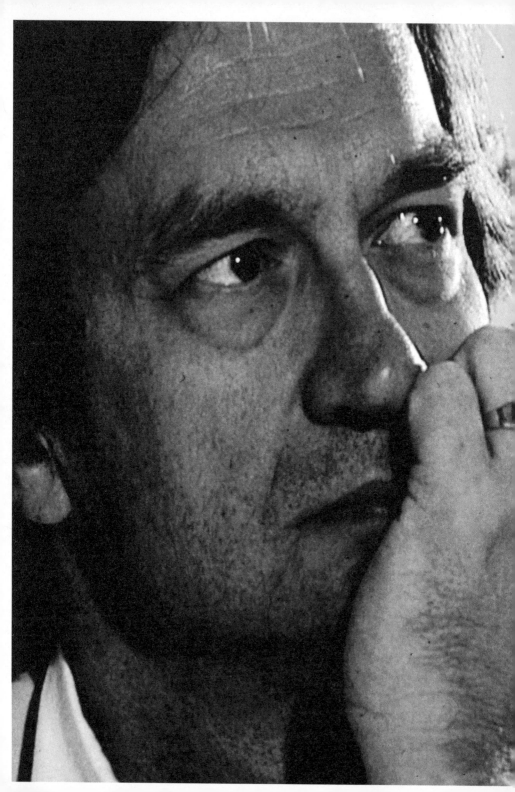

WIM WENDERS

Culturally, the digital image seems to be a logical development

Wim Wenders is a German director with a world-wide reputation. The only one to win the Cannes Film Festival three times. For more then ten years, he has also directed commercials all over the world, for clients including Danone, Ariston, Cadillac and Pontiac.

His cinematographic sensibility of sound and vision, makes his advertising films little treasures and art pieces of the commercial world.

He has also directed music videos for U2, David Byrne and Lou Reed.

I met Wim Wenders during the preparation of the European Summer Academy "The Art of Advertising" and interviewed him several times in Los Angeles and Berlin.

▷ Hermann Vaske: Wim, some years ago you started shooting commercials in addition to feature films. Your first experience in the commercial world was shooting a campaign for Ariston in Italy?

◁ Wim Wenders: Yeah, I shot three spots at once – for a washing machine, an electric stove and a dishwasher.

All three were based on the same idea: people from paintings and murals became alive and moved around. The task to link the warm elements of art and the cold elements of technology interested me a lot. That was something I had never done in feature films in such a way and it's quite a challenge.

▷ Also in terms of effects?

Wim Wenders: Yes, especially in terms of effects! We used classic film making technology, but it was also the first time that I was sitting in front of a "Henry".

▷ What are the differences and what are the similarities between feature film and commercials?

◁ If I were just able to define it that easily!

As much as these two genres have in common, the energy of each is very different.

In feature film we have scenes where dialogue goes on for five minutes, whereas in commercials every set-up lasts between one and three seconds. So it's a different economy in both genres. Since my movies usually tend to become too long, in that regard I can still learn from the strict economy and time frame of commercials.

In addition to that I also did some music videos, which is sort of a sub-art of commercials. Some of them are paced quite slowly, but some of them are already rather fast in editing. Again, the main difference to a feature film is the rhythm in editing. I think nowadays, one cannot say anymore that advertising is imitating movies or art. The opposite is the case. More

Stills from the U2 video

and more it works the other way around. I think it is important for a director these days to know how commercials are done, and that's why I find it imperative to do them myself. You cannot any longer afford to have this attitude where you think "I won't do this, because this is a totally different profession and discipline, I would rather not touch it." Maybe that was a possible attitude in the seventies and eighties, but things are changing.

▷ Isn't it very difficult to get a decent performance out of the actors in this short time formats?

◁ Yes, that's a bit of a problem. In commercials you can't achieve much with "motivation" or psychology. Here, you have to work much more with the presence and simply the physical appearance of the actor, and immediate reactions become very important. As far as actors are concerned advertising, compared to film, seems to be a complete different profession.

▷ How do you go about the casting?

◁ For my movies I've hardly done any casting. Usually most of the roles were already cast, before I started writing them, because I wrote them with a certain actor in mind. The process of casting is something I don't particularly like. It is not very satisfying to look at twenty or fifty people and then choose just one of them. Most of the time you already know when the person enters the room, whether he or she is right. And then you want to be polite, making small talk. Therefore I think casting sessions aren't very pleasant, for the director or the actor.

▷ Adrian Lyne once said to me that he regards "reality" as the most important element for actors in commercials. It's the director's job to bring across the feeling that the old guy on the park bench, drinking beer, has been doing this before, and is not just sitting there because the beer company paid him a lot of money to do that.

◁ In that regard, commercials are not very different from movies. You expect similar things from an actor in a movie, except that he is supposed to bring across that he has been sitting on that bench for three years already. This is the difference, in a movie he has to be believable for even longer.

▷ Commercials are a new challenge, not only concerning the craft of acting, but also concerning the craft of directing.

◁ Especially for somebody who normally takes too much time for everything, like me. I have a track record of making very long and slow films. So commercials are a good lesson. In addition to that, the craft of directing you have learnt and need in feature films is very useful for doing commercials. A commercial follows the same process and goes through all the same

Wim Wenders

phases as a movie: conception, writing a script, storyboarding, searching for locations, casting, shooting, editing, post-production, music, final mixes, colour grading.

▷ How important are punchlines and unexpected endings in commercials?

◁ From a dramatic standpoint you have to build it up, so that it's funny and works. You can tell a joke in many different ways, but not all of them are advertising related. In advertising it is important to do things differently from how they were done before. The cinema is much more conservative and, there, the opposite is the case. Often in cinema, you have to tell things following certain recipes or formulas, in order to get through to your audience.

▷ Are commercials well told jokes?

◁ Sure, they can be like that. But they can also be like interestingly told short stories or emergency calls.

▷ Emergency calls?

◁ Yeah. Somebody calls you, and you feel like you have to do something right away.

▷ Do you think that humour is a great tool to sell a product?

◁ Yeah, I think it's the best tool. But what do I know about how to sell products?

I know how to tell stories. Often it is already enough to tell a story in an ironic way, not taking yourself too seriously. But ,I think, humour always has a strange taste when you realise it's used as a recipe. I don't feel like laughing when I see that in a movie. Humour has to come out of the people, out of the story itself. It just doesn't work if it is simply "written into" a screenplay, by some writer who thought it was about time to make the audience laugh again. That's terrible, when you feel so spoon-fed.

Stills from the TV campaign for Ariston

▷ Do you agree with Marcel Duchamp who once said "A painting that doesn't shock isn't worth anything"?

◁ Well, shock tactics are just another fashion. Shock works only for a while and when people have had an overdose, they will want something different. Seeing Pulp Fiction was a great experience, but seeing all the imitators is painful. Very seldom the copies are as good as the original.

▷ Let's talk about sound. Some people say that sound is 51% of a movie.

◁ That's relatively understated how you put it. When I go to a movie, I sometimes think sound is almost everything and the screen is just decoration for the wall of sound. The bulk of the filmic experience nowadays, is sound. The movie even goes on if you close your eyes.

La Scala, Mailand

Of course the sound literally exploded over the last 20 years. It's only 15 to 20 years ago that we mixed in stereo, then on four tracks. There had been only mono before, and optical sound just had the ability to go up to 7000 maybe 8000 hertz, so that really limited the range of what you could do modelling with sound. Now you can do everything with sound, it can come from the front, it can come from the side, it can come from the back, and you can have it coming from everywhere. In different layers, you can create landscapes of sound.

▷ How important is the experience of listening for you?

◁ In cinema? Enormous. I like good sound design very much. Once, I was my own sound engineer for "Tokyo-Ga". There were only two people, the cameraman and me.

I listen to a lot of music. Sound is a very important part of what a film director does today. Sound takes up more time than the picture. These days you expect a director to edit a movie in a couple of weeks. Then it takes twice or three times as long to work on the sound. So you dedicate much more time to sound than to the image.

I remember when I did "The Goalkeeper's Fear of the Penalty" the sound was finished one day after we had the edit, and when we mixed it in mono, the sound had four different tapes. Today, twenty, twenty five years later, one would need sixty, seventy or eighty tapes, and it would take months to work on it and accomplish the mix. You have to think much more about the sound of a movie than you used to.

▷ Why are you creative?

◁ Every person has certain needs and desires. Most of these needs you already know when you're a kid. Some kids just sit there for hours and hours and draw and are happy. After a while they forget about their happiness, so they don't become painters. But basically I think all children are creative and it's the question of how much you stay in touch with curiosity and creativity. A lot of people learn to do things out of anguish or fear, which certainly are enormous sources for creativity. This is not what drives me so much. I would rather do things, because I like people, places and stories. I get most of my stimulation from travelling, spending time at places I don't know, being somewhere where I've never been before, seeing things I never heard of. Most of my movies come out of the passion and urge to let specific places tell their own stories.

▷ For you personally, who are the gods of creativity?

◁ Nobody, and certainly not any kind of institution. But the media and especially television regard themselves, by definition, as substitute gods. That's why they don't tolerate any other gods next to themselves. But the media are entirely and strictly man-made. The media, in a way, are the golden calf that Moses saw down in the valley when he came down from Mount Sinai.

▷ That brings me to the next question: "Thou shalt not worship false images."

◁ The media are all about "image". Image in plural and image in singular. They are selling images in order to create a specific image of something. Every commercial or ad constantly creates "false images". The fact that you have to advertise a product basically means that there is something wrong with that product. If the product were as good as they want us to believe it is, it wouldn't need any advertising. A great product can sell itself. The worse the product, the more you have to advertise it, and the more lies you have to tell.

▷ What about these images you created for BR 4 Classic Radio? Were these also false images?

◁ (laughs) That, of course, was an exception! But seriously, we showed very ordinary houses and places, but never the product. The product is invisible, out in the air, a programme of classical music. You can't have anything better on the radio than a radio station that only broadcasts music and no commercials. Fantastic. So we didn't show radios, only houses with music coming out of them. Unfortunately, BR 4 Classic Radio won't need another commercial for quite some time. I could film houses and streets for years and years and put music to it.

▷ What about the digitalisation of images and the worshipping of a digital future?

◁ Well, I think, culturally, the digital image seems to be a logical develop-ment. The more we move away from the idea that a picture represents a certain truth, the more we are gonna need self made images, man-made images. No reproductions, but a production of our own. Nowadays every digital image is more a production than a reproduction. You don't necessarily have to go outside to film something. From the desktop of your computer you can create whatever you want.

Fifty years after nuclear physics was able to separate every element into its smallest particle and even further, we are finally able to do the same with sound and images, and dissect them into their tiniest bits and pieces. They are like the atoms of images, so you can decompose and recompose them as you like. That seems to be totally logical and reflecting our image-culture perfectly.

▷ So is the digitalisation of images also a democratisation of the means of production, because more people have access to them?

◁ It's both! Democratisation and the opposite: total dependence. I can get totally hooked on images. On the one hand you are given access to the production of every image, but on the other hand you almost simultaneously become a slave of these images. In that regard it's hard for me to talk about democratisation. I would rather call it a quasi-democratic-slavery.

▷ What about the Internet in that regard?

◁ Well, there you can hardly do anything without being bombarded by ads. Okay, at least you can click out. In the beginning the Internet seemed to be such a great communication tool, but like all great communication tools, it is already being commercialised and being abused.

▷ Where are your creative influences? What about your parents?

◁ My mother and my father encouraged me, or they gave me something that fostered my creativity. I wouldn't say, "my father was creative" or, "my mother fostered my creativity", but they encouraged me which was already a lot. I think it has got a lot to do with the fact that creativity was appreciated at an early phase when I was a kid, so that you think it is welcomed. I think, it's very difficult to be creative if it isn't appreciated. Sometimes, of course, there are people who are creative, precisely because it was never appreciated. They are rebels, they had to be rebels, and that became the main source of their creative energy. Parents can help kids immensely, to be creative. Not by pushing it, God knows how to be creative. You know, there are these terrible parents, too, who think that their son is Michelangelo just because he's drawing. I mean, to actually enjoy your kids' storytelling, just listen to your kids' fantasies, kids feel that right away and react to it in a positive way whenever they are encouraged, and one is really interested in their drawings.

A lot of adults just say, "oh, that's beautiful" and you really know very well as a kid, that it means, "oh, don't bother me with that." Not many adults are able to actually appreciate kid's fantasies.

▷ How important are awards for you?

◁ Once they stand on a shelf, they're nothing more than kitsch.

▷ Collecting dust...

◁ Yeah, exactly, collecting dust. Basically they're nothing more than that. I feel uncomfortable in places with lots of awards. At the moment of the ceremony they probably mean something, but already a week later they are not worth anything, especially in the world of advertising. So I recommend for the people who win them, to put them on their desk for two weeks, or take them to bed with them, and then to clean them and give them away to children.

▷ Let's talk about sex in the media. Does sex sell?

◁ In advertising, nothing works better than sex. That's why commercial spots like to play with the theme of adultery. Advertising likes the sex theme, because it is temptation in its simplest and easiest form. I'm mostly bored by sex in advertising. I mean, you couldn't sell anything to me with sex. It's this one dimensional thinking that bores me, and mostly it's so predictable.

If you want to sell me a car with a girl that has hardly any clothes on, then I know that the car itself can't be very interesting.

□

HUGH HUDSON

You've got to catch the eye with the television set

Hugh Hudson is one of the "Famous Five" among British directors who made it in Hollywood. Whatever their differences may be, they have one thing in common: they all have their origins in advertising. None of the "Famous Five" however, has won as many Oscars for a single film as Hugh Hudson did for "Chariots of Fire" in 1981. The film was made with an all-British team and produced by David Puttnam.

Apart from "Chariots of Fire", Hugh Hudson has made several other feature films: the critically acclaimed "Greystoke" starring Christopher Lambert, and one of the most expensive Hollywood productions to date "Revolution" starring Al Pacino and Nastassja Kinski.

Hudson's work in advertising has produced quite a few global blockbusters: there is the famous "Smiling Face" commercial for British Airways, and another BA spot in which a whole island was given a Christo-like "wrap-up" treatment. I met Hugh Hudson for a talk about past, present and future in the London Museum of the Moving Image, which has Hudson on its board of directors.

▷ Hermann Vaske: Hugh, Richter says that film is the only art form developed in the 20th century.

◁ Hugh Hudson: I would say it's the most powerful art form of our century. I mean, in the way it has developed, and the speed with which it develops, it's staggering, and this is a kind of a tribute to it, certainly to movies anyway, and television. I'd say advertising as well.

▷ So you think that advertising belongs inside a museum too?

◁ I would say so, yeah. I mean I'm sure they haven't ignored it. I mean it's all part of our everyday life now.

▷ How did you get into film?

◁ I started out as an editor, in France, in Europe, in the late fifties, early sixties. Then I left the editing and started to produce and direct myself in England. I started my first company, making documentaries, and just by chance we met somebody who wanted a documentary made. Mainly these were sponsored documentaries for Pirelli and Ford and various other companies in England. So that's where I began, and then slowly, and then very fast, advertising took over, because there was the advent of television advertising in the late fifties, early sixties. So I've really gone right through it in the last thirty-five years: I worked with Ridley Scott in his company, RSA, when it began, in the early 70s. I was the first director with Ridley, and so that's really how I went into it, and finally went into feature films. I'd always been wanting to go into feature films.

Stills from the Benson & Hedges
commercial art directed by Alan
Waldie, directed by Hugh Hudson

▷ And you certainly succeeded in doing so. You belong to the bunch of English advertising directors who managed to break through the 30 seconds barrier and finally conquered Hollywood.

◁ Well, Alan Parker began first, he was the first person to make a film coming out of advertising. I was just slower. Although I began in film school before Alan and Ridley. I was making commercials and documentaries early in the sixties. But I got much later into films for some reason. Alan was the first person in, with "Bugsy Malone," and then Ridley came in after that, and then I came in, and then Tony came in. Alan made a feature film before me. He made "Midnight Express", which I did the second unit for as a friend– because he was a very great friend. He wanted some work done in Turkey, but he couldn't go because of the nature of the travelling. I shot some material for Alan's film at the same time while I was making a documentary in Turkey. Ridley, who I knew well, having worked with him in the early 70s in his company made "The Duellists," then he made "Alien," and about that time, just before he made "Alien," I made "Chariots," because I met Puttnam, through Alan. Having worked on "Midnight Express" – Puttnam was the co-producer of "Midnight Express" – and then this film came up. But I'd been trying, well, many years before I made a feature. I made a very famous film for Pirelli called "The Tortoise and the Hare," which was a sponsored documentary of forty minutes, that was a great success around the world, and from that they asked me to go to Hollywood and they sent me scripts, but there was nothing I really wanted to do.

▷ What was the storyline of the Pirelli film?

◁ It was the fable of the Tortoise and the Hare. And it was a truck, a big truck, like a big Mac truck, and a sports car, and it was completely silent, it was a silent movie.

▷ What do you think of Billy Wilder?

◁ Wonderful, he's a very great director. Billy Wilder, yeah, great. Can't get a job now. Maybe he's too old, doesn't want to, but I mean, certainly, he finds it difficult. His kind of films don't get made, that's the tragedy.

▷ But Wilder's unique way of saying it with a smile would be great for commercials.

◁ I think it's a very good way. Well, it always was in my time when I was doing advertising in a very condensed way. I do it much less now, but humour seems to have gone away from advertising. In the 70s when Parker, Ridley and myself were at our sort of heyday – in the height of commercial productions, humour was used very much. You know, the little thirty-second situation comedy, coming out of Collett's usually , with Frank Lowe who was running Collett's. Most of the films were like

Hugh Hudson

288

that. They were wonderful. It's different now, it's completely changed.

▷ Today post-production, technique and equipment seem to be most important.

◁ Yes, you make a thirty-second commercial, it might take three days to shoot it, but you have everything, all the equipment in the world if you want to use it. Not only this mechanical equipment, but you have all the video now and digital equipment at your fingertips that's used in films but also mainly now used in commercials. I mean the industry, the digital industry is so vast now, certainly in London it is, and in Hollywood everything is now geared to that. I think maybe a bit too much, I mean the human element has gone. It seems to me that the human element... you know, the relationship even in a thirty-second commercial seems to have been removed from advertising, on the whole at least. Even in the ones I do, you know, there are no human situations any more. These boards are not presented to you, or very rarely. It's changed, everything changes. I think it's gone a little bit too far perhaps. I think it'll probably come back into more relationship-driven forms. Films have lost it. Films have gone away from it. Films have been influenced by commercials and video, and I'm sure you agree about that.

▷ The "Natural Born Killers" phenomenon?

◁ Yeah. Well, all Oliver Stone's films, which I admire very much, but it's not particularly "Natural Born Killers." Just all these action-driven films and the violence-driven films, particularly Quentin Tarantino. I mean, we'll see how long Quentin Tarantino lasts. Can he go beyond the kind of film he makes? Billy Wilder, he was dealing with the world of comedy, dealing with, essentially, human drama. The only thing that's interesting really is the relationship between one person and another; the development of a relationship, the continuation and the breakdown of a relationship, that's the only thing that really interests us. So why is advertising moving into this arena? I don't know why. Is it because it sells better? Because that's the only thing that's important for advertising, isn't it?

▷ But in order to sell you have to grab people's attention.

◁ Yeah, and that of course is the vital thing. You know you've got to catch the eye with the television set. And then the consumers stop doing something else, and they look, and they get the message and they're going to buy that, and in a way in films you've got to catch people. I mean that's what they always tell you in Hollywood, that you've got to catch your audience in the first minute, or five minutes maximum in a film, and if you don't... So that's why, you see, most of these scripts you get, or that are made, have a sequence at the beginning that catches you.

Blockbuster commercial
"Smiling Face"
for British Airways

▷ How important is music?

◁ I think it depends on what you're doing. I've made silent films, and then you've got to be very strong with your images. Well, of course I have not made silent films. I'm not in the silent era obviously, I'm too young....(laughs). But I've made some films that have no dialogue. I mean "The Tortoise and Hare," the first documentary, had no dialogue at all. I made a film called "Revolution," which had a disastrous passage in its history. It's virtually a silent film. It was about the American Revolution, and it's done like a silent film in a way; very minimal dialogue. And it was attacked for that, it was an experiment, I suppose, rather an expensive experiment (laughs).

▷ Well, a mass audience expects mainstream and not experiments.

◁ Sure! It's such a mass audience, and it's so expensive, that is one of the problems, I mean, commercials are so expensive. You know, half a million, three quarters of a million dollars for a thirty-second commercial I often spent. I mean, I've spent it on British Airways spots...It's a lot of money! I think the average film now is thirty-eight million dollars in Hollywood. Now, in order to get that back, you have to have a lot of ticket sales.

▷ I think the British Airways film is one of the best commercials of all time.

◁ Thank you. Do you remember the Benson and Hedges film? With the helicopter and the box, and the blizzards, the iguanas, purely visual? I mean you could call that shock, visual shock.

▷ I would say your Benson & Hedges film is the first really surreal and artistic commercial.

◁ Well, maybe it was surreal. I mean, we're back into the surreal age again, aren't we? Tony Kaye and all that, you know. They think they've invented surreal cinema. Well of course, Buñuel...

▷ ...the "Andalusian Dog"...

◁ ...the eye, cutting the eye. There's no greater image of horror than the eye, the razor, the cut-throat razor going over the ball of the eye. But do I find it really shocking? I certainly find the eye of Buñuel electrifying, and it catches my attention. Am I appalled by it? No, I'm appalled by the images of Dachau and Auschwitz, that's shocking. That really is shocking, that's truly shocking, and poverty in Central Africa, truly shocking, those images. I don't think this image of the cut eyeball is there to shock, and it is deeply disturbing, and it gets right into your nerves, and yet it's a very fabricated image.

▷ People are still talking about "Chariots." Was that an English production?

Hugh Hudson

◁ It was an English production because we were all English, Puttnam, myself, all the actors. But it was not one penny of English money. Half of it was Fox America, and half of it was Egyptian: Mohammed al-Fayed, who owns Harrods, his family put the other half in. So it was completely non-English, although he would like to be considered an Englishman. He should be allowed to be an Englishman actually, but he's not, he's not allowed to be an Englishman, he's not been given a passport. But, anyhow, he lives here. So, his money wasn't from England.

▷ How much did the film cost?

◁ Six million dollars; twenty years ago. And it grossed seventy-five million dollars in America: twenty years ago.

▷ Good profit for Harrods.

◁ Yeah, not bad.

▷ Did "Chariots" build the bridge for Puttnam to America?

◁ Not really. No, Puttnam was always trying to get money from America, and eventually he went to run Columbia. But well, it was a sort of injection into British cinema for the time, and it had an influence, people loved the film. It's a classic movie now. It changed music. Vangelis's score definitely changed film music. There was before Vangelis and after. And it did a lot of damage too, of course. Think of all the musicians, the orchestras, you know. They started mainly to use synthesizers. It's changing back again actually, I've noticed.

▷ What made you pick Vangelis?

◁ Well, I'd known Vangelis for many years before, working in documentaries and features. So I brought him in. This was the first big film he'd made.

▷ Which directors influenced you?

◁ Fritz Lang! Fantastic! Brilliant.

▷ Do you know the book "From Caligari to Hitler"?

◁ I do know the book, I do, very good book.

▷ Do you agree with the theory expressed in the book, which says that German expressionism and its aesthetic influenced propaganda movies like Riefenstahl's and through that prepared the soil for the dictatorship?

◁ Prepared the soil? I think the Versailles Treaty prepared the soil for the dictatorship. I mean, the terrible reparations that were put upon Germany prepared the soil for Hitler, and the way the French and the British demanded the money from Germany. That's the most important issue. I think the cinema only reflected certain things of the times.

▷ What do you think of the Benetton campaign?

PURE GENIUS

Stills from the Guinness commercial "Pure Genius"

◁ It is absolutely unacceptable.

▷ Why?

◁ I don't think it should be censored, we're in a censorship arena here. I don't think it should be censored, but I won't buy under those circumstances.

▷ Should anything be censored at all?

◁ I think it's a very interesting and tricky problem because I think if you 're dealing with advertising and you're benefiting, you know, somebody is benefiting from that and making money out of somebody else, and if it's done on the back of the potential of others. Well, there are standards that control what's put on the screen. And I think that is probably right, a lot of people would disagree with me. But I think the Benetton ads actually are quite irresponsible. But then you could carry the argument further, you could say that the cinema should also be censored. If I said that to you about advertising, you could quite rightly say to me, well there should be censorship in the cinema. Which, of course, in most countries there is in some kind. There certainly was in Nazi Germany – censorship, absolute categorical censorship of everything: burning of the books, destroying of art.

▷ Is advertising propaganda?

◁ Yes, it usually is. I mean, I've made political films which were pure propaganda, and been attacked for it. I've made a film about the British Labour contender to be Prime Ninister, Neil Kinnock. I made a film, it became very famous, called "Kinnock, The Movie." It was human, because it went into his background and his views and his family. But it was ultimately accused of being manipulative. Well, ultimately, it was propaganda. It was manipulative, I suppose, it used music emotionally, and it was a history of this one man over ten minutes, and it did change people's view of this man. So it was advertising, definitely, and it was propaganda.

▷ Would you have made a film for Hitler if you had lived in Germany at the time?

◁ Very interesting question, yeah. I'm far from being rightwing, but I think I probably would have done the Olympic Film. You know, I had the offer to do an Olympic Film, for the Olympics in Barcelona and I regret not having done it because we had a very interesting approach. It should have begun with the Battle of Marathon. It's fantastic, you have a whole battle scene, the Persians against the Greeks, and then the man has to run to Athens, to give the news, and he collapses. That's how the whole film would have begun. And we went right back into the history of the Games, and then we would have brought it up to date, obviously, in

Hugh Hudson

292

Barcelona. It was a wonderful concept. We'd written the script and we were going to make the film in Barcelona. I pulled out the week before, because they didn't have the money to make the film that we'd all agreed to make. So many good things don't happen in the industry of film.

▷ Why are you creative?

◁ Oh, I don't know why I'm creative. It's in my genes, I suppose. But I want to learn about myself, and about the world, and that's why I make films. Why I make commercials has another reason. I make commercials to practise my craft, and to make money, and that's a perfectly fair answer about commercials, because commercials are made only to take money from you and give it to me. So why shouldn't I take money from the advertiser and put it in my pocket if he's taking any money? So it's a money issue, commercials. But it does serve as a training ground, which is what it was for me when I was young, and it does serve as an experimental ground, to keep up to date. But why I make films is to find out about myself really, and discover more about other people, and the world. That's why I'm creative, I think. I don't know how else to answer it.

□

TONY SCOTT
I don't shoot from the hip

After Tony Scott had become one of the strongest "visual" commercials directors in London, nobody was surprised that he was able to get a foot in the door of feature films. His first attempt, "The Hunger", was a vampire movie with Catherine Deneuve and David Bowie. From then on his collaboration with the most successful independent producers in the world, Don Simpson and Jerry Bruckheimer, began.

With "Beverly Hills Cop", "Top Gun" and "Crimson Tide", the trio pulled off some of the most successful Hollywood productions of all times. After "Crimson Tide" Tony Scott did "The Fan" with Robert de Niro and became an established Hollywood director. I interviewed Tony Scott a couple of times, when he was editing "Days of Thunder", when he was at Marlboro PPM with Michael Conrad and when he was editing "The Fan".

▷ Hermann Vaske: How did you happen to break the borders, coming out of Soho, London to become an important Hollywood director?

◁ Tony Scott: With gross difficulty. It was very tough, yeah. The process of actually making any form of film, whether it's commercials or documentaries or features, is the same – it's making choices as a director. There is a whole psychological difference and the difference is in the length – the duration of the piece of film that you're making. Thirty seconds, one hundred minutes, whatever, directly corresponds to the physical and mental duration of doing something for such a long time frame. When you're working on a film that averages somewhere between... well, this last film I did was five months of shooting, six days weeks, that's tough. And it's that psychological step, that leap that you've got to take. You know I think my first movie suffered because of my years in advertising. It was a film called "The Hunger"; the film tended to look like a series of thirty second commercials. I wasn't able to step back and take an overview of one hundred minutes.

▷ You mentioned "The Hunger". How was working with a musician like David Bowie?

◁ It was for me a brilliant experience because he was always my hero, you know, as a musician. I'd also seen him do a film called the "Man Who Fell To Earth" and he was brilliant in it. The director, Nic Roeg is particularly good at using non-actors and making them feel comfortable and he got a great performance out of David. As it was, David was really playing David more in the "Man Who Fell To Earth" than in "The Hunger" where he was doing a full-on actor character piece.

▷ In general, is there a different psychology to working with actors in commercials and feature films?

Tony Scott´s rain sequence with Gene Hackman in "Crimson Tide"

◁ No, the psychology for me is the same, it's just a longer time frame, so you can afford to be sweeter with people. You have to work a little bit harder if it's a shorter time frame, you're not looking at working with someone for six months, and normally commercials aren't as performance oriented. The ones that I got were all visually-oriented, even though I used a lot of stars in the commercials that I did.

▷ How was it working with Robert de Niro?

◁ I always wanted to work with Robert and he is tireless in his pursuit of trying of get things better and trying to make the character better, and make the story better, make the situation better. So it's a constant process throughout the shooting of the movie, but he did a huge amount of preparation and homework in terms of finding his character, you know – the character on the page. We then sat down and looked at sixty hours of tapes on these guys who were stalkers including the guy that killed John Lennon. We looked at one hundred hours of police tapes and then we sat down with knife salesmen, did a casting session of knife salesmen from all across America, these guys came and sat and we did one hundred hours on them and then we transcribed all these tapes, highlighted them and I watched de Niro build his character out of a little bit of each guy. We sat in a six hour hair cut session...actually it was three sessions of two hours, cuts a little bit here, cuts a little bit there. And what it is – it's not insecurity, it's formulating his character. I watched him build through this whole process and I watched him build through his wardrobe as well, you know, and he works very much – because I began my life as a painter – he works very much like painters do. He prepares his paint and he then starts putting it on the canvas and I watched him build his character in a way that a painter would build a canvas, and it was a totally new experience for me. His father was a painter so I presume that's where it's all coming from.

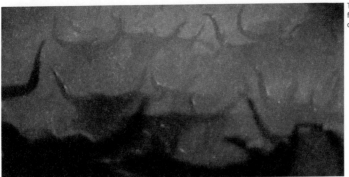

▷ You once compared commercials with sprints, and feature films with marathons. Are these sprints a healthy exercise between feature films?

◁ Yeah. I still love both and I still do both. I love both the fact that I can run a marathon which is a feature film and then the fact that I can change my pace of life and do sprints and do commercials and both are equal art forms to me. So my struggle and my endeavours are just as strong in both features and in commercials 'cos I have a passion, a huge passion for both and I'm able to do things in commercials that I can't do in features and also it's funny how I always bring something from features to commercials and vice versa.

For instance in "Crimson Tide" there was a sequence at the beginning of the movie with Gene Hackman in the rain. Gene Hackman addressing the troops like Patton in this horrendous rain storm, yeah, and then I came to do these Marlboro cowboys so it was a stampede, it was 750 head of Long Horn stampeding and I turned it into night and turned it into an electric storm with rain and each time it gets a little better. For me, I felt totally in control, I knew what I was doing and by the time I came to do Marlboro I could do something that was a little different from what I did in Crimson.

▷ I presume the rain was artificial.

◁ Yeah, it was all artificial. that's tough to do because you imagine an area that 750 Long Horns cover when they are in full gallop – so you have to have that rain spread over that area and it's at night so you've got to light that area, yeah, and then you've got to try and control the Long Horns and our worst worry was that things were going to stampede and trample people to death and run off into the wilderness. But our main, main problem was they wouldn't move. They just stood there. We had shotguns and explosions and 750 head of cattle just stood there. We were firing cannons and they wouldn't move until one of the cowboys picked up this black screen that they used to cover up one of the trucks, and one of the steers saw this black screen and went aaaaaahhhhh and took off into space and we had 750 Long Horns blasting across. And of course none of the cameras are running. But after that we knew what we had to do....we got 100 feet of this black plastic and did that with that and the herd would do that. And you never get that luxury of time, which requires money, in feature films.

I love working for foreign agencies, European agencies, because they leave you alone. They trust you. They're very detailed in terms of their pre-production, and they want to have a very clear understanding of what you're going to do, and then they let you do it. What I hate about American agencies is they never leave you alone. And the British agencies lie somewhere between American agencies and what I call European agencies: France, Germany, Italy. And you get to do some weird stuff... some of the most interesting stuff on my reel is foreign stuff, French and German stuff. I do commercials now between features and I love them because I see features as mountains and commercials as friends. And one is a totally different art form to the other. I think it's a better life when you're shooting commercials because it's less pressure. In film the pressure is enormous, physically and mentally.

▷ Commercials can be pressure as well.

◁ Oh sure. But compared with film, it's a day on the beach. You know, I spent eight years in art school. I spent five years as a painter and then I got a scholarship to the Royal – to the film school. In my last year as a painter I produced a half-hour film which the British Film Institute financed and then, based on that, Albert Fenney gave me money to make an hour-long movie which I wrote and directed. Then I got my diploma from the Royal College and I came out of the Royal College, after eight years as a student, owing a lot of money. And I got side-tracked into commercials. But I got into it, I loved it. I loved it as a way of life. I loved the fact that I was shooting. Shooting 100 days a year, two days a week, and I loved it, I loved the fact that I was getting to shoot film twice a week and it was great.

▷ You shot two commercials a week? That's really a lot.

◁ Yeah, but I didn't do it for the money. I did it because I loved it. I had a great life doing it. I got a reputation as a director, you know, shooting on tops of mountains, underwater. I also shot a lot of cosmetics stuff with pretty girls and rock 'n' roll and jeans and stuff, so I had a whole variety of stuff to do and was pulled and pushed in different directions all the time, which was great. And so I had a great life doing it and that's why I stuck with advertising.

But after ten years I thought I wanted to go back to a longer format. So then I came to Hollywood and chased one film for a year, and spent nine months down in Chile, we built a hotel eleven thousand feet in the Andes for a hundred and twenty men crew. But Paramount pulled the plug on the movie. Then I spent a year trying to get other scripts to do. And two films came up – "Flashdance" and "The Hunger." Adrian Lyne and I were up for both, though I was in a better position on "The Hunger" than he was. And he said that neither of the scripts were very good but beggars can't be choosers. So Adrian directed "Flashdance" and I did "The Hunger."

▷ "The Hunger" was a very good film.

◁ After "The Hunger" I couldn't get arrested. They hated me, they thought it was an indulgent, esoteric, art movie. What happened after "The Hunger" was that it took me two years to get another movie, and again I give credit to Simpson and Bruckheimer. They had just made Adrian famous with "Flashdance" – they produced "Flashdance" with Adrian. They like to take new young directors so they feel they can control them. They didn't like "The Hunger," but they cut through and they could see that I knew my craft, understood my craft, knew how to work with actors. So they gave me "Top Gun." And when they offered me "Top Gun" I read it and I thought, "This isn't for me," because my vision of my movies is always something that's darker, I wanted to make "Apocalypse Now" out of "Top Gun". So I went back to them and I said "I want to make it much darker and down and dirty and psychological." And they said "No, you've got to rethink it." And so I didn't want to do it. As a director you've got to find that hook, because film is so hard. It's like going to war every day. Unless you have a passion about what you're doing you shouldn't be doing it, because once you roll over you're dead. I've had a passion about every film I've done. I always have my hook. And each day when I'm sort of failing, I always go back to my hook. It was funny. I have Bruce Weber's book, original black and white coffee-table book, and there's one picture in there, just in the corner of the frame is this one guy sitting there, and he's a Navy Marine, and in his time off he looked a little bit like James Dean with his haircut and he was great-looking. It was almost like a 50s period piece. And all of a sudden I knew who these characters were, the characters I wanted to portray in "Top Gun."

And I went back to the boys, Simpson and Bruckheimer, at the studio, and I sold my soul in a way, but I didn't because I had a passion for it. I said this film is about the rock'n'roll stars of the skies, and I see silver jets against blue-black skies and it is an audio-visual experience.

▷ Visually it's a great great piece.

◁ Storywise it's predictable.

▷ Storywise...is exactly what I wanted to ask you.

◁ Predictable. That's why I turned it down originally. Because there was no mystery for me in the story. I could predict there was no mystery for me in the story. I could predict where all the beats were. But in the end what Don and Jerry, what Simpson and Bruckheimer did, was they made movies that they want to see. And I loved working with them because they had a tremendous passion about what they do. But they made a particular sort of movie. It's what I call a hard-core entertainment movie. And they weren't interested in trying to re-do "Apocalypse Now" with "Top Gun," and they were right and I was wrong. They had a particular film in mind and they got what they wanted in the end, and I kept fighting it. I understood, or I came to terms with understanding what they wanted. But I still had a passion, a passion I had to re-direct, to re-focus.

▷ What was the exact reason you compromised?

◁ When I say compromise it was re-direction. It's a different vision. When you say "compromise," I suppose my first compromise came when I said, "I see these guys as the rock'n'roll stars of the skies". I got a different hook...

▷ That's where the hook came from...

◁ Exactly, and rock 'n' roll music and great-looking guys. I no longer saw Sean Penn all wrung out down in the belly of an aircraft-carrier smoking a joint. All of a sudden I got a fix of Tom Cruise who is great for this piece in the way I re-focused it, and he became the Guy in the Bruce Weber photograph for me. And all the other guys. Val Kilmer, I think, was great in the movie. Val's got a darkness and a strangeness but it worked for that particular role as Ice-Man. In the end, I haven't committed to anything I haven't really had a hook or passion for.

▷ Certainly there are different levels of passion. As you said it's the rock 'n' roll passion, the rock 'n' roll of the skies.

◁ Exactly, yeah.

▷ Do you know who James Hosney is? He's sort of a film critic at the American Film Institute. He described "Top Gun" as the most homo-erotic movie mainstream Hollywood has ever produced.

◁ (laughs) Really?

▷ Yes, did you hear that comment?

◁ No. (laughs) But I know that "Suck" magazine in San Francisco, the gay magazine, voted the volleyball sequence there as its favourite sequence in any movie over the past four years. But to be honest, that sequence – we shot the volleyball in half a day. They gave me half a day to shoot it, so I didn't have the chance to style it or design it as I wanted to. So really in the end I just got three cameras and had to grab it. But the guys are great looking guys and we oiled them up, and there were the haircuts and the dog tags and the slo-mo.

▷ But this scene could also have been a commercial for some sneakers, if you had put some close-ups in there. The way it's cut it's brilliant. One thing which goes back to "The Hunger" is the use of the light. There's a very particular use of light and smoke. Did you choose this intentionally because of the esoteric approach you wanted to bring over?

◁ Yes. I think you'll find in all of the films I've done that they change a little bit according to the subject, but I still have my stamp on it. "The Hunger" was the most out there in terms of the mysterious and strange and that atmosphere has lent itself to a lot of smoke. At times you're aware of smoke and it should be just atmosphere as opposed to smoke, but I like the way light hangs in that environment, hangs in the smoke. So that's why I used a lot of smoke in that particular movie.

▷ Are you an adventurer?

◁ Yes. I rock climb. I've climbed much of the big north walls in the Alps.

▷ Like what?

◁ I've gone on the Eiger twice. That was my claim to fame. We didn't get up there though. We got up to the top of the Pillar, they call it, which is only 2000 feet up the wall and then the weather broke. I climb in the Dolomites, so most of my climbing is on the big walls in the Dolomites, the Italian Alps. I've climbed the China Grande and the Chubetta, the Mamalada. Basically all the big walls in the Dolomites.

▷ When you were kids back in England where did you and your brother get the inspiration from? What did you do for adventure as kids?

◁ As a 13-year-old kid I started to climb with an organisation that enabled us to get out of the bleak Northern working-class town where we lived, the North of England, the North-East...

▷ You're from the North-East?

◁ From Newcastle. The North-East is bleak and depressing but has enormous character. Within ten to fifteen minutes we could be out into the beautiful moorlands. So as a kid I always took off. I played rugby and hung out with all the boys and drank a lot of beer and got fucked up. And in the summer, in the second part of my childhood, I was within fifteen minutes of a small crag which was a hundred feet high. I'd go there in the summer evenings and run up and down it.

▷ Did you play together with your brother, team up?

◁ No, Ridley's older than I am.
Ridley and Alan Parker grew up together and Adrian Lyne and I grew up together. So Ridley and Parker are sort of a generation ahead.

▷ How many years older than you is he?

◁ Can't tell you, he'd kill me. (laughs) He's a little bit older than me.

▷ When you're brothers one is sometimes stronger. Was there this type of relationship?

◁ Yeah. Ridley and I have a production company called RSA. RSA is in London, New York, and L.A. and the two of us run this company. Rid is really the businessman, he's an excellent businessman. He's very strong and he's hell with business, he's a killer. But he's the best, and he enjoys it, he gets off on it. I'm not a businessman, and so I suppose my strength is keeping the people happy. On a day-to-day basis I stay in touch with the people who work in the company. There were three of us, three boys, and Ridley was in the middle, Frank was the eldest. Rid used to occasionally beat me up, and Frank would step in and beat Ridley up. There's a two-year difference between Ridley and Frank so they're much closer in age, and so they tended to do things more together than I did. I used to go off on my own. It's funny coming form the North-East, there's nothing creative within the family background. My great-grandfather was a blacksmith. He did write a book of poems, poems which he got off the miners down in the pits. He was a blacksmith in the pits. He used to shoe the horses. He wrote this book of poems. My dad occasionally did water-colours but they were terrible. That's about it. So it's funny that the two of us came out of that sort of environment.

▷ Why are you creative?

◁ I think it was the milkman (laughs)

▷ The what?

◁ The milkman. That was a joke.

▷ The milkman?

◁ The milkman. What I was alluding to was that the milkman made love to my mom. (laughs) The milkman was a painter. I don't know where it came from. Rid as a kid was always, from the age of six, was always drawing. He would sit for hours and just draw, and at the age of 13 was a brilliant draftsman. His drawings as a 13-year-old were like that. Do you know Moebus? French illustrator? There's a magazine called Heavy Metal. At the age of 13, I remember he was drawing the way Moebus draws, it was very beautiful. My in-roads into art, there was a very cute art mistress at school, I felt very sexually attracted to her, and she initiated me in all sorts of things other than art (laughs). But even before that I was the same as Ridley, I was always drawing. I didn't quite have the same passion that Rid had. I preferred the climbing or whatever, Rid would sit there and draw for hours on end. And then slowly I started watching what Ridley was doing. He inspired an interest in me to continue on and go to art school. I wanted to be a painter, what I wanted to do was paint. Slowly, my painting became more and more graphic, and then I was spending more of my time in the photographic department. Then I made a short film on my own shot on 16mm which I paid for with my own money, and produced with my flatmate. A strange, offbeat dream film, 'ten-minute one'. And based on that the British Film Institute gave me money to make a half hour move called "One Of the Missing" based on an Ambrose Bierce short story which was inspired by a film that I'd seen called "An Incident At Owl Creek."

▷ How would you describe yourself?

◁ What are my strengths? Very tenacious, very wilful, and I have a great talent for manipulating people. These movie guys say "you're not gonna do this". I say "okay, okay, okay" and then somehow I always, nine times out of ten, manage to get my own way. I found that in the beginning I'd have stand-up fights and say "Fuck no, I'm not gonna do it that way!" But I learned, especially with film, just to smile and say "Yeah." It's not a definite "yes," and then slowly I manage to get it back round to the way I want to do it.

▷ Somebody said never give up.

◁ Yeah, exactly. But also I work with people I want to work with. I enjoy what I do, and now I've got a crew around me which I've worked with for ten years. I spend time with these guys on and off the set. They're all oddballs, they're all strange offbeat characters. They give blood for me. They give blood for me because they see the passion I have about what I

do, and it instils a passion in them. I suppose that's one of my attributes.

▷ You've just manipulated the question into the positive, into the strengths. What are your weak points, then?

◁ My weak point?...God...sex! (laughs). Women are my weak point. My weak point is if I feel I haven't got someone on my side and they're not with me in terms of trusting... I don't like beating people up and saying "Just fucking do it." I want people to work with me, not against me.

▷ How do you work with actors on the set?

◁ The same. I get them on my side. I come to the set...I always do a lot of homework because I'm not good shooting from the hip and I need that preparation to be comfortable with the day's work. I storyboard everything. Every morning before I shoot I do two hours preparation before I come to the shoot and I storyboard the day's work and it's not just to show visually what I want from the scenes, it's therapeutic. It helps me work out what I want from the actors, what I want from the visuals, what I want from the overall tone of the piece.

▷ Do you give many directions on the set?

◁ Yes, constantly. My directions are very basic, I'm not an intellectual so I say, "It's too broad, it's too big, come down smaller, if you think it right you communicate it right. I'm just talking in basic terms.

▷ Some say if you cast it right you don't have to give directions – in commercials that is.

◁ But in film it's different. Film is a medium of control. Whether it's performance, light, art direction, whatever, I believe the director is there to control every element. Ten years ago people could afford to say "I'm a people director, I'm an actor's director" or "I'm a visual director." But now, both in film and commercials, you can't afford to be just pigeonholed in that category. You've got to be good at everything, it's too competitive out there. You've got to be an actor's director, a visual director, you've got to know what you're doing with your sound. You really do have to cover all bases.

My background is visuals so I started out hiding the camera. Especially when you get big-time actors. I'm still intimidated by them. My intimidation normally comes out of respect. Respect for people like Robert Duvall, Eddie Murphy, and therefore it's great when I find that they trust you. I like a good atmosphere on the set. A lot of directors like anxiety on the set. They like fights, they think they get a better performance. I think the opposite. I think you get a better performance when people are happy and relaxed and they can focus on what they're doing better. The best work I ever got on film I always relate to good days.

▷ Sometimes I figure producers can also be an ass.

◁ I've been fired many times.

▷ By producers?

◁ By producers, by studios. And re-instated the same day, fortunately.

▷ What was working with these guys Bruckheimer and Simpson like?

◁ What they did was they made me realise what I was capable of doing. They opened up my avenues, and I was capable of doing a comedy, which I never thought was my forte, but I got a hook and a fix of what I wanted to do with "Beverly Hills cop II."

▷ Basically they persuaded you, said you should do it?

◁ Yeah. At first I said, "I can't do it, comedy isn't my strength." I love Murphy, and I wanted to work with Murphy, but I read the script and I said, "I don't think this is for me." They said, "No, no, you can do it, you can do it." And I was intimidated by Murphy because I love what he does. He's one of the funniest men out there and I love what he does and I felt as if I was ill-equipped to direct him. In the end it worked out. I'd put him in situations and I was able to say "It's a bit too, it's too small." And it became a great two-way dialog. I really enjoyed the experience.

Don Simpson was the head of production at Paramount, and when he left they gave him the script for "Flashdance." It was a terrible handshake, not a golden handshake, because the script was awful. Adrian came back and said he didn't want to do it. He said, "Fuck, I don't want to do this thing." Then he kept watching his daughter watch MTV...MTV had just begun then. I think it was in the evening, two hours in the evening. She

Shot from Marlboro commercial
directed by Tony Scott

Tony Scott

used to be glued in to this rock 'n' roll station and he said "It's MTV, it's ninety minute MTV." And that was his hook, that was his fix, and the boys supported it. Paramount was terrified of it but Don and Jerry supported it.

▷ The death of Don Simpson must have been an incredible loss for you.
◁ Don I've known for twelve years. Twelve years. Was a friend, a very close friend and as well as being a business partner you know so, out of the twelve years I must have spent six years on a daily basis with him, yeah, so it's a huge loss when it actually happens, you know. It wasn't a surprise to me but you can never anticipate the ... the pain is a bad word but I guess it's a very, very clear word. You know, you can never articulate the pain that actually happens and it was really sad, very, very sad. He was one of Hollywood's greats you know, like John Barrymore, and in terms of party animals, in terms of characters, Don Simpson was one of the all time Hollywood characters and there are very few of those guys left in our industry today. You know in the industry, living has become much cleaner and healthier so that we don't get the same sort of characters as there were before – because previously there was drink or drugs to produce the madness in these people that made them what they were. But Don was very smart, very articulate and also very sweet and very loyal to his family, and that family was a very close circle of people with whom he worked. And he and Jerry Bruckheimer, they were, it was, right arm, left arm in terms of producing movies. They seemed to compliment each other in terms of their talents, yeah, and ah they were brilliant together.

▷ Tell me about "Days of Thunder", the only flop that you produced with Bruckheimer and Simpson.
◁ It was too fast. I had twenty day in post-production. I had three weeks in which to edit. The studio had a guaranteed 83 million dollars if we released on a particular date, which was June 27th. That was a big cheque, so they said 'we've got to get it done'. Because it was Tom Cruise behind the wheel of a racing car, everybody was lulled into a false sense of security, thinking that Cruise is enormous as a star, so whatever he did whether it was sit in that racing car and smoke a cigarette for a hundred minutes, was gonna make a lot of money. I think "Thunder" would have made a lot more of a monetary success if it had been released not surrounded by all these other big blockbuster movies. I felt disappointed, more with the post-production than the script. In post it became silly. I'd got lots of footage that I never got a chance to edit into the film because we ran out of time. For instance Cruise, in the middle of the movie, the turning point in his life is when he crashes. The car flips and there's this end-over-end, I shot it with 360 frames and 500 frames and the stunts were done at 140 miles an hour – I've got to say, definitely the best crash footage that had

ever been shot. After I'd edited the sequence I presented it to one of the executives from the studio, to Don and Jerry, and the show of hands dictated that all the slow-motion footage would come out. The sequence took me a week to shoot, and a show of hands and a thirty-second conversation and it was pulled out.

▷ How did you feel at that moment?

◁ Terrible, because I loved what I had. I fucking loved it. No movie has ever shot a crash like that before. Nobody has ever had the money, had the reason, or the time.

□

TONY KAYE
I invented Hype Art

Tony Kaye won many awards as an art director before he started his career as a director.
As a director he has won a phenomenal amount of awards.Breaking new ground has become his trademark. First with his British Rail ad "Relax", then with his Dunlop ad "Tested for the Unexpected" with a Velvet Underground soundtrack, then with his Volvo ad "Twister". All this before he took on Hollywood, where his first film was nominated for an Oscar.
Then he took on the bastions of the art establishment, such as the Tate gallery in London.
Nothing stops Kaye. He wasn't allowed to exhibit his work inside the Tate, so he exhibited it outside, in the street. (Where it got more media coverage than the work inside.)
I interviewed Kaye in London and Berlin.

▷ Hermann Vaske: Is it hype art exclamation mark or is it hype art period?
◁ Tony Kaye: No, it's hype art period, yeah.
What hype art is – hype art is basically any work of art, its value is accrued by how much hype it's had.
For example every gallery owner that sells a piece of hype art has to keep a record of all the hype on floppy disc or whatever, so that when a potential buyer comes into the gallery and buys it, you get so many points for ... you know, being on the television, or so many points for being in a news-paper or whatever. And the good thing about hype art is it never loses, it always goes up in value, because the minute the person buys it, it gets more press, you see, and it gets more points. So the value goes up.
So for example this piece of work here, which is not hype art, but I could turn it into a piece of hype art by stopping the taxi, right, and throwing it through that window over there and breaking that window, smashing into the shop. I'll do it if you want. And ... because then the police will come and I will be taken to the police station and tomorrow it will be in the newspapers and this piece of work will become more valuable as a result of that. Do you understand?
▷ Yeah, in the London advertising world, Tony Kaye is notorious. Some say he's truly crazy, others say he's just pretending to be in order to attract attention.
◁ There's a film I saw ages ago, about that bloke who has a plan to commit murder. The plan is that he kills a person, and he gets off on the grounds that he is insane. He reads all these manuals on these types of cases, and works out exactly what he should say and exactly how he should behave

VOLVO

Stills from Volvo commercial

in court. And his plan is that he is put in an asylum, and then, after six months, he lets on that he's recovered so that they review the case and let him out. He's released. So he does it. He walks up to the guy standing in the middle of a public place, goes up to him with a gun, kills him and goes to court. The court finds he's completely off his trolley, he gets put away. They do all these tests and after six months they say, "Yes, he's definitely off his trolley." The point comes where his plan was to go back to normal. They think, "Blimey, he's mentally recovering." They put him to all these final tests, and then, at the end of the tests they say, "No, we're terribly sorry, you're completely off your trolley." And the fact is that he's mad. To go to those lengths and do all that, you're completely around the bend. That's my only analogy. Sure, I've done lots of mad things, purely to attract publicity. But sometimes I think to myself, there must be an easier way. Do you understand the point I'm making? So I totally agree with the people who think what I've done is mad.

▷ He who attracts attention shows off. He who does not set himself apart doesn't get noticed.

◁ I think you should get noticed for the work you do. I don't think I'm terribly good at what I do. I do work very hard so I hope that the effort will produce results, and occasionally it does. Do you know the stunts I've done?

▷ Is it true you climbed up on the roof of Saatchis'?

◁ I'll tell you what really happened. It was a self-promotional stunt. I gave the cab driver who took me to Saatchis' a camera and some money, and he photographed everything. I went up on the roof and threw down some leaflets that said "You have to work with Tony Kaye". While I was doing that, they were having a meeting with the Conservative Party, and they rushed out and said "What are you doing there?" I said I'd come to check the railings and climbed out the window. Then I got chased all around the building. I made some prints of the cab driver's photographs and sent them around to people. And it worked. I did more work for Saatchis' than for anyone else.

▷ Let's talk about the hundreds of promotional letters you sent off to people in the business.

◁ I just like receiving peculiar letters, peculiar parcels. It's quite exciting, really. I'd arrive home bored in the evening, because I didn't get any scripts when I started out, so I started doodling at home. I started putting them in envelopes and sending them out to people. That's how my first production company, "Wandering Jew", started.

▷ Then, when no breakthrough came, you did your Hitchcock self-promotion on double page spreads in the daily newspapers. How did you get the chutzpah to compare yourself with Hitchcock?

Tony Kaye

◁ Because I thought he was the most important British director. I had to pick someone good.

▷ Does it bother you that since "Furry Friends", some people see you as an animal director?

◁ They see me as an animal. I don't know ... Hitchcock used to treat actors like cattle, so I don't see what difference it makes, really.

▷ In your case, you didn't work with cattle, but with a dog, a cat and a mouse. Was that difficult to shoot?

◁ The animals got along brilliantly, but not the trainers. They had different owners for each animal, and they hated each other. They were arguing throughout the entire shoot about everything. And while they were arguing, the three animals were getting along really, really well.

▷ How do you work with actors on the set?

◁ The actors do whatever they want to do. I pick them because they are right for the part, and I don't give direction at all. I believe in using what's already there. I think that if a director has to work too hard with an artist in front of the camera, then he's cast the wrong person. Casting and editing are the two most important things about directing.

▷ Do you rehearse with your cast?

◁ No, I'm too frightened that when I'm rehearsing and not filming, I might get something great and miss it. So I film everything.

▷ How did you hit on the idea of directing?

◁ I really don't know. I only learned about film-making from the directors' standpoint. Before I started directing, I'd never ever, in any shape or form, shot a piece of film. I've never even worked on one.

▷ So you plunged into the deep end?

◁ I picked up everything along the way. I've kind of learnt it the hard way, if you know what I mean.

▷ You started your learning process as an art director?

◁ Yes, at Collett Dickenson and Pearce.

▷ And you worked on Heineken?

◁ Yeah, I did that because it was easy and a big campaign. It was very visible. I was a sort of junior art director while I was there. It was an established campaign, which isn't difficult to work on. It was a way of getting noticed the easy way.

▷ Is that why you went to Colletts?

◁ No, I went because I was a designer and I wanted to work on radio and film. And being an art director gave me that chance really. Colletts was sort of the academy of advertising at that particular time. It was just a brilliant place to go and learn from people whom I kind of worshipped. It's incredible the people who came from there. David Puttnam ... Alan

Stills from "Tested for the
Unexpected" for Dunlop

Parker ... Charlie Saatchi ... Alan Marshall ... they all came from C.D.P. Incredible. The founder was a guy named John Pearce, whom people know very little about and who is, in fact, a genius. I don't know if you know a magazine called *Picture Proof*. It was a fifties photographic magazine. I'm not sure, but I think he was the founder of that, and he was also the founder of the Eagle Comic, which is one of the greatest British comics. And he formed the agency to do great work from the beginning. The atmosphere in those walls is really interesting.

▷ Was C.D.P. a means to an end, to get into film?

◁ Absolutely, from the minute I walked in the door. For no other reason.

▷ Where does your film obsession come from?

◁ You just start working with images, and you want to explore the entire process. Film is the ultimate, isn't it, because there's movement and there's sound and there's talking.

▷ Richter said in his book that film is the only art form that the 20th century has developed.

◁ Brilliant.

▷ And that means that anyone with an artistic ambition has no other choice than to do film.

◁ I would agree with you there. I have no choice.

▷ I once read that when you started out, you wanted to make a feature about the life of George Grosz. Why?

◁ When I was at art school I found out about him and I thought he was brilliant. And Berlin in the early thirties was the most artistic and brilliant period of all time, really. I mean I really like German painters. I don't know that many German people. My father comes from Gdansk, he came to England when he was about 12 or 13. In fact, my name is Kliegermann. It was changed to Kaye. I'm totally fascinated with that Berlin whatever it is. That rawness.

I was fascinated by the drawings, the brothels, that sort of stuff. I wanted to make a film that was all storyboarded by him and his work. The colours, the intensity of colours. It was not really going to be about George Grosz, because George Grosz's life isn't that interesting. He was a very quiet, subdued sort of bloke, I think, but it was his work ... it would have been like making a film about Berlin as if he was making it storyboarded by his own drawings. From his eyes, with Weill music, Hindemith and all that. That was five years ago, and in a way I've been proved right, because a lot of film-making, and particularly advertising right now in London, has gone to that Bauhaus German. That's what people are really, really into now. So I think maybe I was on the button some years ago. There was a band called Frankie Goes To Hollywood. Their whole philosophy and image

Tony Kaye

has that sort of Teutonic approach. It's never been exploited in the movies. It's something I'll do at some point. It will take a long time to be in that position, but I will do it.

▷ Isn't there always the danger that the copiers do better work than the avantgarde originators who started the trend?

◁ The copiers are always better than the originators, because when the originators do it, it's always a little bit raw and rough around the edges. They don't know how to perfect it, because they haven't got anything to bounce it against. That's what makes me sick about a lot of advertising. Something's borrowed from a Pop video or a feature film, and it's like cheating. Ads are getting awards for things like that. How can you give an award to something that is a direct rip-off of something else? Sure, it fulfills an advertising brief, and it might even do brilliantly for the product. But just because someone's taken an idea from an obscure source and made an advertisement out of it, and just because the public thinks it's brilliant and goes out and buy lots and lots of the product as a result, you can't give an award to that. Something's been stolen.

▷ Tony Kaye, can you honestly say you've never ripped off an idea?

◁ Who, me? Oh yeah, I do. But I'd say I'm inspired by something rather than ripping it off. I repackage it a little, so it's totally unrecognizable, and that's different, I think.

▷ How do you comment on the crossover of advertising and feature film directors?

◁ Anyone involved in film-making of any kind who turns around to you and says, "I don't want to make a feature film", is lying. They say that because they're worried about obtaining their next script from an advertising agency. They're just not being honest. 90 percent of commercial directors are only in it for the money.

▷ Did you ever turn down a script?

◁ No, I haven't. Now I would, but I would have done everything I've been given in the past. There's always something to be learned. I'm not saying that now I'd turn things down because I don't have anything left to learn. But now I'm in a position to say, there's no point in putting 59 billion decibels of energy into something if there's no point to it at the end of the day.

▷ You did commercials and music videos. How do they mix?

◁ In video, it's the song. If you get a crappy song, it's like getting a crappy script from an advertising agency.

I also believe that the sound track is 51 percent of film. When you're watching TV, it's the sound that fills the entire room. The sound fills every corner, yet the TV screen is just a little square in the room. Even the sound

Stills from British Rail commercial "Relax"

of an actor or actress's voice is important to how good that line sounds. You can have the worst bit of dialogue in the world, and if people are saying it with the most brilliant voices it sounds just fine. Watching a film is exactly the same. The sound fills the theater, and the screen is only a flat bit of canvas on the wall.

▷ If you look at *The Untouchables* dubbed, Robert De Niro loses all his Brooklyn charm.

◁ Right, exactly. Charles Bronson was a huge hit in the Middle East for years. The person who was dubbing his voice died, and they had to make a change. With a different dub, Bronson immediately flopped. It was that voice.

▷ Sound is important, but film is a visual medium.

◁ It is. It's a total medium of sound and picture, of which the sound is 51 percent.

▷ What about silent movies?

◁ Well, there was always the piano accompaniment. People are too sloppy with sound. It's a lack of respect, they don't know how important it is. They think it's important, but they don't realize it is more important than the picture. If they knew that, then they'd give it a lot more respect.

▷ Why are you so sensitive when it comes to sound?

◁ Maybe it covers up all the mistakes I make on the picture. I don't know, really. I listen to the radio when I sleep, so when I open my eyes during the night there's at least a bit of sound going on. (He looks at the tape recorder.) You should have one with you all the time, and turn it on whenever you're talking to someone. It will make a good conversation more interesting, particularly if you're chatting up a girl. It will make her pay more attention.

▷ Is sound the reason you decided to do rock videos?

◁ It's a longer form. I work within four minutes. There are a lot of techniques that I want to explore that I haven't been given the opportunity to do with commercials. I'm given that opportunity when I shoot a Pop promo.

▷ Do Pop promos need a story?

◁ Not always, but it helps. It depends on the strength of the song. It needs some kind of linking material, and that can sometimes be a story. When you're watching a film, you really shouldn't notice how it's cut, how it's photographed, how the performance is. If there's good music in there, you should be totally entrenched in the story ... carried along. If all these things are working at their most effective level, you're not actually aware of them. True, if you watch it three or four times, you're going to start picking up on things. But at a first viewing, you shouldn't be aware of any one thing.

Tony Kaye

▷ You also worked with Malcolm McLaren. Could you elaborate about that?

◁ I called him up and told him that we'd do the video to the wrong song. He said, "Great, when shall I send you the record?" I told him that I didn't want to hear it, because I wanted to do it to a different song. We never shot that idea, but I did two other videos for McLaren and CBS. My work with McLaren ended in a total dispute.

▷ Why?

◁ I think we were too much alike.

▷ Did he want to play director?

◁ Yeah, but I don't mind that. I don't mind working on a very close level. When I work with agency creative teams, we are unbelievably close. We talk about every shot, work hand in hand.

▷ What do you think is the best training for a young director?

◁ Short films. I think directing commercials can be very damaging if you want to make features, because most commercial directors become capable of only executing style. They have no idea of concept and content at all. There is no way that 90 minutes of film can just live as a piece of style, there has to be content and concept. That's why very few, if any, commercial directors have gone on to become great film directors. England hasn't produced any ... I suppose people would say the Scott Brothers and Alan Parker. I think Ridley Scott is a commercial director. Then again, the man has made Blade Runner and Alien. For me, both of those films are quite boring. You see, when you make commercials, you get pretty good budgets. Generally speaking, you have the ideal circumstances. It's kind of surreal. That's not what film-making is all about. I think that if somebody wants to make films, they should begin by making short films for themselves, not commercials.

▷ What are the components of a good film?

◁ A good idea, and an excellent collection of people. Characters and ideas. Characters come first and the idea comes second.

▷ What about the execution?

◁ The character is the execution.

▷ Sure, casting is a key element. How do you go about casting?

◁ My casting with each person lasts about 30 seconds. I just get a feeling sometimes I'm talking to them, sometimes I'm watching, sometimes Im listening. For my Pepe Jeans commercials, I interviewed 1000 people. I had to find the one person that I needed. Extraordinary people are one in a million.

▷ Why are you creative?
◁ I'm not.
▷ Marcel Duchamp once said: "A painting that doesn't shock isn't worth anything." Would you say that about advertising?
◁ The Mona Lisa doesn't shock, but it's still a good painting. There are different ways to get attention. Marcel Duchamp was talking about his own experience. He wasn't into execution, he was more into the concept behind the picture.
▷ Some people think you are the Enfant Terrible of British film directors. Do you see that as an obligation?
◁ I'm not the Enfant Terrible any more. I'm not extraordinary, this business is just very conservative. If you sneeze a little louder than someone else, people notice.
▷ Do you have an advertising complex?
◁ Well, advertising as a whole is a bag of shit. It's only that little bit of cream on the top that is brilliant. It worries me that I've spent a lot of years of my life doing it. But then again, it has given me everything I have.
▷ What was your funniest commercial?
◁ The Wickes Drills one. We did that with Mark Williams and Hayden Morris, and while we were making the commercial there was one shot that we thought would make a better commercial than all the rest put together. So, after the client bought it, we made our own one and entered it in the British Television Awards. It won a gold and somebody found out about it. Saatchis' had to pay loads of money, because the awards people make up a reel with all the gold winners, and Saatchis' had to pay for all the reels to be redone without the Wickes spot. But it brought the house down on awards night. We were there, so we picked up the award.
▷ What is your biggest wish?
◁ Give me a fucking script, you bastards.
□

ALAN PARKER
No creative work ever comes out of committees

Alan Parker started as an award winning copywriter at Collet Dickenson Pearce in the sixties. When he decided to become a director it was almost unheard of. Directors came from the film side of the business, not the advertising side. Then he did another thing that was unheard of, he used people with working class accents to sell products. His advertising films for "Birds Eye", "Silk Cut" and "Benson and Hedges" were breakthrough advertising to put it mildly. He soon became the hottest director in town. He didn't send you his reel, you sent him your scripts, and he'd see which ones were good enough. His first major success in feature films was "Bugsy Malone". Then "The Wall" with Pink Floyd and Bob Geldof, "Midnight Express", "Birdy" with Matthew Modine and Nicolas Cage, "Angel Heart" with Mickey Rourke, Robert de Niro and Charlotte Rampling and "Mississippi Burning" with Gene Hackman and Willem Dafoe followed. He shot "Welcome to the Paradise", then "Road to Wellville" with Sir Anthony Hopkins, the youth drama "The Commitments", and then his biggest production so far "Evita" with Madonna and Antonio Banderas. I met with Alan Parker on the Evita set of Shepperton Studios.

▷ Hermann Vaske: You've been away a long time shooting „Evita". You shot in Buenos Aires, in Budapest, and now you're filming in Shepperton. Your colleague Tony Scott described commercials as sprints and feature films as marathons. Do you agree?
◁ Alan Parker: Well, it's even more than that actually. I've been on this since June of last year. Actually I've been on it before, if you count writing it. So I've already been on it a year and a half, and I'll be on it another six months before it's finished, so that's two years compared with one day on a commercial.
That's quite a difference, isn't it.
So it's not about how good you are, but for how long you can be good. It's kind of an everyday job.
We film six days a week. I work seven days a week, so – it's hard work.

▷ Tell me about your relationship to Frank Lowe. You started at the same time in advertising, worked together successfully and are still friends today.
◁ I started in advertising, and met Frank, in an agency called Collet Dickenson Pearce.
He was an account man and I was a copywriter. And everybody thought

we would hate one another because of his very strong personality, and mine, but actually it was quite the opposite, it worked very well.

I went off to direct commercials and then, from commercials I went off into feature films. The first film I did was "Bugsy Malone" and I was thinking about music and Frank suggested Paul Williams, actually that was Frank's suggestion.

So we left for Las Vegas to find him. That's the story of the music of "Bugsy Malone".

▷ And the mission to Las Vegas was successful, you found him and he did it?

◁ Yeah, I mean, Paul Williams hadn't done a film at that point .

He was a quite popular songwriter and a singer at the time, and he was performing on stage in Las Vegas, so there was never any time to talk to him. That seems a long time ago.

So I could never really get him, I stayed there for about three days in my hotel in Las Vegas. Finally we got to have a meeting with him, finally read the script and it worked out very well.

▷ In the sixties and seventies you were the avantgarde of advertising and managed to break into feature film. Was that a magic moment in time?

◁ Yeah, I mean I'm of the opinion that there isn't a natural progression to go from advertising into feature films. Not really an obvious progression. It just so happened at that particular time we had a lot of people who became feature film directors. Myself, Hugh Hudson, Adrian Lyne, Ridley Scott, Tony Scott, so we made a transition.

But there have not been hundreds and hundreds of commercial directors going to feature film, quite the opposite was the case.

Almost every one of them failed, that's the truth.

So there isn't a natural progression at all, because we happened to be around at some period in time, and we made that jump.

But a lot of people automatically assumed that it would be an easy jump, but in fact in twenty years very few have made the change over.

I think they've very different worlds.

▷ Mike Figgis once said that he never saw a commercial that influenced feature film. Would you agree to that? Is there no mutual traffic between advertising and feature film?

◁ I don't know, I don't know anything that was influenced by a Mike Figgis film either, come to that.

I mean most commercials are really about things that happened in the rest of the world last year, whether it be entertainment, comedy or film. That that's always in some way pastiche of what's been done before. Originality, creativity, doesn't really come out of commercials.

The originality, creativity of commercials is how to use things that already have occurred in the world, in entertainment, or anything else.

I think that, on the other hand, when we first started, certain things did influence film, certainly in regards to light.

At that point in time, cinematography completely cracked way open and it was not just the influence of stills photography.

A lot of stills photographers were going into commercials using the same light that they'd used in their stills, and that actually influenced a whole generation of cinematographers that came out of commercials then.

I remember it 20 years ago, I don't see much of it now. But certainly to my mind that's the only thing that influenced cinema.

> ▷ What is the relationship between the narration in your "Murphy's" commercials and "The Commitments"? They seem to be very similar.

◁ You know, originally I was gonna do the Murphy's commercial. I haven't done a commercial for so long, like 14 years, isn't it ? So it's not something I do all the time, I did it really as a favour and I quite enjoyed doing it.

Stills from
Murphy's commercial

What they wanted to do originally was, they wanted some commercials for Murphy's based on "The Commitments".

So I thought I'd prefer to do them instead of having somebody else copy them, and maybe I wouldn't like it.

So I did them. And as it turned out, they didn't use the kids from "The Commitments" because they were too young to do beer commercials. So I kinda got into it, I thought I was actually gonna work with the kids in "The Commitments", who would star again, so, yeah, it was based very much on "The Commitments". They seem indeed very similar.

▷ What you got out of that commercial in regard to narrative performance and humanity is amazing for a commercial.

◁ It ought not to be difficult. There are plenty of directors who could do it. Unfortunately those directors normally don't work in commercials. It's difficult because in commercials there are too many people involved, too many art directors and copywriters and producers and clients.

They are the ones that mess up commercials.

Because they've all got a whole lot of opinions, and no great creative work ever comes out of committees like that.

That's what actually messes up most commercials, and that's why commercials aren't nearly as good as they used to be, because the freedom is gone for people to make them, you know.

Which is one of the reasons why feature film directors don't do them.

▷ Didn't you feel you were destroying your own legend by imitating yourself shooting "Murphy's" based on "The Commitments"?

◁ Well, better for me to copy myself than someone else to copy me, they're not gonna make the money.

There are enough people copying what I do all the time and making fortunes out of it, I thought maybe for once I should make some money out of it.

You know, I'd done three Murphy's commercials, I did a Sprite commercial for Frank Lowe, that's it, actually, in 14 years.

That makes four, so there's not very many.

▷ Dave Trott once said to me, you were the first to use people with working class accents to sell products?

◁ When we started in doing commercials, because it was the beginning of commercials in this country, we were searching really for another language that wasn't just everybody being handsome and everybody beautiful and everybody speaking with a middle-class accent. We used unattractive people, we used ordinary people, not unattractive people but people with character. I mean, probably the commercials I did were the first to do it in the area of advertising.

It wasn't really such a breakthrough because in the area of drama, in the theatre, in television, and even in film, that was already happening. So in a funny kind of way what we were doing was dragging advertising into the 20th century.

Alan Parker's early commercials and the introduction of the working class accent

Because it already was really backward, the whole of advertising in those days was based on class, particularly in Britain.

That you have to be upwardly mobile in order to buy that product, you know. And that kind of class thing was actually getting in the way.

And what we proved was actually, in order to sell things to people, maybe they should recognize what is said in the commercial. In those days that was quite revolutionary.

▷ Between the "Zulu"-commercial and "Evita", there are a lot of years and a lot of milestones films; like "Mississippi Burning", "Angel Heart" and "Birdy". How long are you shooting in Shepperton now?

◁ We've been filming "Evita" now for 14 weeks. Before that we recorded the music for three months, last year. Then we prepared the film and we have 1 more week of filming, and then I'll spend 6 months editing it. So we're close to the end of filming, fortunately. It was very long this one.

▷ The inevitable question: How was working with Madonna?

◁ Very easy. She's very good in the film. She did surprise a lot of people. She's in fact quite brilliant. She's a very smart lady, very talented. There are a lot of people who are gonna make a decision on that and they're going to be surprised. She's extraordinary, very easy to work with.

▷ Because some people are quite cynical about her acting, you know.

◁ Sure, well those cynical people are going to be surprised.

▷ Could you tell us something about the press coverage of the shoot in Argentina. When you and Madonna arrived there were demonstrations and, at the end of the shoot, you were invited by the President. Was that a natural progression or just clever PR?

◁ What happened was, we arrived in Buenos Aires and we drove from the airport there was this sign saying "Go home Madonna!" and "Go home Alan Parker!" and they were signed by some people called "The Commandos of the Peronista" and President Menem.

The ruling party at the moment is also a Peronist Party, and Eva Peron is either seen as a saint or a whore, depending on what your political point of view is.

So we were never gonna please them all.

And certainly a small group wasn't just pleased with us making the film at all.

So it was quite dangerous when we first started, and we were kind of fearful that it would be difficult, and with all this political graffiti obviously. And because of the celebrity of Madonna there were newspapers around a lot. So we were rather fearful that the Commandos of the Peronista might set up a bomb or something while we were filming, or just even demonstrations which could have been difficult and interrupted the work process.

Stills from
Zulu campaign

But in the end there was more of us than there were Commandos of the Peronista, so they left us alone.

In the end there was no trouble at all, and finally the President gave us the Casa Rosada for filming.

First time ever anyone has ever filmed in the Casa Rosada, using the balcony which was very important to me.

So when it started out I wouldn't have been surprised if we had to leave after two weeks.

When we did leave after seven weeks we felt quite triumphant – and alive!

▷ Madonnas sex book was regarded as very controversial. Do you agree with Marcel Duchamp who said "A painting that does not shock is not worth anything"?

◁ No, I don't agree with that.

I think that a good painting that shocks can be worth something, if it is a bad painting and it shocks it isn't worth anything.

With regards to Madonna and her book, you know, it was an expression of something she wanted to do, it was a creative decision that a lot of people didn't like.

But that's not all she is, and that's not all that she's done.

Evita won't shock, it is a highly original, musical film.

It won't shock.

I mean, this is not the Madonna of the sex book.

This is a very serious woman, you know, she's 37 years of age and she's put her heart and soul into it.

And she's somebody quite capable of changing herself.

She transforms herself in a creative sense, and has done so ever since her career began.

And this is a Madonna no one has ever seen, and it's a very serious Madonna.

And I think largely talented one.

This may sound like publicity, but people are gonna be surprised how good she is.

▷ We spoke about provocation. Is the element of provocation paramount for you to become interested in a film idea?

◁ Yeah, I think provocative is probably a better word than shocking.

I mean the fundamental sin of any creative work is to bore people.

It's my job making a film to shake people with regards to the normal, boring kind of films that have been made.

I hate pretentious filmmaking. The hardest kind of film to make is a film that has its own voice and its own spirit, that also has integrity, that also reaches a large audience.

That's the most different kind of film to make. That's what I endeavour to do all the time.

Stills from "Evita", starring Madonna and Antonio Banderas

▷ Are you as director always looking for the truth?

◁ You know, as a director, the one thing I always constantly said, if you're watching a performance, is that if it's not honest, then it doesn't work. If it's dishonest then the viewer, the observer, will detect that.

That honesty is integral to the creative process in my opinion.

▷ Were do you get your creative stimulus from? What about reading?
◁ I've just been given "Brave New World" which I started to read lunch time, which is an old book by Aldous Huxley.
I hadn't read for a long time, so I started to read that.
When you're making a movie you get very little time to read.
I actually finish here at the studios at 11 o'clock at night.
It's about time to go home. I hardly have the strength to eat let alone read.
So reading will start the moment I finish shooting next week. I got a lot of catching up.

▷ It's interesting, in preparation for this interview I re-watched "Angel Heart" and "The Commitments". That was as marvellous as reading a book you liked for the second time.
◁ Well, you see other things each time you look at a movie, I suppose. When I'm making a film, I probably will see it 20 to 30 times before anybody else sees it. Actually, truthfully, I only ever see it for real, when an audience sits there, you know, when I'm sitting amongst an ordinary audience, and suddenly it takes on a different way. There are things that you might not have seen before, even though you've made the film.

▷ Frank mentioned to me that you always arrange an exclusive sneak preview for the Lowe agency before your films come officially to the cinema?
◁ It's a tradition. I'm very superstitious, and every time I finish a film, you know, I wanna show it to certain friends first. I always show it at Frank's agency, as Frank has always been a supporter and helper to me outside of business. He's also my friend, you know. So it's rather nice to continue the tradition.

▷ Frank's obligatory set visits are part of that tradition as well?
◁ Yeah, Frank always sends champagne to every film that we've done, and sometimes he forgets and we have to remind him. On "The Commitments" he arrived on the last day. This year, he was quite early actually, so we had quite a large share, he sent five cases of champagne, so every day on the call sheet I raffle two bottles, so there's a winner each day of Frank Lowe's champagne. They don't have any idea who Frank Lowe is, the crew, but they're just personally sent champagne.

▷ And Frank told me that he forgot to send his champagne tribute on "Road to Wellville".
◁ There you go, you see? He better keep sending his champagne on this one, so hopefully it'll work.

▷ Your lead actor on "Road to Wellville", Sir Anthony, is now also directing. Do you think it's a healthy progression for actors to direct?

◁ I think it's very healthy, yeah. I think, that there are lots of very good examples of actors who can direct. He's a highly intelligent man, and therefore I'm sure he'd be a good director. It doesn't always work, I think most actors are lazy, and actually being a director is hard work.

So I think they're always surprised how hard it is.

With regards to the intelligence and the creativity necessary, surely a lot of actors are quite capable of directing.

Whether they are capable of getting up every morning, every single day, for six days a week, for a year and a half, I'm not so sure about that.

□

JOE PYTKA
All good ideas come from God

No other director in the world has won so many Lions and Clios as the "leader of the gang" from Venice Beach. Apart from leading the commercial arena, Pytka found time to direct the feature film "Let it Ride" with Richard Dreyfuss, and the box office hit "Space Jam" with Michael Jordan, Bill Murray and Bugs Bunny.
I interviewed Joe at Cannes, and in LA.
Despite his rough and tough image Joe has a big heart and terrific viewpoints, so that talking to him was always a learning experience for me.

▷ Hermann Vaske: Joe, you did 2 features "Let it Ride" and "Space Jam" and you had the privilege of working with Bugs Bunny which not everybody has.
◁ Joe Pytka: Pain in the neck.
▷ Why?
◁ Should have said pain in the ass. He's a pain in the ass. He doesn't care about anything.
▷ Bugs Bunny?
◁ Nasty. Nasty critter.
▷ Why?
◁ No, I'm just kidding. Buggy was funny. He was great. Bugs was funny. Worked with him a lot. Did two commercials and now we did this movie. So, we've worked with Bugs a lot.
▷ How was the production?
◁ Beyond belief. Pre, during and post, very difficult. Drives you crazy. You have to focus so clearly on things. It's difficult. You're shooting on a green stage to separate the live action people from the background people the movie I'm talking about, the commercials we kind of shot mostly on live sets but on the movie we shot on a green stage with little dots, and after a while you think you're in prison because everything is green, and you're there and you have little guys in green suits with the different sizes of the characters and you're doing little sketches and you have to be very aware of that and you have to kind of pump up the performers to make sure that they are up to the level. And the performers too, it's difficult. Michael Jordan did a great job.
Oh he's really terrific in this movie. Fabulous. Shockingly fabulous.
▷ Is it true that you built an basketball court especially for Jordan?
◁ Oh, the studio did that. They did it, in order to keep Michael fit for the coming season they built an entire basketball arena. It was air conditioned they called it the Jordan dome. It was a cloth building. But full size basketball court, it was a cool place. Fabulous. A lot of great basketball players came here to play with him and then while we were filming we had some

great basketball players doing the filming.

▷ You played with them as well?

◁ Yeah, sure I played with them a lot. I have to keep modest! Everybody else gets out of his way, I trod on him, to block him from going to the basket. I trod on a few feet! No. He's a brilliant, brilliant human being.

▷ Could you elaborate about the storyline of Space Jam?

◁ The storyline is very similar to the commercials we did for Nike. Michael Jordan is retired from basketball, Bugs Bunny in the Loony Tunes character faces a big dilemma from outer space and the only person that can save him is Michael Jordan. So, half the movie is Bugs Bunny trying to persuade Michael Jordan to help and the rest of the movie is Michael Jordan trying to help and it's pure entertainment.

▷ Does it bother you to have the reputation of being passionate and sometimes rude?

Frank Mettman Jr.
October 1999

◁ No, why? You know, something happened to me recently. And this is what happens when you've got a certain bit of power or certain respect. I was working on the set recently and one of the actors was making a conscious effort to disturb during the takes. It was a very complicated set and everything had to be very precise. And everybody was working

SAVE THOUSANDS on MEDICAL BILL

Mettman HOME SURGERY KIT

incredibly hard and it took about 6 or 7 hours to rehearse the shot. And this actor was not concentrating. He kept missing his marks and doing something silly each take. And after about three or four of these I went after him and I just screamed at him. Because he was purposely being a jerk. And there comes some point in time where you have to call attention to the fact: "This guy is an asshole." And he wants to behave like an asshole in front of everybody. And everybody in the crew knows he's an asshole. And the only person who doesn't know he's an asshole is him. I'll be the person to tell him. I showed him that the first five or six takes, where he was just making these stupid mistakes, were just a matter of him being a jerk. Costing everybody a huge amount of money, costing 50 or 60 people a huge amount of discomfort. But using violence? No, never! Violence is never an answer to anything.

stamps.com
Postage from your printer.

▷ "Say it with a smile," as the English commercials director Paul Weiland says.

◁ Oh, that's the British way. The English have a great tradition of dealing with things with wit and humour. That may work in England, but sometimes doesn't work here. Because we don't know what wit is in the USA. We are kind of a primitive nation.

Commercial for stamps.com,
Gold Lion Cannes 2000

▷ A good example of American wit which is on you is that T-shirt, done by Fallon McElligott.

◁ "Fuck you." The front said "Fuck You." The back said: "Joe Pytka's School of Charm." David Mamet once told me a funny, funny phrase. And it explains "Fuck You." There comes a time when behaviour is so absurd, so ridiculous and so insulting you can say "Fuck You. End it right now". Nothing ends any kind of stupidity quicker than "Fuck You." Occasionally you have to do that. Because sometimes people under the pressure of this business get so irrational that their behaviour destructs everything and causes chaos. And there comes a time when someone in charge has to say STOP THIS RIGHT NOW. The quickest way to say this is to say „Fuck You."

▷ You've done hundreds of commercials. What was your funniest story on the set?

◁ It's a tough one. Funny things don't happen that much. You know, weird things happen. I just think that the funniest thing that ever happened on a set, and I don't want to talk about the circumstances, that comes to my mind quickly, goes as follows: I had a client who locked himself in his car in the parking lot and refused to go back on the set because his feelings had been hurt. So I had to go out to talk him back into the set.

▷ And he sat in his car with all the locks down?

◁ All the locks down and the windows rolled up. And the funny thing was, the producer convinced me to talk him back into the set. And I went against my best wishes and I went out to the parking lot and he was sitting there in his car. It was a big Cadillac and I remember he was sitting in the middle of the front seat like a little boy. And I came to the car, and when he rolled the window down he rolled it down like about half an inch. So we talked through the window and he finally came back on the set.

▷ What do you think of American advertising?

◁ They are very conservative, very profitable, I guess. It's very conservative here. Maybe cable or MTV or something like that. But even MTV is just noise. Some cable stuff is not boring. We're getting very conservative in our advertising.

▷ What about your work?

◁ For my work I don't care. I try to push limits. I talk about advertising in general. The opportunities to do good work are narrowing down considerably.

▷ With Hal Rhiney you produced one of the most interesting TV campaigns of the last decade. How did you hit upon the Ed and Frank concept for Bartles and Jaymes?

◁ Hal worked on that for years before they did it. Quite a long time. Within other jobs he was working on the concept for Bartles and Jaymes. It took a tremendous amount of effort on his part. He created the entire campaign, the whole mystique about the guys. Hal and Jerry Andelin, the art director, worked it out. Worked out the packaging. All those things. So when we got together and did the stuff it was very easy for me because

they worked out all the hardest parts. The first time we shot we shot about 10 or 15 commercials. They are very easy to shoot. They are quick jokes. They were the most witty things I've ever heard. I mean the writing in them was brilliant. It's never been done before, and it never will be done again.

▷ What do you think of Wieden & Kennedy, Oregon's creative hot shop?
◁ I love Wieden & Kennedy. They do fabulous work.

▷ How did you get into the business?
◁ I started at the end of the first creative period in American advertising in the early seventies. I started doing commercials seriously in the early seventies. Late 1971. Up to that I was more involved with documentaries and things. And with occasional commercials here and there.

▷ Is broadcasting your background then?
◁ Yeah, I worked in public broadcasting. At that time it was called the National Education Television Network. And then I did myself documentaries.

▷ What kind of documentaries?
◁ Everything. I did documentaries on conductors, symphony conductors. I did a documentary on air pollution. I did a documentary on industry workers. I did a documentary on my hometown. I did a series of documentaries for the National Aeronautics and Space Administration. Lots of subjects. But I got frustrated by the form.

▷ What do you think of innovative documentaries like "The Thin Blue Line?"
◁ I absolutely love "The Thin Blue Line." It's very crude but it's actually not crude enough. If it were a little cruder, like the documentaries of the sixties, it might be even more effective. But the subject matter is so

powerful and it's so unusual, I think it's the most interesting film I have seen in about five years. I tell you it's an incredible film in many ways. If you can get the audiotape of the music it's mesmerizing. You listen to it in your car, it's almost like an opera. Oh, it's fabulous. They've taken the best parts of the film and put them on tape with the music and it's almost like an opera. It's just an audio cassette. It's Philip Glass. It's the composer. You listen to it in your car. It's totally captivating. The rhythm, the speech and everything is just phenomenal. It's not the Philip Glass music that makes it powerful. It's the people, what they say. The rhythm of the speech and the truth and the power of what they say. If there are ways to honestly get the documentary form in a dramatic film, it would be ...

▷ ... worth an experiment.

◁ Yes, I tried in the video that I did for Michael Jackson to make the opening of the film like a documentary. It's called "The Way You Make Me Feel." And the first half of it is docudrama. A lot of handheld spontaneous things. A lot of the performances that are sort of documentary nature. It sounds like you're hanging around a street corner with these guys. And we put it to a music track. And it's very powerful. But it was misunderstood by a lot of people.

▷ It's really interesting how the viewer decodes documentaries. There is a book that tries to answer the question if there is any such thing as an objective documentary. The author analyses a documentary film about mine workers in Bolivia. Take-by-take and frame-by-frame. He uses lots of inserts to compare the results. If you, for instance, shoot the mine workers in their folklore costumes with a lama in the background you immediately associate happy indios and a package tour of Thomas Cooks Travels. But if you pan to the right and put the camera in a slightly different angle and shoot the mine workers in their working gear chewing coca leaves, the viewer thinks of hunger, starvation and poverty in the Third World. The quintessence of the book is: there is no objective documentary.

◁ Yes, there is no objective documentary. There can't be. There is no such thing as a true documentary. It might document people but it's still from the point of view of the filmmaker. I manipulated my documentaries. I put music in to intensify the emotional moments. And they polarise people. When I did a documentary on workers I used songs like Bob Dylan's "Maggie's Farm" and some of the Richie Havens stuff just to give an emotional viewpoint. Because the film didn't have it. What the people were saying wasn't sharp enough emotionally. What they were doing had to be underscored. And I wanted the documentary moments to give a strong viewpoint about my viewpoint about these people. I did not want to leave the audience the chance to perceive something about this on their own. What I found is that you always have to prepare an audience for a film or a commercial if you try to do something breakthrough. If you

gonna just rehash some clichés , you can just do it like it's been done before. But stuff like the new Lee jeans commercials we did and some other things we had to sort of do groundbreaking. People were kind of angry at first when they saw them because they felt they were disturbing, which is exactly what we are trying to do.

▷ Did you want to make the people angry?

◁ Anger, oh wonderful ...

▷ ... said the old dadaist.

◁ Dada exactly. That's exactly what we are trying to do. We're trying to break down on editing, sound and formal composition. I kind of laugh at people who think that photography for example, good photography is strictly beautiful compositions. A sunset, a range of mountains, a beautiful girl. And things like that. Those are easily absorbed pieces of beautiful compositions, but when we are talking about Man Ray, I'm sure that many of his compositions aren't that formal and beautiful but still wonderful photography. Henri Cartier-Bresson was a great photographer. But his compositions and his choice of subject matter weren't necessarily beautiful. He certainly was a far greater photographer than Ansel Adams, who did these big formal landscapes. But if you show Ansel Adams' work and Cartier-Bresson's work together to a general audience they will say that Anselm Adams is the better photographer because he's shooting mountain ranges and stuff like that, which are easy to absorb. We are talking about manipulation here. It's very easy to manipulate a mass of people. And you find that today in totalitarian societies.

▷ The soul of the mass audience and the rules of their manipulation and leadership as described by Gustave Le Bon were perfectly adapted by the Nazis.

◁ "The Triumph of the Will" and the movie about the Olympic Games are perfect examples about that. Another piece of propaganda is "Battleship Potemkin." That is a beautiful film, but it's still propaganda. It's the same as Olympia 1936. I find that Potemkin is a piece of propaganda. I can't watch it or its filmmaking because I get polarised by the propaganda. I can see it in the film. So if people call it a great classic movie, I kind of say it's nothing but a commercial. Except it's for the Bolsheviks instead of a soft drink. It's the same as „Triumph of the Will" and the Olympic film. Propaganda is nothing more than a glorified commercial. All the commercials are propaganda. The films that I like are films that deal more with human elements, usually of a very primitive nature.

▷ For instance?

◁ Well, a modern film would be "Chinatown." The thing that intrigues me about a film like "Chinatown" is not the political stuff and the water and politics and the real estate deals in Los Angeles, but the thing that intrigues

me is how those two people fall together, get together. It's so polarising in the beginning and then they fall in love. And that's the most interesting thing about that, and that's what the film is about. The closer you get to those elements, the better, but as soon as you get a political content in the film, it sort of gets more commercial. You know I grew up in the fifties. And I became aware of film in the fifties and early sixties. When I was at college I started to look at European filmmakers like Truffaut, Godard, Fellini and Antonioni. And the experiments that were done in music and jazz. Coleman and John Coltrane were totally free. I mean that they were free of any type of worry about the dynamics of economics or making trillions of dollars. "La Dolce Vita," "La Strada" and things like that were magnificent films. I mean when we saw for example "Breathless" for the first time, we went "Oh, what's this?" And it made you angry. We went to see the film, and all off a sudden it was like a new vocabulary we didn't understand anything about and said "What is this?" I dont't think things happen like that now. Anyway I'm excited about "Sex, Lies and Videotape" for what it represents in terms of ... It's a personal film, done for a small amount of money.

▷ Yeah, 1.2 million.

◁ That's what they say. But I admire the fact that it was done and it was done for that kind of money. And it has that fresh approach.

▷ Let's talk about your other movie "Let it Ride."

◁ In that film I had to fight to keep everything so people could see that kind of reality in performances. And I've been criticised for that.

▷ Some of your critics were missing a motivation in the main character.

◁ How can they miss a motivation? Dreyfuss as a positive gambler. It's a sickness. That's his motivation. He's compulsive. He's like a dope addict. If they wanted some articulate motivation, then they should go to some other film. This film starts in the middle of the story. It doesn't start at the beginning of the story. See, most stories say this is the guy, this is what he does, this is what happens.

▷ Yeah. Shakespeare's beginning, middle and end. Like in real life.

◁ Yeah, and this film is the middle of a story. You come in in the middle of a scene. The main character is a compulsive man. As soon as you see Dreyfuss you know he's a compulsive gambler who as soon as he gets a tip goes crazy. You see it, he explodes. He's almost like a junkie who hasn't had drugs for a long time seeing a guy on the streets with a bag of heroin. And he has 50 dollars in his pocket.

The first scene in the film sets up the fact that Dreyfuss had a bad time. He had problems with his wife. He promises he won't drink and gamble anymore. The second part of the film sets up the fact that his partner is a weird guy who tapes conversations. He sees these two sinister figures in the back of his cab and they are saying something about a horse. The guy is such an idiot. He's taping conversations. Weird conversations in the back of his cab. Sex stuff and things like that.

He goes to play Trader, who is Richard Dreyfuss' character, the tape of the sex conversation and he rewinds it too far. He plays the other conversation. As soon as Dreyfuss hears one snip of the other conversation about the horse he knows that is it. That is the tip of a lifetime. That's the motivation. I can't believe anybody who does not see this. That's why you cast a guy like Richard Dreyfuss. You cast a neurotic compulsive actor for this role. If you cast Tom Hanks for this role you would have 3 scenes to show how Tom Hanks got there. If you cast Richard Dreyfuss, as soon as you see him you know exactly what's going on.

▷ Not every actor is a Richard Dreyfuss. What do you do if you have to work with difficult or bad actors?

◁ I don't get upset with actors too much. It doesn't pay to get upset with most actors because they just get upset with the work. Instead of screaming at an actor I scream at one of the crew members. And then apologise to that crew member. I have certain selected crew members who understand that. Because sometimes you work with an actor who's really not up to the standard. Especially in commercials, when you sometimes don't have time to work with the actor a lot. Editing could shape the performance better. When we shot "Let it Ride" we always did half a dozen takes of a thing. And I tried to shoot with multiple cameras as much as possible. So that if in fact a specific performance among the players didn't work, we had enough coverage to cut it and edit it properly.

▷ How do you work with the creatives on the script? Do you sit down and work with Hal Rhiney and other people?

◁ No, not with Hal. Other ones yes but not with Hal. I work with some other writers but Hal is a concept writer. He's the "auteur" of his commercials. Hal's scripts are perfect. He works the scripts out himself to the level of a great playwright. It's perfect. The demands he puts on himself are far greater than the demands you put on him. But sometimes we work with other writers, they may not have the power of control of their work. So, generally speaking, what I try to do when I get scripts that I want to do and I see their weakness is over the writing, I try to talk to the writer about changing them.

▷ What about storyboards? Do you take the big marker and change the pictures on the storyboard as well?

◁ I don't pay attention to storyboards at all. I never pay attention to storyboards. I only pay attention to the content of the story. The script is more important than the storyboard. I'd rather just get a script. Don't tell me how to shoot it, don't tell me what the compositions are, don't even tell me what the location is. Just give me the script and then all the other elements will dictate how it's shot. There used to be a kind of habit in directors, especially in commercials, where there is an established pattern of commercials. First shot is the big spectacular shot. Show where you were and then the rest of the stuff is ... That doesn't interest me anymore. The scene is the only thing. David Mamet once wrote that anything in the frame, or anything in the play that is not further to the drama, is destructive. And this is a fault in a lot of filmmakers. A lot of directors, particularly commercials directors, put people in such a visually over-stimulated environment that you lose sense of the drama quickly. In truth most commercials makers have no sense of drama or dramatic content because most commercials don't have it. It's not that they can't deal with it. It's just that most commercials don't have proper emotional content. That just doesn't exist. It's so much effort in selling something that there's not enough humanity in there.

▷ What does a commercial need to get that sense of humanity?

◁ Human drama. People say human drama, which is comedy. Comedy is drama in a way. But it has the humanity. And humour that comes out of human relationships is more important to me than jokes. Some of the commercials that I worked on that I think are ideal for human drama would be the John Hancock commercials. Because they are only involved in human content. You are seeing a dramatic moment between people and then the advertising message is contained in the cutaway stuff.

▷ That's very emotional.

◁ Yes, because when you're seeing it you see people in emotional moments. And over here you're seeing the hard, dry reality of their exi-stence. The problem here and there the facts. There is a tremendous power there if you get it. Europeans didn't get it at first. When they first saw the campaign they hated it because in many ways Europeans are much more protected with their personal lives than Americans are. We really do tell people the darkest secrets of our lives. Whereas the Europeans are generally very reserved, particularly the French. They are reserved about how much money they make, they don't tell you how much their car costs, they don't tell you how much their houses cost, things like that. Well, Americans they blast these things out. But that's what these commercials were; they are not meant to be obnoxious, but they are like observations of these people. There's a dramatic moment between these people. A moment about their lives, a moment about a conflict in their lives. A moment of happiness, whatever. But there's the hard reality of their existence. And if you get it, it's wonderful.

▷ Your background as a documentary filmmaker shows in the Hancock stuff.

◁ We tried to make the performances and the filmmaking as realistic as possible to get away from the normal conventions of commercials. We tend to look at things in different ways. The Hancock campaign was very successful. Now it's been copied a lot and it's been corrupted. And it's been sort of parodied. And it lost perhaps its power. But the writing has always been brilliant. The writer Bill Heater is a brilliant writer. He is able to write convincing realistic dialog. Because he not only writes the essence of what people say, but he writes the style in which they say it. Heater writes the way people pause, the way they mumble, the way they say things in an eccentric manner. And very few people write like that. Rhiney writes like that in a very stylized way. Heater writes like that in a very natural way, as does David Mamet. And when you hear that dialog it's so rich and it's so shocking because of its unusual quality. And that to me is the best example of that type of emotion and realism in commercials.

▷ Believe it or not, I've heard people in agencies say: "Hey let's do a Joe Pytka style commercial. Let's use some inserts."

◁ That's not the essence. It's not an insert. It's tied together like this. It may be shocking visually. But see, they only look at the surfaces. It's curious, I lecture a bit in universities and stuff. And we discuss things after the talk. I don't have any particular philosophy that I try to look for. But the thing that always upsets me is that people only talk about the surface way of how they do stuff. What film stuff you use, what lenses, what cameras. Do you use a dolly? Do you use a crane? Things like this. They never talk about things we talk about, the emotional quality of it. What the writing is, how to change a phrase so that it sounds better, that it sounds real. Is this actor convincing in this role? How do you get a con-

Pytka's Pepsi commercial with Shaquil O'Neil

vincing actor? How do you get a performance out of a non-actor? They never ask those questions. They always ask superficial questions. That's why if we go to see films nowadays all we see are films for technique. It's all actors stumbling around on camera with crane moves and steadycam shots. Where the performance is to me tremendously lacking. The films that are popular are the films that seem to be trendy and predictable.

▷ You are not always dealing with a student audience. How did you feel when you were on stage at the Palais du Festival in Cannes and you heard the boos?

◁ First of all I'd been forewarned by a journalist that there was gonna be some booing at the festival. So what I did when they started I just lifted the Grand Prix and I had the Palme d'Or in the other hand. And the booing stopped a little bit. And when I just looked around the booing faded tremendously.

▷ So looking them straight in the eye worked?

◁ Yes, I walked to the front of the stage. And when I looked people straight in the eye they stopped booing. It's the only way to deal with

Joe Pytka

that. And it's an image they will never forget, the image of me holding the Palme d'Or and the Grand Prix up in the air in front of them as long as they live. Because it doesn't matter how long they live, the Palme d'Or and the Grand Prix are sitting next to the other Palme d'Or and Grand Prix that I won. And these guys go back empty. The final picture is me. In many ways I feel like Duchamp. It was shocking to them. Work that has this element of controversy when people love it or hate it. Work that is totally accepted by the public tends to be mediocre. I think if the public totally accepts your work without bitterness, without controversy you're successful. Because what you are doing is making too many people satisfied. I can't imagine doing a piece of work that makes everybody happy. I can't imagine that. Because in order to do that you have to take away all the elements of quality.

▷ A German award-winner who was booed at the award ceremony told his critics later: "Your booing gave me an erection".

◁ Ha, that's fabulous. Remember the group of German writers and painters that got together 15 or 20 years ago? And they would meet periodically and be absolutely honest with each other about their work. It was Günter Grass and the others.

▷ Gruppe 47, yes.

◁ They were just brutally honest. We're not like that here. There is too much diplomacy. There comes a time when creative people should get together and say: „This is good, this is not, this is shit". Directors here don't talk to each other. When I meet other directors they talk about money, they don't talk about their work. They worry about this, they worry about that, they worry about their fees. It would be wonderful if we could get together and have some food and have some wine and talk and be honest with each other. And say: „Your criticism gave me an erection. Your script made me puke. Your photography was wonderful. How did you do that?" Whatever is honest.

▷ Why are you creative?

◁ Why am I creative? What is creativity? Creativity implies something godlike. I'm not sure if this word should be used, "creativity." Creativity is a word that is misused and abused. I think creativity comes from God. God creates. Nobody else can create. Man can ...sort of... I don't know. It's not creativity. It's not making something from nothing. There must be some other word for it: But I won't argue about semantics. But I do what I do because I like making things, expressing myself. It's not necessarily creativity. I like expressing my viewpoint about things through my work. And I think it's just an extension of carpentry or masonry. If you build a building or build a wall or something you try to be your best. What I do best at this point is filmmaking. And the elements are the drama, the photography, the music. Those are just parts of how you express yourself. Plus what we use. Cements or stone or brick or whatever to build a building or a wall or something. What I do is just a matter of building the best wall I know how to make, with the tools I have at my disposal. And as I get older and more experienced, I know how to use my tools better and my people better. The actors, the crew and things like that. It's just the stories I can tell or the images that could be done become more imaginative and more interesting. I tell a story in a different way. I don't want to repeat myself. It's really a bluecollar way of expressing yourself. It comes from a kind of gut thing as opposed to a head thing. I think most of my work comes from here (touches his belly) to here. Rather than from here (touches his head) to here. It comes from an emotional quality to my hands and to feelings in my body, but not from an intellectual standpoint.

▷ So communication is not an intellectual sport for you?

◁ It's not intellectual at all. It's more of a craft. It's a very high craftsmanship as is music. And inspiration in it comes from God. It's funny that I find most good ideas come from God. I was thinking about this the other day. Because we were arguing about a commercial. And the commercial was incredibly well written. It's perfectly written. And I have to tell you the writer doesn't understand his own commercial. He wrote the commercial and he doesn't understand the people in it. He doesn't understand how good it is. He doesn't understand how perfect the idea is. It's a perfect idea perfectly written. And he doesn't understand it. All he did was write it down on a piece of paper. And somebody else gave him the idea. I don't know where it came from. But he doesn't understand his own work. It's frightening. So what happened was some inspiration came in. He was somewhere and happened to be fortunate enough to write it down before it disappeared. You know things like that, right? You get an idea or something comes from whatever. Get it down on paper.

▷ The filmmaker Joe Pytka as a transmitter of divine ideas.

◁ Yeah, there's no question. I've written about six or eight screenplays. In every instance when the idea came, it came out of nowhere. It did not come out of thinking about it, it came out … it just came. And I went back and wrote it down. If there was a problem to be solved in a screenplay the idea would come from somewhere. I don't know where, when we worked on Hancock I was talking to Heater. He was writing something so beautiful: "So where did the idea come from?" I asked him. And he said: „I don't know. It just came". It just came. He doesn't articulate it, but I'm sure it comes from the same experience. But sometimes I see some work that is so perfect from some people and sometimes they are not capable of writing this. They wrote this, but they are not capable of writing. I say: „Where does this come from? This is such a brilliant idea". But how did this come to you??? It's like the gift of tongues. You know it came down and I'm God-blessed and it came out of ...

▷ Let me mention something that is interesting in that context. Years ago I saw a panel where people in the communication industry were asked what, in their opinion, the most creative book was. And you know what turned out to be the most creative one: the Bible.

◁ Well, it has to be. If you read the Bible it's really a terrific book because of the drama in there. There's a lot of human drama in there. War, pestilence, everything. It's there. It's hysterical. My wife, as a gift at Christmas, will always give me a very rare edition of the Bible. And this sounds strange and bizarre. But I have a beautiful collection, actually a fabulous collection of Bibles. They are going back to near the time of Gutenberg. The first printed Bibles. Not Gutenberg but ...

▷ ... very old prints.

◁ Very old, very old. The works of art in the editions is so wonderful. But the other day I was trying to look up something. Because the screenplay I was working on had to do with a quote from the Bible. I went back to find the quote. And I read the book Thessalonians. And in it there was the phrase: „Don't drink to excess. Don't become drunk," and "You will not eat, if you don't work." Ha, that's very primitive. But it had to do with being paid for not working and stuff like that, which is a big problem we are facing in society today. There are a lot of people who want a job but they don't want to work. It's very difficult to motivate people anymore. People want to get a job and it's hard to make them work. It's hard to make them earn their money. This is true everywhere. You can't get people to work. You can't get people to function. You know that from advertising. I mean how many people are really functional in advertising? A writer and an art director can really get by without doing a hell of a lot.

▷ What do you think about "The Last Temptation of Christ" and the outcry about the movie?

◁ The fact that Martin Scorsese made the movie is a tremendous achievement in this day and age. It harks back to the films we talked about earlier in the late fifties and early sixties. Great and shocking films. I've not seen it. But the very fact of getting the movie done shows a tremendous amount of courage and moral fibre in Martin Scorsese. He is really a filmmaker that I admire tremendously.

▷ Unlike Scorsese's movie, the Bible doesn't have a soundtrack. There are people who say that 51 percent of the movie is sound. Would you agree?

◁ Well, it could be as important and not important depending on what you wanna do. It depends on the movie.

▷ You would not generalize.

Pytka´s Durito commercial for BBDO New York

◁ You can't generalize. Because some films depend on their imagery and some films depend on the spoken word. I would say "51 percent of a film is sound" is silly because if you think about certain films, e.g. "Lawrence of Arabia," I think the imagery is infinitely more important than the soundtrack. If you think of a movie like "The Maltese Falcon," if you think about the lines of dialog, the sound is much more important in that movie because it's about intellectual relationships, verbal relationships. I think that a film that depends too much on one element over another is faulty overall. I think there has to be a wonderful balance.

▷ But in your Lee commercials you are using sound in a very experimental way?

◁ Yeah, in our Lee commercials we use sound outrageously. We have different sounds and things like that. But in the Hancock stuff, for instance, the sound is very detached and minimal. It's mostly normal sound from a distant perspective. Reductive sound.

▷ How do you work with Pop promos?

◁ Well, I've done some for Michael Jackson. We were kind of bombarded by the critics for the first one. We mixed natural sounds, music and dialog in a somehow incoherent way until we got into the song and nobody understood it. Because they were used to convention. They just couldn't accept this. So the second video is just pure music and effects. No experiments.

▷ You've done that spectacular Pepsi commercial with Madonna.

◁ Well, that's just a song. There is no experiment in sound in that. It's just images against the song. Surreal images.

▷ How did you feel when it was …

◁ … pulled. Actually, I kind of liked it because it makes it more special and dramatic. It's kind of nice to say: "Oh, that's what it was." You know what they would have done? They would have made a 60-second version, they would have made a 30-second version. They would have diluted the quality of the original production. But now it's only in this original form, its pure form, the two-minute version, it tends to have a sort of charisma that it might not have had otherwise. Some things should only be seen a few times. Now, when people see it they say: „Oh, I love it. What was all the furore about?"

▷ Actually, what was it all about?

◁ As far as I know, the public was confusing the video and the commercial. There was so much publicity about Madonna and the song, which was identical in both forms. When the video started running it was very controversial. Religious statues coming to life and things like that. Enough people called Pepsi thinking that was the commercial. Even people in advertising who should know better thought that the video was the

Joe Pytka

commercial. Even though there was not a hint of Pepsi Cola in the video. So as soon as it started to run the Pepsi Cola Company was attacked by some religious groups. They boycotted the product. And they decided not to run it for a while until the furore would die down. And it just never did.

▷ And your commercial never came back on the air. Is it true that it took 5 million dollars to shoot it?

◁ The whole thing was much more than that. If you talk about the amount of money spent on everything. It must have cost a huge amount of money to run the commercial once all over the world. So if you put all those figures together it's obviously more than 5 million dollars. But the amount of publicity they got from the whole thing is worth probably much more.

▷ Was it always planned to run the commercial worldwide?

◁ I think it's truly the first global commercial ever done. When they really ran the commercial all over the world in its original state. And we got the control. Some of the Apple things I have done were adapted in other languages. But Madonna ran all over the world. So it was an attempt to try worldwide advertising for Pepsi Cola.

▷ You just did another celebrity commercial with Ringo Starr for Oldsmobile.

◁ Yeah, very funny. He's wonderful.

▷ There are mixed and conflicting views about the Oldsmobile campaign in the States. Some people say about Oldsmobile that it's a bestselling car campaign that brought up the Oldsmobile sales, and there are researchers on the other hand that say using these celebrities might take the attention away from the car.

◁ That might not be a bad thing.

▷ What do you mean?

◁ Ringos commercial is not like other commercials. Ringo's commercial is more just a bit of entertainment. It happened to be entertainment for the public that has the product involved. And what I try to do when I make the commercials, whether it's Michael J. Fox or these guys, what I try to do is make the celebrity look and perform as well as they can. One of the things I love about Madonna, what she did for Pepsi, was that she gave a full performance in our commercial. She didn't hold back anything. It's not like some commercial where you see celebrities walk on, say a few words and walk off. I demand that these people give a performance. When Ringo Starr's script was presented to me, it did not demand a performance out of Ringo. I wrote the script so it demanded a performance from him. And he did a fabulous job. He has fabulous talents. Remember Jacques Tati and his performances? Ringo has that quality. He's wonderful. He just walks across the room and makes you laugh. It was thrilling to work with him. I didn't know what to expect. Because since the Beatles have broken up the roles of the various Beatles have become kind of muddled. You know, the businessman, the producer and so on. And Ringo recaptures the flavor of the original Ringo from „A Hard Day's Night." That's what the commercial is all about.

▷ The commercial also plays with the "Fab Four" in conjunction with the four doors of the sedan.

◁ Oh yeah, but that doesn't work quite as well. The stuff they say about the car is not very clever. I don't think the writer was up to the standard that she should have been for those things. But the power of Ringo's presence in the commercial overpowers all that.

▷ You haven't answered my question yet. Does Ringo put the attention on him or on the car?

◁ I can't talk about the campaign. I'm not that interested in the campaign.

▷ But what about the Ringo commercial?

◁ I think the only thing that Ringo does is call attention to the car. And I think that's all a television commercial can do, call attention to the car. Make it stand out from everything else. In other words: you might not be thinking about an Oldsmobile, but if you see Ringo and his daughter in an Oldsmobile commercial that is entertaining to you, you say: "Ah, Oldsmobile, that's a nice looking car." And maybe if you want to buy a car you go to an Oldsmobile dealer to see what the car is like. And then it's up to the dealer to convince you that it's a good car. I understand that. But if you can only recall that you saw Ringo in a commercial and you can't remember, whether it was for Fiat, Chrysler or Volvo, things look slightly different.

◁ No, they remember it's an Oldsmobile because the brilliance of the concept of that campaign is the line: "It's not your father's Oldsmobile." And there is no doubt in your mind it's an Oldsmobile commercial that finished. It's not like a celebrity "What was that car?" You will know it's an Oldsmobile commercial which is the brilliance of the concept of Leo Burnett Chicago, the agency which created the campaign. So that you use celebrities and you still get the fact that it's Oldsmobile. I mean you think about it — "It's not your father's Oldsmobile." Father daughter. Father son. "It's not your father's Oldsmobile." You are clearly left with the impression it's an Oldsmobile commercial, which is not the same for other commercials. I saw some of the other commercials recently. A celebrity was singing. And she was singing about the car and I can't remember what car it was. I remember her, but I don't remember the car.

▷ Who was she?

◁ If I told you who it was, the people would get upset. But I saw her and it was awful. She was uninteresting and the car was uninteresting. And I don't know what car it's for. But if you see any Oldsmobile commercial you know it's for Oldsmobile.

▷ The Oldsmobile campaign for me is in some sort of sense an upside down adaptation of the Pepsi concept into the world of cars.

◁ That's an interesting idea. I sort of like that.

▷ A bit more twisted.

◁ Much, much more twisted. Well, you know, the Pepsi stuff, especially the stuff with Michael J. Fox, started using celebrities in a less patronizing manner. When I did the first commercial with Michael J. Fox, I think that was the first time when a celebrity acted in a commercial as an actor rather that a celebrity. Remember, when he goes to the copy machine and did a copy? You know, this is not a Michael J. Fox presentation for Pepsi, this is Michael J. Fox playing a role as a performer, using his charisma and his abilities as a performer. So that was the first time it was used it set the tone for a lot of stuff.

▷ Don Johnson, Tina Turner, David Bowie and a lot of others followed.

◁ That is Phil Dusenberry. He did it.

▷ I think that it's a great concept, and whoever they are using it's always refreshing. If you look at the commercials of the last five years the Pepsi commercials definitely belong ...

◁ ... to the best.

▷ How did you guess I wanted to say that?

◁ No question. They are always high quality. They are always well produced. They are always entertaining. They are always fresh and, as you said, refreshing is the best word. They are always larger than life. They are very much like Steven Spielberg.

▷ If you look back on your life what do you still want to achieve that you haven't achieved yet?

◁ I don't think that I'm ready to say what I'm gonna do yet. I think that in many ways I'm at the beginning of my career. So that in many ways I don't think that I have reached the point where I can look back yet. I'm still looking forward. The only thing I can say is: The best has yet to come.

□

JOE SEDELMAIER
Everything's relative

If you ask icons of the English and American advertising who influenced their advertising style the most, many come up with the name Joe Sedelmaier. The King of Slapstick Comedy influenced late 20th century advertising like no other director. Federal Express, Alaska Airlines and Wendys' are timeless classics of their genre. Joe can truly be said to have a style that many have tried to copy, but no one's managed. Every creative with a so-so script knows that if only he could get Sedelmaier to shoot it, it would be an award winner. There are many good directors, who fit on the conventional stylistic scale and can be measured against each other.

Joe Sedelmaier isn't one of those. No one can come close to Joe because he didn't improve on what others were doing. He invented something totally new.

I talked to Joe in Chicago, which he refuses to leave.

▷ Hermann Vaske: Well, pal, after you made us roar with laughter through the cascades of humor in your commercials, what is your final verdict: Does humor sell, yes or no?

◁ Joe Sedelmaier: There's one thing I've learned in this business: There is no yes, there is no no.

There is no right, there is no wrong, only opinion.

Rube: That's the business.

◁ And everyone has a right to a their opinion.

Rube: That's the business.

◁ Whatever works, even if it doesn't. Everything's relative.

Rube: That's the business.

▷ But there's no greater satisfaction in this business than doing things yourself.

◁ Or being involved in making them.

▷ So, why not involve yourself in this situation. We're sitting here and we're doing this interview. That is the situation, you even have the same coloured shirt as the chair you're sitting on. And my shirt's nearly the same grey as this leather chair. So, how could we turn this situation into an ad for a Sony tape recorder? How could we make it funny?

◁ I don't have the least idea. That is something where I'd have to sit down. I couldn't just do it like (snaps his fingers) that.

▷ What about accessories, like putting glasses on?

◁ No, that's not where the humour comes from. Humour is something completely human: it comes from the tension between people, between

When it absolutely, positively
has to be there overnight.

Areas served, delivery times, and liability
subject to limitations in our Service Guide.

Stills from
Federal Express commercial

those trying to make the best of a situation and those who are completely humourless.

▷ What about dialog? What about our voices this machine is recording?

◁ If you listened to this tape recorder and put it down on paper it would make no sense whatsoever. The only thing about tape recorders which is interesting is, it can help you with things that you might have forgotten, but that's it. Too many people use it as the thing. To give you an example: if someone transcribed me on tape it would be an absolute bolixed-up mess. You would wonder what the hell is going on. It's also a good dialog. Good dialog doesn't read well. I was reading the Nixon things, they had these tape recorders and then they transcribed them and you then tried to read them and people were saying the man doesn't even know how to speak English. No, no, they missed the whole point, that's good dialog. Because that's what's wrong with dialog in most commercials. It all points to the end, to the product. There should be little mistakes. When you finish things, when it's all put together, it makes sense. I'm sitting here talking to you and I know I'm making sense to you, but I think if you just came in cold and you had this transcribed you'd wonder what the hell I'm talking about. There are a lot of things going on, like sound, a lot of things going with it. And that's too often what they miss in commercials, in film. You get a good script and hey, the script is only the beginning.

▷ What if instead of using a tape recorder we used a camera?

◁ You'd have the same problem. It all comes down to the "magic moments." And you don't know the magic moments, if you haven't been around to see them. It's like what they do nowadays, they shoot all the footage and then someone else takes the footage and does something. That's why I always have to look through the lens, because when I'm looking through the lens I'm seeing it entirely different from the guy who is sitting over here, or over here. It's a whole different thing, it's like it's on the screen. Also I'm thinking about the cut, where I can go from this shot to that shot. And I think now; with videoassist, then you're beginning to see what the camera is seeing, although I will not use videoassist, it becomes a monster. What the lens sees is entirely different from what you see over here, because first of all you look at a flat two-dimensional plate, it's composed, it's just by the way you place the guy in there – it's saying something. When they had this whole thing, truth in film, it was a cliché. All this cinema verité stuff, they were documentaries that were supposed to be absolutely truthful.

▷ When documentaries are of course subjective.

◁ That's my point, I'm saying that once you pick that camera up and point it, it's being subjective. For anyone to say that it isn't he is either a fool  or a liar. I think it's fine to try and be objective but still it's gonna be your point of view, that's why I always like fiction. I've always liked fiction to read, to see fictional films more than these so-called documentaries, they're such shit, because they mix the two, and I'm amazed how unsophisticated people are when they watch these things.

▷ Did you ever appear in a commercial yourself?

◁ No, I can't see me. I like to be able to see, and look. I can't be a viewer if I'm in it, because basically I'm a viewer person. I'm directing it, but I'm also the guy viewing it sitting in the theatre. I found when I first started  shooting, it was down on State Street, and I wanted this guy to walk through a crowd of people, and I thought I would feel rather uncomfortable shooting with all these people watching me, people looking at you while you're doing this. But once I put that camera to my eye they were no longer  there, they were all actors. They were performing for me and I was no longer there. I think that's the feeling I get when I look through that lens. I've had that scene when everybody was freezing to death on a 101 degree day. Then you see it later put together and you think you weren't even there, that's a cool day. You weren't even involved. It's real. One time  looking at it after being put together it becomes real to me, it's almost as if I wasn't even participating. I didn't even have anything to do with it. Don't you find that in writing too? You write something, you go over it and over it and then all of a sudden, later, you look at it and it always lives on its own.

▷ Let's go back to our situation with the tape recorder. Could we make this funny with batteries?

◁ First of all we're going about it the wrong way. What are we trying to say? We don't know what we want to say. To me the humour comes out of the problem. It's like getting on a plane, and I always think what am I gonna do next, you have a problem with the plane, what can be the problem? Too often a lot of the problems in commercials are not real problems, they're unreal problems, they are created and then solved. And there were no problems to begin with. People have to be able to identify with the problem.

"Fast Talking Man"
commercial for Federal Express

▷ What could be the problem?

◁ For instance, when you are on a plane, what would happen if you had to pay to go to the john? Ok that opens up...my god, you need coins, I never have coins, I'm always looking around for change. All of a sudden it's a very real problem and this guy is reacting to it very real. But I'm thinking things that happened on the set you're not planning, is when

KAY
JEWELERS
The diamond people

"That's the business" -
Sedelmaier for Kay Jewellers

the guy says, "Can I get a dollar change?" When he came in there was a shiver in his voice, almost as when a kid has to go and urinate there's that little shiver. That shiver was there and all of a sudden it seemed as if it was part of the thing. It was the "magic moment" you were waiting for and you go on from there.

▷ What if I'm sitting here wanting to interview Joe Sedelmaier, the big star in advertising, and the batteries don't work – that could be a problem! Too boring?

◁ No, it could lead to something. I was thinking if you got done and there were no batteries in it from the beginning or you lost them, which sort of reminds me. Have you ever been in a car and needed directions and there was someone in the car with you when you were asking for directions. You say, "How do we get to...?" The guy on the street says, "You take route 4 to 5 to 6...", whatever, he goes through the whole thing. And you say thank you and start driving away and the other person, the one next to you says, "Where is it?" And you go, "I don't know, I thought you were listening." Neither one was listening.

▷ What if I thought I switched it on and we sit through the interview and in the end I notice it wasn't even turned on?

◁ Except that still does not do it, because how do I know that you didn't remember you have to set it up... That's the other thing, a commercial has to be so fast.

▷ You mean the viewer should be involved and know that I didn't have batteries in it from the beginning?

◁ Even better yet, you never wanted to buy a hearing aid. Let's make it for a hearing aid. Why do you buy a hearing aid? Well, what do you need a hearing aid for, it's like I don't want people to know that I have a hearing problem. So what I do is I take a tape recorder and as the guy is talking. I'm nodding my head but I don't know what the hell he is saying. I always take the tape recorder to someone who types it out and then I read it. That's it. So next time buy a hearing aid!

▷ Did you just make that up?

◁ Yeah, as we were talking. One thing led to another... all of a sudden I turned you into a deaf person. We got something going then. It always depends on what you want to sell. We could go further and say you don't want to reveal that you don't know how to speak English. You know some basic words like "Let's begin" or "How do you do" or "I've got a tape recorder." It's like you won't appear as if you don't know English, so you take the tape recorder and you have someone translate it after you play it back. You're on. And what happens? The tape recorder never works. But this gets complicated. Basically we still don't have a product. So often I think that what happens is the funny stuff never comes from the original, I have guys that come in from the agencies – what I like to do is sitting down to have a pre-production meeting and let's sit down and discuss what we're trying to say and they come in with these ideas, none of them really that great, I learned to say, "What are the ideas that you threw out?" It's amazing how there's something in one of those ideas they threw out. You started there and that gave me the idea of you being deaf, then you might go one step further and say something and then we'll... and we'll arrive at something.

▷ What about this chair we're sitting on?

◁ But there's no reason for the chair, it's like in this Federal Express commercial where the guy wakes up in the morning. He goes: if you wanna do anything, you gotta do it yourself. It's like there's a reason. First of all his alarm clock doesn't work, second thing he has a flat tire. He goes to the elevator, it doesn't work. This guy was not a real good actor, but I like his voice, he was an old comedian but he couldn't remember anything: "Hey Joe, don't worry we're gonna get this thing done right away, this is gonna be one take, I'm a one-take guy." Well, you know right away he is not a one-take guy. Did you ever see the commercial – "Promise him anything" for Federal Express? This guy is one the telephone "tomorrow" and his wife is saying "sure" and he says "early" and she says "sure" and this goes on. I used him for the first time. I went through that take I don't know how many times to get it. You work with these people and sometimes it can take a year and a day to get it out of them, but it's worth it. Most people don't wanna put up with that. They wanna go with the guy who gets his lines right, but they don't realize the guy who did his lines right doesn't have any magic. Anyhow, this guy was in the elevator and the next thing he is going up the stairs. I said, "Pretend, like it's heavy," and he'd go up and it looked too easy. So what I did is I put these weights on him, and this guy he almost dropped the load going up there. I always think that funny stuff, it's interesting, because commercials don't follow the same rule that the feature does. I'll give you an example that you could not use in a feature. The guy is sitting there with his wife on the front lawn, and he is struck by lightning and the guy gets blown up. In a film after that you wouldn't believe anything. You have to keep the tone straight. People say it has to be possible talking about features. Now, giving a good example – did you see Blue Velvet? Ok, I enjoyed that. Remember, at the end of the film, when these cops are standing there and they've been shot and the bullits coming out of them and they keep

Stills from
Wendy's commercial
"Russian Fashion Show"

standing there – totally impossible – but he put it at the end of the film. If he had put the shot in the beginning of the film, this would have broken the whole film up. That was the trouble with a lot of the later James Bond films. The earlier ones, they played it straight and there was this villain: what's he gonna do now? But toward the end, when the other guy was playing Bond, there was a scene, this was like in the middle of the film, and Bond is being chased around this mountain and these guys are behind him and he swerves and they go flying right off the cliff in their car. Ok, we cut to this peasant in his little cabin and he comes out and sites down with his bread and his wine, and just when he sits down, this car goes right into his cabin and he just looks around – it's a funny shot – the door of the cabin and the guy that was driving the car comes out like this. Ok, it's funny but it kills the rest of the movie, you don't believe anything after that. They went for that easy laugh and it just throws everything out. If you had that at the end of the film it would be okay. You accept things then.

▷ Do you have idols?

◁ For me Bernbach is an interesting figure. What I particularly like about him is that he hated everything that had been done before. "It's the client's money," he used to say, "but it's my work!" That's a great line! And I'll tell you something else, they talk about the golden age of advertising, which is also a lot of bullshit, there never was a golden age of advertising. There was Doyle, Dane, Bernbach and there was Doyle, Dane, Bernbach and there was Dane, Bernbach and it was really Bernbach and there is still Bernbach that was the great stuff. That Doyle, Dane is a joke today. You know when I started in the business, agencies had styles, they had a point of view. You could tell Y & R, they always had consistent quality. You had Doyle, Dane they always stood out. Then for shock you had Ted Bates. Ted Bates was the epitome of shock, they did the things with the knocking on the head and all that. But today there is no style. It's all mish mash. You can find something good and something that's a piece of shit in the same unit. You hear of these hot shots but I notice where they really make their mark. It's not in commercials, it's in print.

If I worked for someone else, if I had worked for a studio, I wouldn't be in the place. They tried to buy me one time, it was a studio on the coast. They said: "Hey, you're very successful." Shit, once they buy you they say, "You know, Joe is very good, but he could be better." That's it. Even though you're always working for someone, your life doesn't depend on just someone.

▷ At the end of the day you have to be an island.

◁ I'm not saying it's playing funny games, but as long as you get your kicks, that's what counts.

▷ It's like famous Route 66, you have to find it in your own eyes.

◁ All the people are always looking for somehting outside of themselves. You gotta do that, you gotta be here. After a while, you say it's gotta happen here. People get intimidated by their environment. Constantly you're looking. Especially today with technology and with communication where it is, you don't have to be looking. With the fax machine and all that you're just so much more available. Most people don't wanna be individuals. They want someone to come and tell them everything is gonna be okay. They wanna climb back into their mother's womb. You can't do that.

▷ Mr. Sedelmaier, your experience with feature films was not a happy one. What do you think of movie directors that make commercials?

◁ I have never seen one feature film director yet go from features to commercials where the result has been worth a damn. It's pretty phony crap.

▷ Even the late, great Fellini was no exception. When I was in Cannes a year ago and they showed his Banca di Roma spots, I dared to say that they weren't all that terrific. And this Adweek journalist started screaming, "But Fellini made them!"

◁ That's a stupid comment. Nothing but a rag anyhow. It's the "National Enquirer" for the ad people. It's bullshit, it's a family. They said when I did this "Russian" thing, for Wendy, "How could you do this?" And this was right at the time when Gorbachev was here in the United States and it was so nice and Raisa even wore this Annie Hall outfit. And then I go and do this thing.

▷ Woody Allen or Scorsese, do you know their commercials?

◁ No. I always find, though, that first of all Scorsese is one of the best, probably the best American feature filmmaker. His films for the most part are the best films made in the last 20 years in America. You know, films like "King of Comedy," "Mean Streets," "Taxi Driver"...

▷ "Goodfellas"...

◁ Yes, "Goodfellas," what's the other one – "Raging Bull."

▷ What about "The Last Temptation of Christ"?

◁ I don't know, I found that was almost kitsch and still all the fundamentalists were upset. It's absurd. I just thought it was so kitschy. By the way, have you seen Altman's "The Player"?

▷ Yeah.

◁ I thought that was terrific. That was not a sad story, that was reality. One woman said, "Well, it was a little exaggerated, but for an exaggerated film it was okay." It was not exaggerted a bit. It was this business. I look at it often. I thought the casting was perfect.

▷ Have you seen any Woody Allen's commercials?

◁ No, he does his commercials in Japan or in Italy. You know what it reminds me of? It reminds me of this man who takes his dog for a walk in someone else's neighborhood. It's like, why doesn't he make commercials here? I don't find that these feature film directors understand the medium at all. I don't think I could understand making commercials if I started the other way – if I had started on the features. When you think about it, you think, "I gotta say this in 30 seconds? It's incomprehensible."What it ends up with is Scorsese making a lot of pretty pictures but there's nothing there. You see Fellini who has his characters but basically it becomes a commercial-commercial. They don't understand there is this small little time problem. I don't think I could go back, I could not do it if I came the other way. It's unbelievable – 20 seconds, 30 seconds.

▷ What could you recommend for someone who is here in Chicago for a couple of days.

◁ You should rent a car and drive around town. Chicago is a beautiful city.

▷ I forgot to bring my driver's license, though.

◁ Then just walk. That can be pretty interesting too.

▷ What do you like best about Chicago?

◁ The architecture. (Points to the picture of the Leo Burnett building in Chicago.) It looks like a vase with flowers. If I imagined a vase with flowers that's what it would look like.

□

PAUL WEILAND
Say it with a smile

Just like Alan Parker and Frank Lowe, Paul Weiland started his advertising career at the legendary London agency Collett Dickenson Pearce (CDP). After chewing pencils for a couple of years as a copywriter, he became a film director, learning his craft at Alan Parker's production house which he later left to found the Paul Weiland Film Company.

By common consent his classic commercials, Hamlet's "Bunker", Heineken's" "Water in Majorca" and "Points of View" for the Guardian are amongst the best ever produced. That's why nobody was really surprised when David Puttnam drew Weiland over to Hollywood to shoot the 40-million-dollar movie "Leonard" with Bill Cosby. The film – one of the biggest flops Columbia Pictures ever had – was torn to pieces by the critics and the beginning of the end for Puttnam as studio boss of Columbia Pictures.

But Paul Weiland didn't give up and turned "City Slickers 2" with Billy Crystal into a success, and followed it with a critically acclaimed European production "Rosanna's Grave" with Jean Reno. In all those years The Paul Weiland Film Company remained one of the finest London addresses for commercials, winning Grand Prix and Palme d'Or in Cannes. As time went by I met Paul Weiland, interviewing him several times in London.

▷ Hermann Vaske: Paul, do you think it's okay for advertising creatives to separate people from their money as long as they give creativity, entertainment and excitement back to them in return?

◁ Paul Weiland: Yeah. I think people want to be entertained. People want to be taken on a journey. It's like you pick up a good book. You read it and appreciate it. But if you are watching something on TV and you get interrupted, if it's not a good commercial, then it's a pain in the neck. So, what we try to do is to make things as entertaining as possible, because no one's really sitting there, saying, "come on, sell to me". It's all working from wherever they are, and wherever you go now.

Now you go into any country, and it'll feel familiar, because there are these same voices selling to you, wherever you go. And it's become part of our lives. And because of that I think that we do need to keep the standards up. My feeling is that it's very hard, because people get worn down by clients.

I think what we need to do is be more creative, and I think that is not really happening, in this country, particularly, at the moment. Things do need to change, there needs to be a new wave, a new approach to how to go into people's homes.

It's not that we can't be entertaining, it's just a question of whether

Stills from Weiland's
Army campaign

we're being boring now because we keep repeating the same messages, time and time again – just dressed up in a different coat every time.

▷ Does creativity pay? Or in other words, is there a correlation between creativity and selling?

◁ I think it depends on what the product is. I think that there have been certain products that have been absolutely face-down in the water, and then through a spark of creative inspiration, someone comes up with an idea, and suddenly the product is completely propelled, and it works and works and works. But it doesn't work forever, and that's the problem. People feel comfortable with someone coming into their home that they think is gonna make them smile or entertain them, and creativity can do this for a product. But there is this other debate. Should we be selling kids toys whose parents can't afford it? Should Sony stop making Playstation, because when they come out on the market there's gonna be lots of children saying 'I want it', with parents who are gonna have to sacrifice something to give their child a Playstation?

But this is our society, isn't it? In one way, it does make people work harder, so they can achieve all these trinkets, and get the new car and the new fridge the new pension plan. But on the other hand they have problems affording it. That's the big debate.

▷ You shot TV-commercials for the British Army. No ethical problems with that?

◁ Well, we did some things for the army, which was a good campaign. Whether that's politically correct is another question. If we recruit people that see the ad for the territorial army and they join up, then go off and get shot... is that my fault? I mean, in the end one could be responsible, to a certain degree. But if you thought about that on everything, you'd be in deep trouble.

▷ How was shooting the Virgin Atlantic Campaign with Buscemi and Berkhoff?

◁ Yeah, I did the Virgin Atlantic commercial with Steve Buscemi and Steven Berkhoff. That was fun, we did a spoof on British Airways. We created a concept involving two spies, Mr. A and Mr. B. Buscemi played Mr.B and Berkhoff played Mr.A. They both tried to figure out the new improvements of Virgin in comparison to British Airways. And that's how we were able to communicate, for example, bigger seats or fitness programmes.

▷ One of your colleagues once said, "commercials are sprints, feature films are marathons". How was your last marathon?

◁ Good. Yeah, I really enjoyed working with Jean Reno, that was a very good experience and I felt pretty pleased with the way it turned out.

Paul Weiland   360

▷ Why are you creative?

◁ Okay. Why am I creative? That's always a hard one, because you always think that you're gonna get found out one day, and you're not really creative at all – you're just pretending to be creative. Creativity has to do with being slightly excluded from things, as a child, wanting to make things right. I like to walk into a room where there's a blank canvass, so that I can feel insecure, so it makes me feel a bit nervous, thinking: "My God, I've gotta make this work". But what makes you creative? I don't know, I think probably goat's milk yoghurt?

▷ With the help of yoghurt you have won quite a number of awards...

◁ The awards, yeah, they all go to my mother's house. She then takes them to car boot sales and we split whatever she gets from them.

▷ These days we are confronted with commercials that present us images of shock violence on a daily basis. How do you cope with that?

◁ Sure I recognise that trend, but that doesn't mean that I agree with it. Violence and culture clashes and whatever can be good, but sometimes they go slightly too far. And sometimes we do commercials that I think go slightly too far.

There used to be a time where, if a promo was banned it would get more publicity by being banned, and I think some clients go for that as well these days. They don't have a huge budget so they make something that is going to be impossible to run. And in a way, I think sometimes probably rightly, that it shouldn't run.

Advertising does have to have guidelines and I think that sometimes you can overstep the mark. All directors get off on trying to do shocking things where it could kill someone, or they could cause a stir, or there's a suicide, you know blood and guts and gunfire. One of my directors did a Pepe Jeans commercial, where to establish a cult image these kids were putting themselves into spin-driers in a launderette and spinning themselves around.

And to me it's fine, but it's not fantasy. I mean it's a reality and then a young kid goes and tries it and dies, and, you know, how do you feel about that? I'm not sure about that.

New Upper Class.
The Business.

virgin atlantic

▷ Wasn't the Pepe commercial banned?

◁ Yeah, it was banned. But I think that they intentionally set out to ban it. I mean they knew it was going to be banned, and that way everyone talks about it, everyone wants to see this commercial that's been banned. But I think it's slightly evil.

Mr. A and Mr. B - Weiland's campaign for Virgin Atlantic with Steven Berkhoff and Steve Buscemi

▷ Don't believe the hype?

Stills from "Comic Relief"

◁ Well, I think advertising really has become hype definitely. I think the days where a commercial stood on it's own are gone. These days everything is a bit like the emperor's new clothes where we're all led to believe that it's art and it's wonderful and it's fashionable and it's trendy, but I can't really believe that everything just appeals to people who watch MTV. I think that there's got to be a bigger market out there.

And advertising tends to follow like sheep. You know, one person does it and it's seen to be successful so suddenly everyone's on the bandwagon making poor imitations. Well, I think it's just hype. But I think it's something that doesn't necessarily build a brand. You know, I'm an old fashioned kind of advertising guy where I always believe that things should grow. It's like you meet someone once and you'd like to meet them again, and then every time you meet them you get to know them a bit better. And at the end of the day you hope that you're going to like this person, so when this person comes into your life, you think ah, it's really good to see them.

These days everything's transient. You know, it's a big hit, a big splash and then it's gone and it's on to the next thing. I mean, it's become a bit like fast food, junk. Is there a recipe for getting people to give away their money to buy things? It has to be down to building a brand, building a personality. If someone goes out on one date and likes the person they go back for another date. If they just buy it once and they're disappointed with it they're not going to go back again. And I think advertising can really help that.

▷ You're regarded as the King Of Comedy. How do you sell products with humour?

◁ I love commercials when there's a response, when there's an emotional response or when there's something that makes you laugh, or tickles you or someone gives a look that stays with you or says something that you remember. Humour has always been something that people need in their lives. I mean we all need to laugh. Commercials are something that we don't need in our lives, so my theory was always that if you can sell to people but also give them a little bonus so that it raises some kind of a chuckle or an emotion, then you're on to a winning ticket.

But I don't think humour is necessarily right for everything, I mean it's right for certain things. But generally I think commercials are moving away from humour. And that's because it's the hardest thing to do. Fashion, stylistic, visual stuff and kind of wobbly cameras are easier to do because basically it's a bunch of photographs.

▷ What's the essence of humour?

Paul Weiland

◁ It's a beat. Humour's about a beat, a time an emotion and some people can do it. It's like great comedians. I mean you can count them on one hand comedic directors are also very hard to find – it's a very small market. But big action movies, that's the huge market.

▷ Do you think universal humour exists?

◁ No. I mean something that I find hilarious, someone in Spain might not understand at all. But visual humour is obviously a universal key to success. You know when I do the Mr. Bean there's no words but the Mr. Bean go out everywhere and basically children love them and grown ups love them. Of course, some people hate it, they find it kind of puerile, but generally it crosses all borders. But there's not enough visual humour used in commercials.

▷ There is a didactical principle in the Talmud which says a lesson taught with humour is a lesson retained.

◁ Yeah, which is what my point was before. I think there's definitely that we don't ask to be advertised to. No-one likes it, so please do me a favour, if you're going to do it make it as painless as possible. And humour is definitely a route to someone's wallet. If I know you've entertained me, I'm going to pay, if you've not entertained me I'm going to keep my money.

▷ You have not only successfully separated the people from their money in advertising, but also directed Hollywood movies. How did you manage that metamorphosis?

◁ Sure, that wasn't easy. Obviously as a director one has an ambition to leave the nest, where you're comfortable and go off for new challenges. The challenges of commercials are hard enough, but feature films are even harder, because with a commercial I only have to amuse you for thirty seconds. That's not that hard to do because you're not getting to know the person. All you're doing is a spontaneous reaction to something. When you have something longer, half an hour, an hour, two hours, then you have to do a bigger job. We have to make the person like the person even more, so basically whatever they do you find them amusing. And as we know from most films that come out, it doesn't work. So one goes off and one learns and hopefully one stumbles upon something that is worthwhile.

▷ How did you like Hollywood?

◁ It sucks. Hollywood is a land of bullies. And it's very difficult, because commercials spoil a director. We're these kind of incredibly big fish in this very small pond. And we all walk around and go with the attitude "change that script otherwise you die". In Hollywood the big problem is you're always working with people that are more famous than yourself, or better

The grown-up soft drink. (Well, quite).
Stills from Weiland´s
Schweppes commercial
with John Cleese

known and it's very difficult as a director because ultimately it is a team effort. But as a director you need to have the last say, it's you that is obviously taking in this whole picture.

When you work with an actor who's also the producer and the star it doesn't make things easier. Basically these people, unfortunately, have not a clue about making films, but they have been very lucky in whatever they've done to get into the movies, and been very successful and then they think that they can tell everyone else what they should be doing.

Generally I think the time to go to Hollywood is when you're really famous and making movies, not famous for making commercials and documentaries. You have to go and be very lucky and make a very successful movie and than you have the power.

▷ Could you tell us about your Hollywood experiences? Was it really that bad?

◁ I'd rather not talk about it, it normally makes me cry and I always promised my mother that I would never cry in anyone else's company than hers. When I left home she said you promise me you'll never cry and if you don't mind I won't really go into it.

But what I will say is, the experience is in lots of ways a good one, because basically if you're doing a big kind of Hollywood product, you get to spend lots of money and you get to work with all the equipment you need, and you learn politics basically. I'm not sure you learn to be a film maker, because the only way to be a film maker is for you to be in control, and ultimately you're not in control. It's terribly flattering because when you think throughout the whole world, I don't know how many thousands of directors there are and you get to be chosen. You know, you've done some comedy stuff and you get to be chosen.

And I think the first experience I had, I didn't know what the fuck I was doing, the second experience I did know what the fuck I was doing and it was a battle from start to finish, but I never got fired, and I stayed the distance because I delivered.

▷ How was it in England? How was working with Rowan Atkinson?

◁ He's a bastard. This again makes me want to cry, because he's so brilliant. I'm so jealous because he's so much cleverer than me. I love to work with people who are cleverer than me, and Rowan is a serious perfectionist. But he's a bastard at the same time because he's so good and, you know, I'm a control freak and I can't bear if he's getting bigger laughs than me, that's the truth. I just love what he is, and he's so normal in real life, and then the minute he's in front of the camera, he's the closest thing to a genius that I've worked with, comic genius.

Paul Weiland

▷ How to you work with him? How do you give him directions?

◁ I have to do it with smoke signals because he's peculiar. Because if I talk it disturbs so I have to get a fire burning and it's a very good process because it's like the old Indian smoke signals and I have this tiny blanket on the set. The trouble is then it makes a lot of smoke on set, which makes it look moody as well, but it works, it works. No he takes direction very well, we get on pretty well.

▷ Do you work with John Cleese in the same way?

◁ I don't work with John in commercials any more. Because the last commercial we did was the Schweppes thing. And there's a shot in that commercial where basically I wanted John to be hit in the stomach, slapped twice round the face and wacked in the stomach, and I thought it was very funny, and we cut the commercial and he came in and he said "I don't like it, get it out". I said, "but John, it's the high point of this commercial you know, it's just so unexpected, so funny". And he said: "you don't tell me what's funny, I'll tell you what's funny, it's not funny". And you know, in the end, I could have either said "look I'm sorry, yeah, you're right", but I kind of stuck by my guns and I've not worked with him since. But for me the joke is, unfortunately, more important than the relationship. I mean it's not art, it just was a very important joke to me and I knew that if it was in, it would go on and win lots of awards which it did do. If it was out it wouldn't, because to me commercials are about tiny moments, tiny moments that sometimes you stumble upon and sometimes that are there in the script. And I think it is those things that people remember and I think if you ask anyone what was funny in that commercial it would be the bit where he's punched in the stomach, because it's painful.

▷ How did you get to know John Cleese?

◁ The first time I ever worked with John, it was the most amazing thing, I was like completely enamoured by the man. And I got a job directing some Yellow Pages commercials and I kind of wangled it that the cab that was meant to take him home didn't turn up, because I'm pretty ambitious, you see, and I thought if I could have a few hours in the car with him, I'd get his next movie. And we started the journey and we're driving and I'm thinking, fuck I've got John Cleese in the car next to me, this is amazing. And I'm thinking, well what can I say? And he suddenly says, "can I ask you something". And I said, sure, sure. And he said, "you don't know anyone do you? I mean anyone particularly famous, and you're quite a normal, ordinary boy aren't you?" and I thought "oh, this is good, thanks". "What do people think of me?" He said, "I want you to be really honest what do people think of me?" And I said, "they think you're an absolute bastard". "Do they really? Go on", and it was like the weirdest conversation, because he wanted just a complete nobody to tell him what the rest of the nobodies think of John Cleese and I thought that was quite amusing. I did tell him the truth actually because even in those days he was a very difficult man to work with.

▷ Would you do a feature these days with Cleese or Atkinson?

◁ Yeah, but then it wouldn't be me, and I've done that twice, and I think that as I've said, it's very hard when you put that much effort – a year of your life – into something and you don't get a mention. And that is what happens, that when you continue to work with famous people, you're grabbing hold of their shirt-tails, and it's a fantastic experience, but for your career I'm not sure it's that good. If the movie is hugely successful and it goes over a hundred million then obviously you do benefit. But we all know that's a grey area, and it's quite a high risk. And at least if you make something that you feel you're involved in, something you care about passionately, and you work with actors that aren't that famous but are very good at what they do, then the whole thing depends on the movie, not the person in it.

▷ Let me come back to your car trip with John Cleese. It was a very humorous story.

◁ Yeah, I think humour grows out of unusual situations. I am someone who seems to attract odd things and when they're happening to you, you think they're kind of weird.

Like as an example, we went to the opera a couple of weeks ago and we went to see the Marriage of Figaro. I'm sitting there with my wife and it's the Royal Opera House, really pucker and suddenly at the first interval, I lean over to my wife and I say to her, "I bet you don't know who Figaro is", right. And suddenly the curtains come up and the guy behind me punches me in the arm, like really hard. I think to myself, Jesus, you know, I'm at the Royal Opera House, right. I turned round to the guy and I said to the guy, "what's going on, I mean, do you think you were at a football match?" And he's going shhh shhh and the lights turned out. I was actually going to get up and smack him, and he was in a wheelchair and he was one of those guys that they wheel in and he's like paralysed down one side. And with his good arm, he's given me the biggest smack. And it's one of those things that you think at the time. You think, well, where has this come from? But this to me is humour 'cos I could have turned round and whacked the guy and then he would have rolled on to the stage. So those things, you know, it's just life and I quite like that, when it happens.

□

DENNIS HOPPER
Advertising is a fingerprint of our time

Dennis Hopper made the film "Easy Rider". The film that is generally regarded as having started modern cinema. The film that paved the way for Francis Ford Coppola and Martin Scorsese. He's an actor, a director, and a producer. But more importantly, to him, he is an artist and photographer. He has a legendary knowledge of modern art, and one of the finest collections in America. His inner circle of friends and colleagues included Andy Warhol, and still includes David Hockney, Julian Schnabel and Ed Ruscha.

In the year 2001, some of the most important museums of the world, like the Stedelijk Museum in Amsterdam and the Museum of Applied Arts in Vienna, will present Dennis Hopper retrospectives. I interviewed Dennis several times, in Los Angeles and Berlin and when we were shooting "The Fine Art of Separating People from their Money"-Trilogy.

▷ Hermann Vaske: What motivates you?

◁ Dennis Hopper: I think it comes from a very unhappy childhood. Not getting enough approval from the house, from the home. Having to report other places. Having the drive to want to be something, want to be somebody, but really not having education because of schooling to be able to do anything but perhaps play sports, fight a bull, race a car, or be an actor. Well, I can't say acting was the easiest, but it seemed to be the most available to me.

I suppose a lot of it is luck but a lot of it is drive to and it's trying to be the best that you can be under whatever circumstances you're working under. And I think it's heart that makes for athletes and makes for actors and makes for anybody that wants something. It's just to keep going, keep hitting it and keep doing it. It should work out if you have a dream.

▷ A couple of years ago you did a movie that dealt with art and commerce, the "Basquiat" movie. What was it like working with Julian Schnabel, who made his debut as a director with this film?

◁ We were in New York filming with David Bowie and Gary Oldman. We were shooting a film about Jean-Michel Basquiat, the black painter who died on heroin a few years ago. Julian Schnabel was directing his first movie. And it is always difficult for a director to get his financing when he is a firsttime director. So Christopher Walken, Gary Oldman, David Bowie and myself, we got together to help him to get his first picture out. David Bowie played Andy Warhol, I played Bruno Bischofsberger the Swiss-German art dealer, Gary Oldman played Julian Schnabel himself.

▷ How did you like playing Bruno Bischofsberger?

◁ Ha, he is Swiss and he wears these knickers with the socks and that was very funny. Julian said I was a little bit like Peter Sellers. It was funny, I had a Swiss accent: "Ja ja, buy ze painting. Zis ist wonderful."

▷ What are the similarities and what are the differences in selling art and selling products like they do in commercials?

◁ Remember Wim Wender's "The American Friend?" I played Ripley in it. I was an art dealer in that. Nicholas Ray was my painter. I was selling the paintings of a supposedly dead painter at auctions. That was my first dig at playing an art dealer and this was my second. You know, today I think, in one way or another, we are all selling something. Whether we are making commercials or feature films, we are still trying to get an audience to see our films. When I directed "Easy Rider," which was the first film I directed, I got most of my inspiration while editing from watching commercials. I wondered why the technique of commercials had not been put into feature films. And if you look at the acid trip in "Easy Rider" it is very quick and it is very much like commercials are these days – not like they were then. Because I went a little further, I pushed it a little further than I had seen it. My inspiration originally came from watching American commercials. I felt that I wanted to make a time capsule – I thought of films as time capsules. But I knew that I would not be representing my time if I had only used the music. I had to use the technique of things that were affecting me, like commercials.

▷ How far can you go in order to grab people's attention?

◁ I saw Damien Hirst's commercial for TNT, where the dead cows are dropping from the ceiling and the guys were eating... and I enjoyed that very much. I do not know how that will work on television for an audience sitting at home. But it certainly grabs your attention. I think today it is very important in advertising that you be able to grab somebody and hold somebody so it does not appear to be advertising even though you might know it is. And then suck them in and show them what the product is. I think it is very attractive and it is similarly effective in film. I think "Pulp Fiction" is a major breakthrough. Of course I think Tarantino's writing is so wonderful. The scene that Chris Walken and I did in "True Romance," the film directed by Tony Scott, is truly a wonderful scene. That was all wonderful writing. It was great working on "True Romance." Especially working with Tony Scott, because he made a beautiful ambiance and then he let us do our dance and work together on a moment-to-moment reality level.

▷ Tony Scott is a commercials director. Was there any difference working with a guy coming from commercials?

◁ Just that he knew exactly what he wanted.

▷ Do you have any other experiences with commercials directors?

◁ I also worked with John Dahl and Rick Dahl on "Red Rock West" with Nicholas Cage. That film took a little more time because they were constantly racking focus, trying to transfer commercial techniques to feature films. I mean, you would pull out a knife and they would have to say, "No, wait!" and then they would rack focus to somebody else. It took a lot of time, there was a lot of details that were like sort of boring and agitating. I like the final result, though. I was aware of what they were doing at the time but Nicholas Cage was getting a little jumpy. He said, "Come on let's get it done." It can be very tiresome when somebody is coming out of a commercials world and wants to use those kind of techniques. But in this case the end result is wonderful. And what they're doing is reacting to changes in the way people see films. Well, I think that is what Duchamp was doing at a time when all the change was happening because the camera was invented. Every artist was running away from the camera trying to find a new world, a new way, a new image to promote, and to try to better understand themselves and the world they live in. In a way these artists with their paints and brushes can be compared to the special effects guys from things like "Industrial Light and Magic Lucas Films." That work they did for films such as "Terminator 2" and "Jurassic Park," the digital work they did making the dinosaurs and so on. That is just an

exciting world, that was just fantastic. I would say there is a "before digital" and "after digital" – that's my way to describe film. Also, I've always liked that Duchamp quote, "The artist of the future will be a man who points his finger and says, 'that's art,' and it will be art." And I think that's very appropriate today when we talk about advertising because I think commercials are art. I always said that the three-minute to five-minute movie will be the thing of the future, that some day it will not be a one-and-half-hour or two-hour movie, that it would really be like a longplaying album of three-minute and five-minute movies. And that has sort of become a reality through MTV. Just because we have an abstract kind of concept at this time of how long a movie is, because it's as Hitchcock said "It's how long people can sit in the theater before they have to take a pee." Haha. That is gradually changing.

▷ Do we need more restrictions regarding the airtime of the so-called shock commercials?

◁ If they put it on with adult programs – there are certainly other programs on television that children don't watch. But I think some of the shock commercials are very funny and very humorous. Censorship is a ludicrous proposition. First of all we live in a very violent society in the United States. If we cannot reflect the society that we live in then we shouldn't be making films at all. And also it is very entertaining, and people are paying a lot of money to go and see these movies. Well, then they say to you, "You're only doing it for the money." But we are doing it for the money so that we can make other films, make different kinds of films and hopefully get back to being able to distribute and have theaters where we can see foreign films again. My biggest problem right at the moment is there is no venue to see foreign films in the United States. The distribution companies that are distributing the movies have built these big complexes with the ten and twelve theaters. In it there should be at least one theater that shows nothing but what I call art films or films from Europe. And they can afford to have this in their complexes and allow people in the United States to see the important European films — also so that people in the foreign countries can have their own industries and be able to be distributed. I find this a little shocking.

▷ What do you think about shock tactics in Quentin Tarantino's earlier films?

◁ "Pulp Fiction" is shocking but "Pulp Fiction" is also funny, you can laugh at the violence. That's also very important. I mean if you go back to "The Wild Bunch" — Sam Peckinpah's film was as violent as anything going on and was a wonderful movie. It didn't promote people going out and blowing people away. People are blowing others away and it is not because of the movies. It's because they don't have jobs, it's because they are living in ghettos and it's because of a lot of problems. But it does not, in my opinion, have anything to do with the films that are being shown. Films are being shown that reflect the society we live in, and also there is an audience that wants to see these films and that enjoy seeing such films.

▷ These commercials like Damien's, if you put it on late at night, what harm could that do?

◁ I think Damien Hirst's film is very entertaining and it also goes back to the Viennese group around conceptual artist Otto Mühl in the late 60s. The Austrian artists of that time that used to paint themselves white and cut themselves with razors. They also did these great performance art pieces and slaughtered animals and did that kind of thing. So this is not something new, it is just that advertising usually gets it about 20 years later and movies get it — if they get it at all — 20 years after advertising. I think that they are just catching up.

▷ You are not only an actor in feature films, you also acted brilliantly in Nike commercials directed by Joe Pytka. What was working with Joe like?

◁ Joe Pytka is a good friend and a wonderful, wonderful director. And he's a tall man, a very big man, and he operates his own camera. He is actually from Pittsburgh and he went to the same art school at the same time that Andy Warhol did. He was a classmate of Andy's. So he is a quite wonderful man. The first time I worked with him I thought I'd never get along with this man. He's a screamer yeller, big bragger, bully, you know "Get over there, dadada." Yet at the end of the day I loved him. Because he is really, at the bottom of it all, very, very generous, very gentle. The people that work with him have been with him since the beginning. They all care for him and respect him, and he is a wonderful guy and really easy to work with and really knows what he is doing. He operates his own camera so you're talking into the camera. I had the same experience with Jan De Bont, who directed "Speed." He's a great cinematographer. And "Speed" was his first feature film, and he operated the camera himself, and it was interesting. But Pytka is sensational. It was a big decision for me to do a commercial, because I've been offered a lot of commercials. And Hollywood is such a strange place because they categorize every-thing. If you do television, if you're an actor on television, you are no longer worthy of being an actor on feature films. And it's a major jump to go from television to feature film – if you ever make it. The other thing is to make commercials. If you do commercials, you are finished in the business. You can no longer go and be in films. They don't even want you on television – it's very strange. I turned down a lot of commercials. When Nike came to me and said we would like you to do this character for us I thought, "Gee, I don't know – I've never done commercials, it's totally against my image, I'm an artist, blablabla." But my love for commercials, which I have always stolen from as a director in my editing, inspired me. I watch them furiously, still do. Also, Spike Lee had done some and all the great sports figures do them. So I thought that I'd be in good company, so I went and did it. And it became very funny and I found a whole new audience for me, a lot of kids who never see me. See, most of my films are R-rated, so they never see me. I got a whole bunch of new fans. Also, it's amazing how I'm recognized in the United States now. So it was fun, and very lucrative pay.

▷ Talking about advertising and humour – is humour a valuable tool to get into peoples hearts?
◁ If we take ourselves too seriously we are in deep trouble. I think humour is a very valuable device in selling. That even in drama, in tragedy, if you get a laugh right before something happens that is violent and dramatic it makes it even more violent and dramatic, if there is humour involved in it. I've especially seen this in Tarantino's work. Because we're laughing at Tarantino I call it blood, lust – snicker, snicker – on wide screen. I interviewed Tarantino, for a magazine called "Grand Street," it's a literature

magazine put out monthly. It was just before he won the Palme d'Or for Pulp Fiction. So I asked him how he came to that violent kind of thinking. He said it was coming from working in a video store, where he watched a lot of videos and got interested in videos made in Hong Kong. How they dealt with violence was much different from our sort of unwritten code of Hollywood morals. He used "Patriot Games" as an example. He said the guy that directed "Patriot Games" should go to the movie jail and be kept there forever and never be released. "Patriot Games" gives the hero every reason to gouge out the eyes and cut off the head of this man who terrorized him, terrorized his family, tried to kill him, tries to kill his children etc. Yet how does he die? He dies in a fight on a boat. He falls off the boat and hits his head on the motor. So it's accidental how the villain gets killed. The important thing is that the hero is not a murderer. "This is this American moral mentality," Tarantino said, "Just get rid of that. I want people to take revenge when revenge comes". He wants them to take revenge.

▷ Good humour and dramaturgy always have something to do with the unexpected. What was the most unexpected thing that happened to you in the past few years?

◁ The great unexpected was what Christo did with the Reichstag. What a great thing! Christo had suddenly created the Eighth Wonder of the World.

▷ At least for a little while.

◁ For a moment. But our life is momentary. That's why I'm drawn so much to graffiti. Any sort of infantile scratches and images on the wall. It's very much like our life. We are here for just a little moment in the whole scheme of things, but we each contribute a little bit to the building block of culture. We scratch our little place and go on.

◻

OTHER TITLES AVAILABLE FROM HERMANN VASKE

WORLD'S BEST SELLERS

THE
FINE ART
OF SEPARATING
PEOPLE
FROM
THEIR
MONEY

Das Werk präsentiert
A HERMANN VASKE FILM
Mit DENNIS HOPPER
Director HERMANN VASKE
CHARLES V. BENDER, HERMANN VASKE
CHRISTIAN LEONHARDT,
STEFAN JUNG, RALF DRECHSLER, STEFAN JONAS
NICK MANLEY MALCOLM McLAREN
NICKY AGER, MARTYN GOULD, JÖRG KESSEL
ALMAP/BBDO SÃO PAULO
PRODUCED BY DAS WERK IN COOPERATION WITH ZDF/ARTE

THE A TO Z
OF SEPARATING
PEOPLE
FROM THEIR
MONEY

A FILM BY
HERMANN VASKE
WITH DENNIS HOPPER

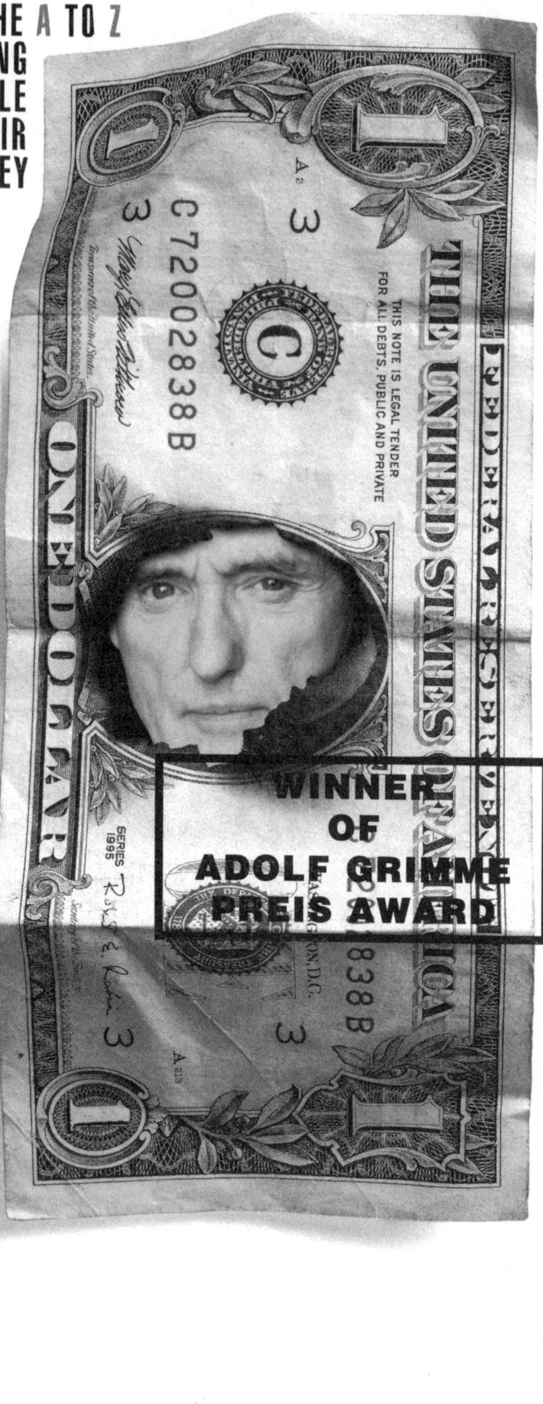

WINNER
OF
ADOLF GRIMME
PREIS AWARD

Nobuyoshi Araki-photographer

Paul Arden-director

Bono-artist

Ian Dury-musician

Abel Ferrara-director

Graham Fink-director

Bob Geldof-musician

Michail Gorbachev-politician

Vaclav Havel-politician

John Hegarty-advertising creative

Teramae Jyoin-zen master

Tony Kaye-director

Takeshi Kitano-director

David Lynch-director

Russ Meyer-director

John Pearse-taylor

Joe Pytka-director

Leni Riefenstahl-director

Leslie Savan-ad critique

Dave Trott-advertising creative

Wayne Wang-director

Mark Williams-director

Dr. Jeffrey Zeig-psychiatrist

Das Werk and Neue Sentimental Film present
A Hermann Vaske Film
starring Dennis Hopper
written and directed by Hermann Vaske
Executive Producers Mark Glaser and Christian Leonhardt
Producers Falk Prahl, Tanja Fredwerk, Barbara Schmitt, Hermann Vaske
Additional funding by ZDF/arte and NRW-Filmstiftung
Dennis Hopper Christian by Hermann Vaske, Risa Mickenberg, Dave Trott
Camera Isabelle Forrer, Stefan Janas, Steven Lee
Editors Philip Kudelhack, Viola Gopel

THE TEN
COMMANDMENTS
of CREATIVITY

Dennis Hopper as Moses

Sir Peter Ustinov as God

FEATURING

Pedro Almodovar
Bono
David Bowie
The Dalai Lama
Nina Hagen
Jim Jarmusch
Milla Jovovich
Tony Kaye
B.B. King
Ben Kingsley
Jeff Koons
Malcolm McLaren
Ed Norton
Sean Penn
Roman Polanski
Joe Pytka
Isabella Rossellini
Tim Roth
Salman Rushdie
Steven Spielberg
Quentin Tarantino
Oliviero Toscani
Vivienne Westwood
Bret Easton Ellis
Frank Lowe
Tim Delaney
and more

A HERMANN VASKE FILM

Director & Script: Hermann Vaske
Producer: Mark Gläser · Stefan Jonas · Hermann Vaske
Associate Producer: Joachim Sturmes
Kamera: Stefan Jonas · Bill Pope · Isabelle Furrer
Stephen Ley · Volker May

Title design: Claudio Fresnada · Ben Losch
Editor: Nicky Ager · Vanessa Rossi · Nadine Fraczkowski
Music: Matthias Willvonseder · Carl Orff · Bono
Malcolm McLaren
Photo: Anton Corbijn · **Art Direction:** Headlab

WHO KILLED THE IDEA?

DETECTIVE STORY

COMING SOON

WITH
DENNIS HOPPER

AN INVESTIGATIVE CREATIVE DOCUMENTARY AND PULP DETECTIVE MOVIE

FOR MORE INFORMATION ON ANY OF THESE TITLES
CONTACT THESE NUMBERS

phone: +49 (0) 69 73 99 180

fax: +49 (0) 69 73 10 21

www.emotionalnetwork.com

If you want to discuss the ideas and topics in this book with the author
you can email him at: www.emotionalnetwork.com

Author: Hermann Vaske
Project coordination - Emotional Network: Anette Krischer

Emotional Network:
Tel. (+49-69) 739 91 80 • Fax (+49-69) 73 10 21
http://www.emotionalnetwork.com

Die Deutsche Bibliothek-CIP Einheitsaufnahme
Standing on the shoulders of giants / Hermann Vaske. Berlin:
Die-Gestalten-Verl., 2001
Engl. Ausg. u.d.T.: Standing on the shoulders of giants
ISBN 3-931126-69-2

Layout: Thorsten Geiger
Cover idea: Marcello Serpa
Production: Hendrik Hellige
Editors: Christiane Löhr, Karla Handwerker
Art Direction: Robert Klanten

Printed by Medialis Offset, Berlin
Made in Europe

Paper: Munken Print. Munken paper is produced in one of
the world's most environmentally friendly facilities for the
production of high grade paper. –→ www.munkenpapers.com

For your local dgv distributor please check out:
www.die-gestalten.de